William Jackson Hooker

The British ferns, or, Coloured figures and descriptions with the needful analyses of the fructification and venation of the ferns of Great Britain and Ireland

systematically arranged

William Jackson Hooker

The British ferns, or, Coloured figures and descriptions with the needful analyses of the fructification and venation of the ferns of Great Britain and Ireland
systematically arranged

ISBN/EAN: 9783743322073

Manufactured in Europe, USA, Canada, Australia, Japa

Cover: Foto ©ninafisch / pixelio.de

Manufactured and distributed by brebook publishing software (www.brebook.com)

William Jackson Hooker

The British ferns, or, Coloured figures and descriptions with the needful analyses of the fructification and venation of the ferns of Great Britain and Ireland

THE BRITISH FERNS.

THE
BRITISH FERNS;

OR,

COLOURED FIGURES AND DESCRIPTIONS,

WITH THE

NEEDFUL ANALYSES OF THE FRUCTIFICATION AND VENATION,

OF THE

Ferns of Great Britain and Ireland,

SYSTEMATICALLY ARRANGED.

BY

SIR WILLIAM JACKSON HOOKER,
K.H., D.C.L. Oxon., F.R.A. and L.S.,
CORRESPONDING MEMBER OF SCIENCES OF THE IMPERIAL INSTITUTE OF FRANCE, ETC.,
AND DIRECTOR OF THE ROYAL GARDENS OF KEW.

THE DRAWINGS BY WALTER FITCH, F.L.S.

LONDON:
LOVELL REEVE, 5, HENRIETTA STREET, COVENT GARDEN.
1861.

PRINTED BY
JOHN EDWARD TAYLOR, LITTLE QUEEN STREET,
LINCOLN'S INN FIELDS.

INTRODUCTORY NOTICE.

By the term "FERNS" here used, we wish it to be understood in the sense in which it was employed by Linnæus and other of the less recent systematic authors, viz. as including what are called more frequently than correctly their *allied* Groups or Sub-orders, to which belong respectively *Osmunda*, *Ophioglossum*, *Lycopodium*, *Isoetes*, *Pilularia*, and *Equisetum*, some of which are as different in aspect and structure from the true Ferns as are many other families of the Flowerless Plants.

The main object we have in view in this publication is to give pictorial as well as descriptive representations of our native species, and we think we have a warrant for the fidelity of our figures in the name of our artist, Mr. Fitch. Of good descriptions of British Ferns there is no lack, from the able pens of many of our predecessors, as well as our contemporaries; but we cannot say the same of plates of British Ferns. Indeed, of those of Bolton, published three-quarters of a century ago, the first series of coloured plates of British Ferns that have appeared, to the latest figures that have been issued, it may truly be said that they do not bear that stamp of progress towards perfectness which the improved state of the art of design, and our increased knowledge of the plants in question, warrant us to look for. There is a lamentable absence, in all, of what is of the first consequence to the correct study of the Ferns, and to every tyro, namely, accurate representations of the parts of fructification upon which the essential generic characters depend, and of the venation. Such analysis, it is true, requires much research and careful and laborious investigation, and space in addition to what is occupied by the figures of the natural size. We purpose to represent these upon such a scale as shall, with the majority at least of our subjects, be truly instructive figures, so that economy and accuracy may be alike consulted. The publisher, Mr. Lovell Reeve, has, and not without good reason, selected the 'Botanical Magazine,' originated by Curtis, as the pattern, with some slight modifications, for the work in question. That work, confined to exotic, chiefly phænogamous, plants of our gardens, has been patronized by the public to such an extent as to have maintained its ground uninterruptedly for a period of seventy-four years, and numbers (at the close of the year 1860) 5,222 coloured plates, with their accompanying descriptions. We are justified then in considering this the model for the publication before us.

As the number of British Ferns, unlike the subjects for the 'Botanical Magazine,' is limited, we can announce with confidence, even should any new discoveries be made during the progress of the work, that it will not extend beyond the present volume, and will include about sixty-four plates. With a view of rendering it as generally useful as possible to British students, the whole descriptive matter will be written in the English language; and in regard to arrangement, it is not unnatural that we should follow (with as little alteration as possible) that of the last edition (the eighth) of the 'British Flora,' by Hooker and Arnott.

The Ferns are general favourites with the lovers of Nature and of the horticulturist, in consequence of the extreme beauty and gracefulness of their forms; with the botanical student, from their peculiar and varied organization, especially in what concerns their fructification. In point of usefulness to mankind, as concerns their *products* and *properties*, they do not hold a very high rank in the vegetable world. It is true that in many parts of the globe, where the arts of civilized life are unknown, many kinds form an article of food, nowhere perhaps more extensively than in New Zealand; though there, thanks to the improved condition of the people, it is rather a habit of bygone days. "*Fern-root,*" says Dr. Arthur S. Thomson, in his interesting 'Story of New Zealand: Past and Present, Savage and Civilized,' "*was* one of the principal articles of food: it was the Bread-fruit of the country. All over the North Island Fern abounds, but the productive edible variety is the *Pteris esculenta*, Forst. This food is celebrated in song; and the young women, in laying before travellers baskets of cooked fern-root, chant: 'What shall be our food? Shall shell-fish and fern-root? That is the root of the earth; that is the food to satisfy a man; the tongues grow by reason of the licking, as if it were the tongue of a dog.'

"Edible Fern," he "continues, comes to perfection only in good soils, and here the plant is ten feet high. Three-year-old plants furnish the best fern-root, and such is an inch in circumference. The deeper the root is found in the ground, the richer it is. In the month of November fern-root is dug up, cut in pieces nine inches long, and is then placed in stacks carefully protected from rain, but through which a free current of air blows. Fresh fern-root is not good; that which has been about a year aboveground is most esteemed. This is only eaten after it is roasted; and before it is cooked it is steeped in water and dried in the sun. The whole root is chewed, and the woody fibre is spit out. The flour is loosened from the woody fibre by beating it on a stone; and seventy per cent. of flour has been obtained from good fern-root. But the present generation of natives only use fern-root as a relish, although they have still fern-root feasts. In taste it resembles ship-biscuits. The pioneers of civilization found a Hindoo domesticated among the New Zealanders who preferred fern-root to rice; and the native stolen away from the Bay of Islands by De Surville (D'Urville?) wept on his death-bed for the want of fern-root."

Now this *Pteris esculenta*, or *edible Fern-root*, is a mere variety of our common Brake (*Pteris aquilina*, L.), and is recorded under that name in Dr. Hooker's 'Flora of New Zealand' (vol. ii. p. 25); and an interesting notice of our own "*Pteris aquilina* as an esculent vegetable" will be found in the ninth volume of the 'Kew Garden Miscellany,' by Dr. Benjamin Clark. The results, however, of that gentleman's experiments were not encouraging. When completely blanched, the root was found an agreeable vegetable, and considered "preferable to garden spinach, and also to have a more beneficial effect on the digestive organs." Garden spinach, however, is a poor substitute for potatoes and corn-bread; and Mr. Backhouse, speaking of the same fern-root as eaten in Tasmania, says: "It is to be observed that persons who have been reduced to the use of it in long excursions through the bush, have become very weak, though it has prolonged life."*

Other species of Fern are used as food; the *Nephrodium esculentum* (?) in Nepal, according to Dr. Buchanan Hamilton, and in other countries *Diplazium esculentum, Cyathea medullaris, Gleichenia Hermanni*, etc. Ferns contain a thick, astringent mucilage, and a little aroma, on which account many are considered pectoral and lenitive: many are bitter and astringent. The rhizomes or caudices (root-stocks) contain starch, saccharine matter, and gum, usually tannic and gallic acids, with more or less bitter matter, and sometimes both fixed and volatile oils, resin. Hence they are considered to possess astringent and tonic properties, and to act as vermifuges, particularly the rhizome of our common Male Shield-Fern, *Nephrodium Filix-Mas*. Syrup of Capillaire is extracted from *Adiantum Capillus-Veneris* and other Ferns. But in general it must be acknowledged the pharmaceutical properties of Ferns are more imaginary than real.

Some of the Exotic Ferns however yield an elastic, beautiful, golden-silky substance, long known and used in Madeira, the Canaries, and Azores, for stuffing cushions, mattresses, etc. This material is found in great abundance upon the rhizomes and

* A better use is made of the common Brake by the English peasantry, who procure an alkali from the burnt ashes, which they mix with water and form them into balls. These balls are afterwards made hot in the fire, and then used to make lye for scouring linen.—*Withering.*

about the base of the stipites of the handsome Fern *Dicksonia Culcita*,* L'Héritier.

Of the commercial value of an exactly similar substance, from plants of a closely allied genus, viz. *Cibotium*, we find the following recent account given by Mr. M. C. Cooke, on *Pulu* and some analogous products of Ferns, in the 'Pharmaceutical Journal' for April, 1860. "Three species of *Cibotium*, viz. *C. glaucum*, Hook. et Arn., *C. Chamissoi*, Kaulf., and *C. Menziesii*, Hook., are described as natives of the Sandwich Islands: all produce *Pulu* (the silky fibre in question), which has now become an established article of export from that locality. Although its use for pillows, etc., has been known amongst the natives from time immemorial, and a little may have been exported prior to 1851, yet, as an article of trade, it only dates back to that year. The Custom-house returns of the Hawaian Islands give the following amount of export in each year :—

1851	2,479 lbs.	1855	82,558 lbs.
1852	27,088 „	1856	247,740 „
1853	12,739 „	1857	260,560 „
1854	34,031 „	1858	313,220 „

It is exported principally to San Francisco (California), though not confined wholly to that port, some being sent to Australia, Vancouver's Island, and other places. Messrs. Harris, the principal dealers in *Pulu*, became by accident engaged in the trade. In 1854 they had a suit with a storekeeper in Hawaii, and judgment being rendered in their favour, about 800 lbs. of *Pulu* was all they could obtain in satisfaction. This material was then worth little or nothing in the market; they however took it, and shipped it to San Francisco, where it realized 28 cents per pound. This circumstance decided them on commencing the trade, and now two-thirds of the exports are supplied by them.

"The Fern which produces the *Pulu* grows on all the high lands of the Sandwich Islands, at an elevation of about one thousand feet in height. Though found more or less on the five principal islands, the trade in it is chiefly confined to the districts of Hilo, Hamakua, and Puna, in Hawaii. The *Pulu* is produced around

---

* Mr. Cooke states that "in the island of Fayal, on Villa Orta, one of the Azores, *Dicksonia arborescens*, L'Hérit., grows round the margin of a lake in such profusion that the silky down of its stems is used by the principal inhabitants as stuffing for their mattresses." Here is surely some error, for the *Dicksonia arborescens* is one of the rarest of Ferns, and peculiar, we believe, to Diana's Peak, in the island of St. Helena. No doubt *Dicksonia Culcita* was mistaken for it, which does grow in the Azores as well as in Madeira and the Canary Islands; and Seubert, in his 'Flora Azorica,' says the substance is largely gathered: "Hæc coma, quam incolæ, uti et plantam ipsam, '*Cabelliutro*' vocant, præsertim in insula Madern, ubi speciosa hæc filix etiam provenit, stragulis farciendis adhibetur, quo factum est, ut hæc planta, quæ sylvas montanas Azoricas mire condecorat, in illa insula rarescere incipiat."

the stalk, where the leaf or stem shoots out from the stock of the Fern, and only a small quantity is found on each plant, amounting to about two or three ounces. It takes about four years for the plant to reproduce this amount.

"Owing to the large quantities that have been collected of late years, the article is becoming scarce in the Hilo district, though in the Hamakua and Puna districts large quantities still remain. But as it is further for the natives to go to obtain it, and as more expense and fatigue is encountered, the cost is gradually advancing, and the probability is that it will continue to advance each year to the extent of a cent per pound. The number of persons engaged in gathering *Pulu* varies: including men, women, and children, probably from two to three thousand are now dependent on it for a livelihood, receiving generally from five to six cents per pound on delivery. The labour of gathering the material is very tedious and slow. When picked it is wet, and has to be laid out to dry on rocks and on mats. In favourable weather it will dry in a day or two, but generally in the *Pulu* region wet and rainy days prevail, so that frequently the natives do not get their *Pulu* dry after several weeks, often taking it to market in too wet a state. The dealers have constantly to contend with the inclination of the natives to sell wet *Pulu*, as it makes considerable difference in the weight when dry. The facilities for drying, packing, and shipping, are improving every year, and the article now shipped is generally dry and in good order, closely packed in wool bales. The trade is reduced to a system, and though there is no probability of any great increase, it will doubtless continue a staple export."

Again, we are informed by the same writer, Mr. Cooke, that a similar fibrous substance has been recently noticed by Dr. de Vry (now on a government scientific mission to the Dutch East Indian possessions, in company with Dr. de Vriese), and the information communicated to Daniel Hanbury, Esq., with some account of the medicinal properties, real or imaginary (probably styptic). There are two kinds; one, *Penawar Jambie*, derived from the rhizomes of *Cibotium glaucescens* of Kunze and of Hook. Sp. Fil. v. 1. p. 83, supposed to be the *Polypodium Barometz* of Loureiro's Flora Cochinchinensis, and consequently the famous *Frutex Tartareus*, *Agnus Scythicus*, or *Tartarian Lamb*,* of the

---

* This condition of the root-stock of some Fern long engaged the attention of early writers on the marvellous, and many strange figures were published of it; but Dr. Breyne, of Dantzig, in a Latin dissertation given in the 'Philosophical Transactions,' vol. xxxiii., for 1725, declared that the pretended *Agnus Scythicus* was nothing more than the root of a large Fern covered with its natural villus or yellow down, and accompanied by some of the stems, etc., in order, when placed in an inverted position, the better to represent the appearance of the legs and horns of a quadruped. He also adds that the down or villus is the "*poco sempie*," or *golden moss*, so much esteemed by the Chinese for the pur-

old botanical writers. The down appears on the young undeveloped leaves as well as on the rhizome, and in such quantities that the native *docheans* (female physicians) pick for years at such a stem without exhausting it. Sometimes these old stems are on sale, in Sumatra, at a Spanish matt (4s. 6d.) apiece. The second kind is called *Pakoe Kidang*, and is stated to be derived from the *Balantium chrysotrichum* of Hasskarl, a species unknown to us, but of which a plantation exists on the sides of the Goenong Gedeh, a volcano in the interior of Java, between fifty and sixty miles from Batavia. The government of Java has exported the product of their plantation to Holland, where it has been sold at a public sale, but under the incorrect name of *Penawar Jambie*.

Of the Club-Mosses (*Lycopodium*) the *Lycopodium clavatum*, or *Common Club-Moss*, is used in Sweden in making door-mats, for which purpose its long wiry stems render it very suitable. Of the properties of the seeds or spores, Dr. Pereira has given a very interesting account in his 'Elements of Materia Medica.' They are used both medicinally and pharmaceutically, and in Poland commonly in the cure of that terrible disease, *plica Polonica*. But its principal use is at theatres, where it is employed in filling flash-boxes, and for producing artificial lightning. And lastly, we have only to mention that a very important use is made of one of the *Horse-tails*, *Equisetum hyemale*, L., of which the cuticle so much abounds in silex that the stems are extensively employed in polishing hard woods, brass, ivory, etc., and for these purposes are largely imported from the Continent (albeit common enough in England) under the name of *Dutch rushes*. By these means the Dutch are said to keep their milk-pails beautifully clean.

pose of stopping hæmorrhages; and this is the very substance now under consideration. Nor can we affirm that this plant of Kunze is not that which gave rise to the tales of wonder, for, although the species was first botanically determined by Kunze from Cuming's Philippine Island specimens, and although it is shown to be a native also of Sumatra, yet we have lately (in ' Kew Garden Miscellany,' vol. ix. p. 334) had occasion to record the fact of our having received specimens of the same Fern from Hongkong, Chusan, and South China, of which country the *Barometz* is considered a native. It is true the words "Tartarian" and "Scythian" are applied to it, perhaps to make it the more wonderful, as Dr. Darwin has done by transferring the plant to the Polar regions, in his well-known lines,—

> "Cradled in snow and fanned by arctic air
> Shines, gentle *Barometz*, thy golden hair;
> Rooted in earth each cloven hoof descends,
> And round and round her flexile neck she bends;
> Crops the grey coral moss and hoary thyme,
> Or laps with rosy tongue the melting rime;
> Eyes with mute tenderness her distant dam,
> Or seems to bleat, a *Vegetable Lamb*."
> *Botanic Garden* (*with a figure*).

Royal Gardens, Kew, January 1, 1861.

CONSPECTUS

OF THE

SUBORDERS AND GENERA UNDER WHICH THE SPECIES OF BRITISH FERNS ARE ARRANGED IN THIS WORK.

ORD. FILICES.

Subord. I. POLYPODIEÆ.—*Capsules dorsal or marginal, surrounded by an articulated elastic ring, and opening transversely and irregularly. Fronds circinate in vernation.*

A. *Capsules opening transversely, arising from the back of the frond; the ring vertical, usually incomplete.*

* Nudisoræ.—*Sori destitute of involucre.*†

1. GYMNOGRAMME.—*Sori oblong or linear, on forked veins.*
2. POLYPODIUM.—*Sori subglobose.*

** Indusiatæ.—*Sori furnished with an involucre or indusium.*

3. WOODSIA.—*Sori subglobose. Involucre beneath the sorus, more or less cup-shaped, and fimbriated at the margin.*
4. CYSTOPTERIS.—*Sori subglobose. Involucre ovate, cucullate at the base, and having its origin beneath the sorus.*
5. ASPIDIUM.—*Sori dorsal, subglobose. Involucre orbicular and peltate.*
6. NEPHRODIUM.—*Sori dorsal, subglobose. Involucre subcordate and fixed by the sinus.*
7. ASPLENIUM.—*Sori dorsal, linear or oblong, rarely curved or somewhat horseshoe-shaped, attached laterally to the veins, and opening towards the midrib.*
8. SCOLOPENDRIUM.—*Sori dorsal, linear, in opposite pairs, and opening towards each other.*
9. PTERIS.—*Sori continuous, dorsal, but at the margin on a marginal receptacle. Involucre formed of the reflexed and generally membranous margin of the frond.*
10. ADIANTUM.—*Sori dorsal, roundish (in many exotic species ob-*

† In this section the genus *Ceterach* has been generally placed, but as that is now found to possess a narrow involucre, like that of *Asplenium*, it is restored to the latter genus.

long or linear). Involucres of the same-shaped portions of a reflexed and altered margin of the frond, bearing the capsules upon them.

11. CRYPTOGRAMME.—*Sori oblong or linear, situated towards the apex of the veins, and covered by the involucre formed of the broad revolute margin of the frond. Fronds dimorphous.*

12. BLECHNUM.—*Sori linear, continuous, parallel with and near the costa, running transversely, with the veins rarely submarginal. Involucre of the same shape.*

B. *Capsules opening irregularly, placed on a columnar or filiform receptacle, and terminating a vein at the margin of the frond, having a transverse ring and included in an involucre. Fronds delicate, membranaceous.*

13. TRICHOMANES.—*Involucre subcylindrical, nearly entire. Receptacle usually exserted.*

14. HYMENOPHYLLUM.—*Involucre 2-valved. Receptacle rarely exserted.*

Subord. II. OSMUNDEÆ.—*Capsules clustered at the margin of a transformed frond or portion of a frond, reticulated, opening by two regular valves; ring almost obsolete. Fronds circinate in vernation.*

15. OSMUNDA.

Subord. III. OPHIOGLOSSEÆ.—*Capsules globose, between coriaceous and fleshy, sessile, forming a simple or compound pedunculated spike, distinct from the sterile frond, and opening transversely by two equal valves. Fronds straight in vernation.*

16. OPHIOGLOSSUM.—*Capsules connate on a 2-ranked spike.*

17. BOTRYCHIUM.—*Capsules free, arranged on one side of a pinnated spike or rachis.*

Subord. IV.—LYCOPODIEÆ.—*Capsules without a ring, coriaceous, sessile, in the axils of leaves or bracteas, 1-celled, 2–3-valved. Stems leafy. Vernation not circinate.*

18. LYCOPODIUM.

Subord. V. ISOETEÆ.—*Capsules without a ring, indehiscent, immersed in a cavity at the base of long subulate radical leaves. Seeds on filiform receptacles. Vernation involute. Aquatics.*

19. ISOETES.

Subord. VI. MARSILEÆ.—*Fructification of two kinds. Capsules without a ring, in globose coriaceous involucres near the root of the plant. Vernation involute. Aquatics.*

20. PILULARIA.

Plate 1.

GYMNOGRAMME LEPTOPHYLLA, *Desv.*

Small Annual Gymnogram.

Gen. Char. Sori linear, elongated, on forked free veins, destitute of involucre.

GYMNOGRAMME *leptophylla;* subdimorphous, small, annual; caudex none; root fibrous, annual; stipites slender, tufted; fronds delicate, membranaceous, fragile, ovate or oblong, sterile ones shorter than the fertile, all bi-tripinnate; pinnules obovate-cuneate, bi-trifid or lobed, lobes obtuse; sori simple or forked, often confluent; rachis winged above.

GYMNOGRAMME leptophylla. *Desv. Journ. Bot. v.* 1. *p.* 26. *Kaulf. Enum. Fil. p.* 81. *Hook. and Grev. Ic. Fil. t.* 26. *Hook. fil. Fl. N. Zeal. v.* 2. *p.* 45. *Newm. Hist. of Brit. Ferns,* 1854, *p.* 11 (*with woodcut*). *Hook. and Arn. Brit. Fl. ed.* 8. *p.* 580. *Moore, Brit. Ferns, Nat. Print. t.* 43 *B.*

GRAMMITIS leptophylla. *Sw. Syn. Fil. p.* 23. *t.* 1. *f.* 6. *Willd. Sp. Pl. v.* 5. *p.* 143.

POLYPODIUM leptopbyllum. *Linn. Sp. Pl. p.* 1553. *Schk. Fil. t.* 26.

HEMIONITIS leptophylla (*and* H. Pozoi, *according to Moore*). *Lagasca, Gen. et Sp. p.* 33.

ANOGRAMME leptophylla. *Link, and Fée, Gen. Fil. p.* 184.

ASPLENIUM leptophyllum. *Cav. Anal. Cienc. Nat. v.* 13. *t.* 41.

ACROSTICHUM leptophyllum. *De Cand. Fl. Fr. v.* 2. *p.* 505.

OSMUNDA leptophylla. *Lam. Encycl. v.* 4. *p.* 657.

Hab. Jersey. "On banks of exposed lanes having a southern aspect, often in company with *Marchantia,* discovered by a lady," about the year 1852 (*Newman*).

I have in vain endeavoured to ascertain the name of the lady who was the first to detect this very interesting plant on British ground; but I can nowhere find a record of it. That it is a plant of Jersey, and not unfrequent there, there can be no question. We have received living plants gathered there at different times, both from Mr. Piquet, of St. Helier, and from our friend Mr. Ward. It there seems to have attained its extreme northern limit, and the most northern of any species of the genus *Gymnogramme.* It is plentiful throughout the south of Europe, and was long supposed to be peculiar to it; but numerous specimens in our herbarium prove it to have a much wider range;

for example, in the Azores, in Madeira and Teneriffe, in the basin of the Mediterranean, in Abyssinia (*Schimper*), Karek, in the Gulf of Persia (*Kotschy*). In India, at Mussoorie and the Neilgherries, in South America, Cuba, *C. Wright;* Mexico, and Vera Cruz. In the southern hemisphere it appears at the Cape of Good Hope, on the east side of the Devil's Mountain; in Australia, at Victoria (*Robinson, F. Mueller*), and at the Swan River and Port Stephens (*Drummond*); in Tasmania, and in New Zealand.

Gymnogramme leptophylla may be reckoned among the smallest and most delicate of our Ferns. On this account, perhaps, it had been long overlooked; and it is likewise, what is very rare among Ferns, of annual duration, like its affinity *Gymnogramme chærophylla*. Thus, in cultivation, if its fallen spores are not carefully protected, it will perish. The fronds in most of our specimens exhibit a great tendency to be dimorphous; that is to say, that the barren fronds are smaller and less divided, and have broader pinnules than the fertile ones. The stipites are slender, and of a chestnut colour towards the base. The whole plant has a very yellow or tawny hue in the herbarium.

PLATE 1. Sterile and fertile, from the same root, of *Gymnogramme leptophylla*. Fig. 1. Fertile pinna,—*magnified*. 2. Fertile pinnule,—*more magnified*.

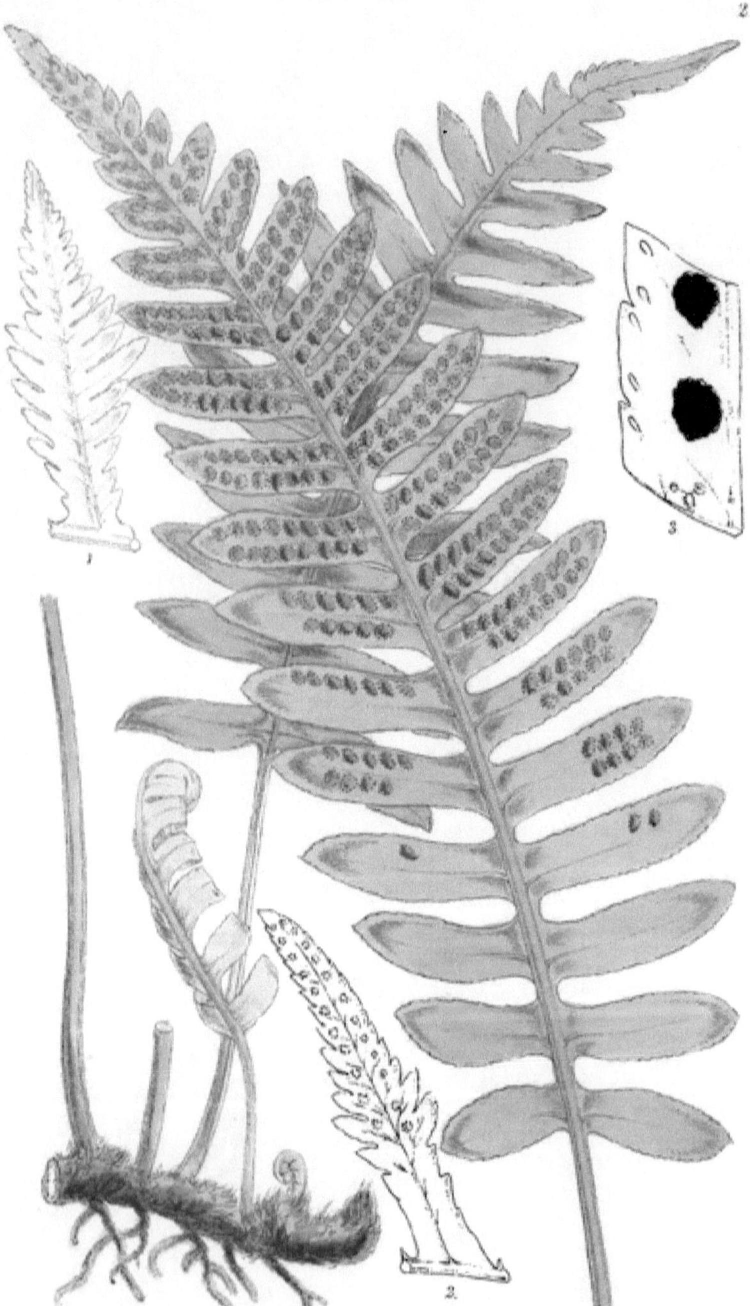

W Fitch, del et lith

Vincent Brooks Day & Son Imp

Plate 2.

POLYPODIUM (§ Eupolypodium) vulgare, *L.*

Common Polypody.

Gen. Char. Sori dorsal, subglobose or oval, destitute of involucre. *Veins* free (as in all the British species) or anastomosing.

Our native species are conveniently divided into two groups:—

1. Eupolypodium.—*Veins bearing the sorus at the apex. Fronds pinnatifid. Stipes articulated upon the caudex.*—P. vulgare.

2. Phegopteris.—*Veins usually bearing the sorus on the back of the vein, more or less distant from the apex. Fronds generally branched. Stipes not articulated on the caudex.*—P. Phegopteris, P. Dryopteris, P. Robertianum, *and* P. alpestre.

Polypodium (Eupolypodium) *vulgare*; caudex long, stout, creeping, very scaly; fronds ovate or oblong, subcoriaceous, acuminate, deeply pinnatifid almost to the base; segments spreading, linear-oblong, obtuse, or more or less acuminate, crenate-serrate; sori in two rows, subglobose.

Polypodium vulgare. *Linn. Sp. Pl. p.* 1544. *Sw. Syn. Fil. p.* 34. *Willd. Sp. Pl. v.* 5. *p.* 172. *Sm. Eng. Bot. t.* 1149. *Schk. Fil. t.* 11. *Hook. and Arn. Brit. Fl. ed.* 8. *p.* 580. *Moore, Brit. Ferns, Nat. Print. t.* 1, 2, 3 (excluding, *I apprehend,* P. Karwinskianum, A. Braun, *and* P. intermedium, *Hook. and Arn. Bot. of Beech. Voy.*).

Polypodium Virginianum. *Linn. Sp. Pl. p.* 1544. *Sw. Syn. Fil. p.* 34. *Willd. Sp. Pl. v.* 5. *p.* 474. *Pursh, Fl. N. Am. v.* 2. *p.* 658.

Polypodium australe. *Fée, Gen. Fil. p.* 236.

Cynopteris vulgaris. *Newm.*

Var. *Cambricum*; segments of the fronds more or less deeply pinnatifid.

P. Cambricum, *Linn. Sp. Pl. p.* 1546. P. vulgare, *var.* serratum *and* Cambricum, *Willd. l. c.*

Hab. Common throughout England, Scotland, and Ireland, on old banks, walls, rocks, mossy trunks of trees, etc.

The well-known "Polypody of the Oak," as our sage forefathers used to call it,[*] is found in the cold and temperate parts of many regions of the globe: throughout Europe, to its extreme south; North Africa, Madeira, the Canaries, and Azores. In Siberia we possess specimens from the Amur, from Manchouria,

---

[*] It was formerly supposed to possess medicinal properties; but Sir James Smith remarks that "they are not enough to make it worth inquiring whether that of the Oak or that of any wall or cottage be most endowed with them."

and from Japan, from Erzeroum; but in the more tropical parts of Asia it seems unknown, even in the great Himalayan range, which exhibits so many European forms. In North America, in the United States and Canada, and in the Hudson's Bay territories, it is frequent. East of the Rocky Mountains the majority of my very numerous specimens are rather small and oblong in outline, with compact blunt segments; whereas westward of the Rocky Mountains, and in California (whence I have only seen it from Benicia, *A. B. Eaton, U.S. Army*), the fronds are larger, much acuminated, yet not universally so. South of California, on the great continent of America, I am not prepared to say it exists. The *P. Karwinskianum*, A. Braun, of Mexico, which Mr. Moore refers to this species, I think will prove distinct. I possess it under that name and as *P. plebejum*, Schlecht., and *P. leucosticton* of Kunze and Klotzsch. Still our species is not wanting even in the southern hemisphere. From the Cape of Good Hope I have received unquestionable specimens from the late Colonel Bolton, and other stations are recorded there by Pappe and Rawson.

Our Plate exhibits all the true characters of this species of the ordinary size and form, but it varies much in the length and breadth of the frond, sometimes being almost deltoid and sometimes it is caudate at the apex. The abnormal form, var. "*Cambricum*," which Swartz calls "monstrosa varietas," is not confined to Wales, as its name would perhaps imply. It is common in Teneriffe, and Mettenius says in southern Europe; but I have seen no specimens from North America. Those who take an interest in the freaks of Nature of this kind may consult Mr. Moore, *l. c.*, who has enumerated seventeen forms.

PLATE 2. Plant of *Polypodium vulgare*,—*nat. size*. Fig. 1, 2. Segments of the frond of var. *Cambricum*. 3. Portion of a fertile segment of *Polypodium vulgare*, showing the venation and the sori from the apex of the veinlet,—*magnified*.

Plate 3.

POLYPODIUM Phegopteris, *Linn.*

Pale Mountain Polypody.

Polypodium *Phegopteris*; caudex very long, creeping; stipites stramineous, glossy-brown below, and scaly; fronds triangular-ovate, pinnate; pinnæ approximate, sessile, confluent above, narrow-oblong, lanceolate, mostly opposite, deeply pinnatifid, hairy, lowermost pair distant, more or less deflexed, and pointing forward; segments oblong, obtuse, nearly entire, lowermost ones adnato-decurrent and triangular; sori marginal, below the apex of the veins.

Polypodium Phegopteris. *Linn. Sp. Pl.* p. 1550. *Sw. Syn. Fil.* p. 40. *Willd. Sp. Pl. v.* 5. p. 269. *Schk. Fil. t.* 20. *Engl. Bot. t.* 2224. *Hook. and Arn. Brit. Fl. ed.* 8. p. 580. *Moore, Brit. Ferns, Nat. Print. t.* 4. *Gray, Man. N. U. St. illustr.* p. 590.

Polypodium connectile. *Mich. Fl. Bor. Am. v.* 2. p. 271.

Phegopteris vulgaris. *Metten. Fil. Hort. Lips.* p. 83; *Phegopt.* p. 15.

Phegopteris polypodioides. *Fée, Gen. Fil.* p. 243.

Polystichum Phegopteris. *Roth.*

Gymnocarpium Phegopteris. *Newm.*

Hab. Moist mountain districts in various parts of England, Scotland, and Ireland, chiefly in woods; rare in the warmer and more sunny counties of the south-east of England.

In Europe this plant is widely extended, but it seems to prefer the cool and mountain regions. We possess it from Iceland and from the Alps of Switzerland; from the Altai and Siberia, as far east as Kamtchatka; Dr. Babington found it in Japan. In North America it seems equally abundant. Our specimens are from Greenland and Labrador, throughout Canada to the Rocky Mountains, and from the northern United States. It appears again on the north-west coast at King William's Sound (*Barclay*).

It is a very distinct species, having for its nearest affinity the North American *Pol. hexagonopterum*, Mich., but the pinnæ of the latter are bipinnatifid, and the basal segments are much more adnate with the rachis, and more detached. It is, too, a much more southern species in the United States, yet I should almost have been disposed to have considered it a southern form of *P. Phegopteris*, but that I find the sori to be quite terminal on the vein, a character really invalidating the most essential mark which distinguishes Fée's genus *Phegopteris* from true *Polypodium*. It is singular that while Moore rejects the genus *Phegopteris*, the cautious Mettenius adopts it. I am content to consider it as a group or subgenus of *Polypodium;* and the present species, which gave the name to the group or genus, may be considered the type of it. Its character, however, does not depend entirely upon the position of the sorus, "toujours," says M. Fée, "au-dessous du sommet de la nerville." Mettenius and others assign to it a petiole confluent with the caudex, not articulated: the fronds are more or less membranous, generally much divided, and resemble many species of *Lastrea*, and even sometimes of *Polystichum*, among the indusiate Ferns.

PLATE 3. Fertile plant of *Polypodium Phegopteris,—natural size.* Fig. 1. Fertile segment,—*magnified.* 2. Portion of ditto, with a single sorus from the back of a vein below the apex,—*more magnified.*

W. Fitch, del et lith.   Vincent Brooks Day & Son, Imp.

PLATE 4.

POLYPODIUM (§ PHEGOPTERIS) DRYOPTERIS, *Linn.*

Tender Three-branched Polypody, or Oak-Fern.

POLYPODIUM (Phegopteris) *Dryopteris;* caudex long, creeping, branched, more or less scaly; frond thin, membranaceous, flaccid, quite glabrous, pentangularly deltoid, tripartito-bipinnate; primary pinnæ long-petioled (especially the terminal one), deltoid; secondary pinnæ mostly sessile, oblong or ovato-oblong, rather obtuse, deeply pinnatifid, at their base sometimes again pinnated; segments oval, entire, or the inferior ones pinnatifido-serrate; sori in two rows near the margin, dorsal on the vein.

POLYPODIUM Dryopteris. *Linn. Sp. Pl. p.* 1555. *Engl. Bot. t.* 616. *Sw. Syn. Fil. p.* 42. *Schk. Fil. t.* 25. *Willd. Sp. Pl. v.* 5. *p.* 209. *Hook. and Arn. Brit. Fl. ed.* 8. *p.* 580. *Ledebour, Fl. Alt.* α genuinum (*his* β *is* Pol. Robertianum, *Hoffm.*, P. calcareum, *Sw.*

POLYPODIUM calcareum. *Pursh, Fl. N. Am. v.* 2. *p.* 639.

PHEGOPTERIS Dryopteris. *Fée, Gen. Fil. p.* 243. *Metten. Fil. Hort. Lips. p.* 83. *Phegopt. p.* 9.

POLYSTICHUM Dryopteris. *Roth, Fil. Germ. v.* 3. *p.* 80.

LASTREA and GYMNOCARPIUM Dryopteris. *Newm.*

Hab. England and Scotland, frequent in the mountain districts; rare in Ireland, said there only to be found in the county of Antrim; and still more rare in the south and east of England.

A very delicate and graceful Fern; and, like our last species, *Pol. Phegopteris*, chiefly confined to moist and mountain districts. It would appear to be found in similar districts in Continental Europe. I possess it from Norway, from the Alps of Switzerland, and from the Spanish Pyrenees, but no specimens further south. Dr. Thomas Thomson gathered it in the temperate regions of Western Himalaya, in the Chanab Valley, Badarwar, and Kishtwar, at elevations of from five to eight thousand feet above the sea-level. It is found in Siberia, Awatschka Bay (*Seemann*), and in Japan (*Wilford*), in Greenland. It is abundant in North America, from Labrador through the Hudson's Bay territories, on both sides the Rocky Mountains, to the Pacific Ocean, in British Columbia; more rare in the northern United States, and not found in the south.

The *root* of this plant is very long, creeping, a good deal branched, scaly with large, brown, membranaceous scales, particularly on the young shoots, and these scales extend a little way up the straw-coloured slender stipes. The *frond* is of a peculiarly delicate and flaccid nature, so that it does not rise quite erect, but has a slightly reflexed or recurved inclination, and is quite glabrous. *Veins* usually forked, the upper branch of the fork bearing the sorus a little below its apex.

The only species with which our present plant is likely to be confounded (and that is so near, if it be really distinct, as often to have been mistaken for it), is *Polypodium Robertianum*, Hoffm., *Pol. calcareum* of Smith and most authors. But as this latter will form the subject of the next Plate, the first in our second number, we shall defer our remarks till its appearance.

PLATE 4. Fertile plant of *Polypodium Dryopteris*,—*natural size*. Fig. 1. Fertile segment, with sori,—*magnified*. 2. Portion with a forked nerve, the superior branch bearing the sorus,—*more magnified*.

PLATE 5.

POLYPODIUM (PHEGOPTERIS) ROBERTIANUM, *Hoffm.*

Rigid Three-branched Polypody.

POLYPODIUM (Phegopteris) *Robertianum* ; caudex long, creeping, branched, scaly ; frond rather firm-membranaceous, glandularly pubescent, at length glabrous, subpentangularly deltoid or triangular-ovate, tripartito-bipinnate ; primary pinnæ long-petioled (especially the intermediate or terminal one), deltoid-ovate ; secondary pinnæ mostly sessile, oblong or ovato-oblong, obtuse, deeply pinnatifid at the base, and then sometimes again pinnate ; segments oval-oblong, entire, or the inferior ones pinnatifido-serrate ; sori in two rows near the margin, dorsal on the vein, often confluent.

POLYPODIUM Robertianum. *G. F. Hoffm. Fl. Germ.* part 2, 1795, *in addend.* Moore's *Brit. Ferns, Nat. Print. pl.* 6.

LASTREA Robertiana *and* GYMNOCARPIUM Robertianum. *Newm.*

POLYPODIUM calcareum. *Smith, Fl. Brit.* p. 117 (1804); *Engl. Bot. t.* 1525. *Willd. Sp. Pl. v.* 5. *p.* 210. *Hook. and Arn. Brit. Fl. ed.* 8. *p.* 581.

PHEGOPTERIS calcarea. *Fée, Gen. Fil. p.* 243. *Metten. Fil. Hort. Lips. p.* 83. *Phegopt. p.* 9.

POLYPODIUM Dryopteris. *Dicks. dr. Plant. t.* 16 ; *and Bolt. Fil. p.* 53. *t.* 1 (according to Sir *Jas. Smith* ; *and of American authors, according to Mr. Moore*). *Benth. Handb. of Brit. Fl. p.* 626.—β. *Wahl. Fl. Suec. v.* 2. *p.* 668.

Hab. Limestone débris, chiefly in the northern and western parts of England. Our most authentic specimens are from Matlock, Derbyshire, Sir *J. E. Smith.*

This graceful Fern, which has so many points in common with our preceding species (*Pol. Dryopteris*), was first distinguished from it by Hoffmann, in his little 'Flora of Germany,' a work unknown to Sir Jas. E. Smith, and probably to many other botanists, and hence he and subsequent writers have not maintained the original name, till lately, when Mr. Newman and Mr. Moore adopted the oldest. It is, however, not a little remarkable that neither of the first describers in their specific character, indicates any good mark by which it can be distinguished from *Pol. Dryopteris.* Take Hoffmann's character, for example : " Fronde triangulari, foliolis ternis bipinnatis, pinnis pinnulisque inferne pinnatifidis;" or Smith's: "Fronde ternata, bipinnata, erecta, rigidula ; laciniis obtusis subcrenatis, maculis fructiferis confluentibus." It is true Hoffmann, in his remarks, adds, what is now considered the most dependable mark, " frons uterque nudo oculo subtili tomento, ad lentem brevissimis glandulis obsita ;" and " odor debilis *Geranii Robertiani*" (whence, of course, his specific name). Smith takes no notice of the glandular pubescence, not even in his subsequent publications, nor is it represented in the 'English Botany' figure,—and in truth it is very evanescent.* What, then, it may be asked, are the essentially distinguishing marks of the species? As far as words can express them, they are very slight. The *differences* recorded by the accurate Mettenius are, "*Phegopt. Dryopteris,* frond glabrous, ternato-pinnate or bipinnatisect; tertiary veins undivided or forked,"—"*Ph. Robertiana,* frond glanduloso-pubescent, bipinnatisect; tertiary veins generally forked." The other characters are nearly word for word the same in both. No one has a more firm conviction of the two being distinct than Mr. Moore, for he says "it is hardly to be supposed that those who have seen tolerably good examples of both would hesitate to admit their distinctness;" and he sums up the difference in these words :—*P. Dryopteris* has a loosely-sprending habit, while the fronds of *P. Robertianum* are rigid and erect, with stouter stalks and ribs, and a less membranaceous texture; the former has ternate three-branched fronds, which is not strictly the case with the latter.† Of less importance, but equally or still more clearly available as distinguishing characteristics, are the perfect smoothness of *P. Dryopteris,* compared with the glandular pubescence of *P. Robertianum*," etc. Now my very numerous specimens, and very good examples too, from various parts of Europe, Asia, and America, rather incline me to an opposite opinion. Many of them have as strong a claim to be called by the one name as the other (and so they are by different botanists); and all those from Himalaya, of Drs. Hooker and Thomson, in our herbarium, which Mr. Moore refers to *Pol. Robertianum,* I have unhesitatingly placed with *P. Dryopteris :* so that my recent very careful reconsideration of these species for the present work, to say the least, confirms me in the view I have expressed in conjunction with Dr. Arnott in the 'British Flora,' viz. that " we consider *P. Robertianum* a very doubtful species." Indeed, from most of the countries given as localities for *P. Dryopteris,* if the specimens are numerous, some may be found exhibiting more or less of the characters of *Robertianum ;* but whether such are due to the presence of limestone débris, as seems to be the haunt of *Robertianum* in this country, I cannot take upon me to say. I have introduced few synonyms because of the difficulty of settling them.

PLATE 5. Fertile plant of *Polypodium Robertianum,*—*nat. size.* Fig. 1. Fertile segments, with glands and sori,—*magnified.* 3. Glands and sorus,—*more magnified.*

* On the contrary, he says in his very latest publication, 'English Flora,' "that the frond is *smooth*, except a minute downiness on the midrib."

† This difference I can neither see in native specimens nor in the respective figures of Mr. Moore, which, being Nature's printing, cannot fail to be accurate in everything save the presence of the glandular pubescence of *Pol. Robertianum.*

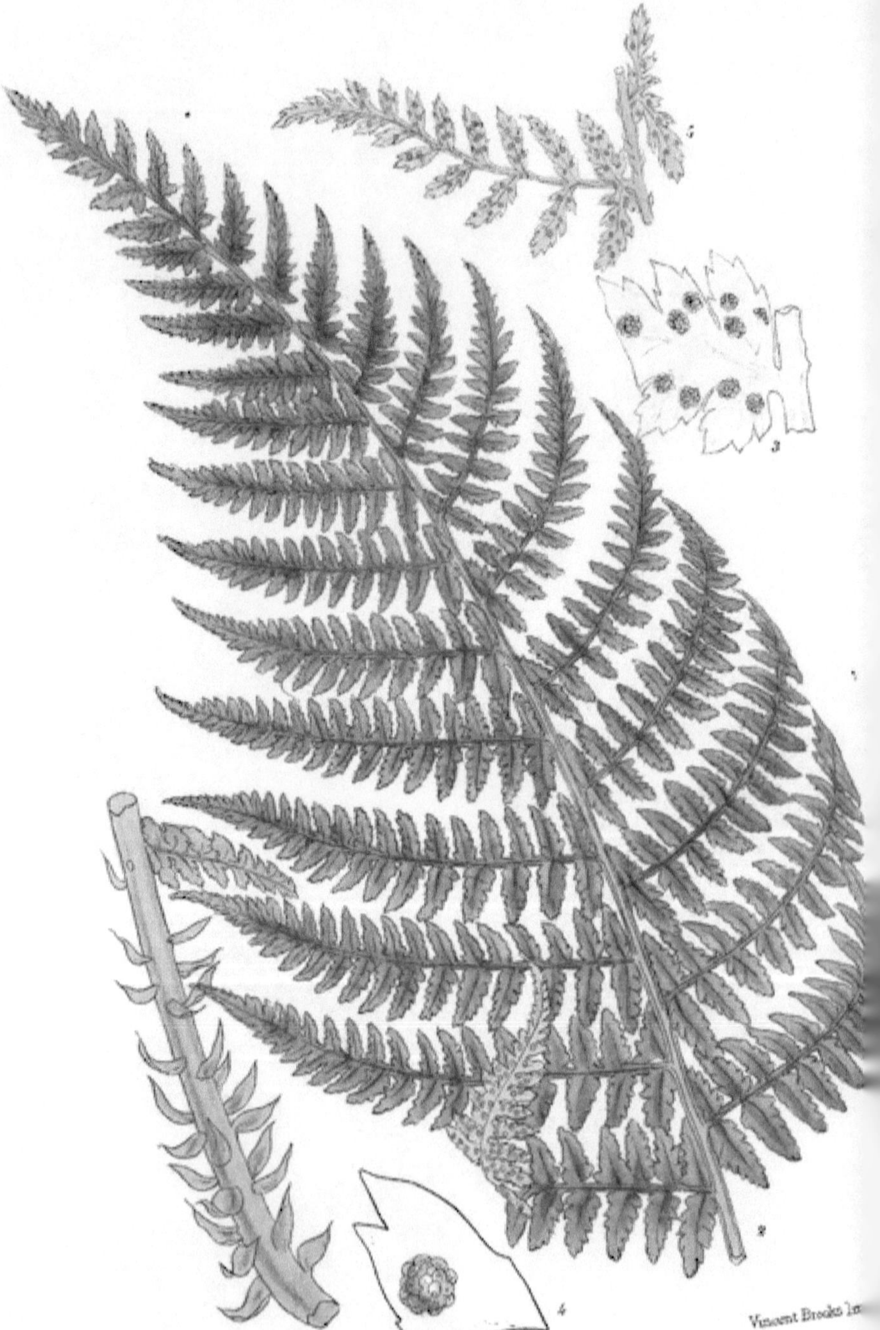

W Fitch del. et lith.

Vincent Brooks Imp.

PLATE 6.

POLYPODIUM (§ PHEGOPTERIS) ALPESTRE, *Hoppe*.

Alpine Polypody.

POLYPODIUM (Phegopteris) *alpestre*; glabrous; caudex oblique, fronds oblong-lanceolate, bipinnate; pinnules oblong-ovate, sometimes slightly falcate, sub-acute, sessile, more or less deeply pinnatifid, segments ovate, inciso-serrate; sori globose, placed near the sinus on the margin; stipes short, with large spreading scales.

POLYPODIUM alpestre. *Hoppe, in Spreng. Syst. Veget. v. 4. c. p. p.* 320. *Koch, Syn. Fl. Germ. v.* 2. *p.* 974. "*Heafrey in Francis' Anal. of Brit. Ferns, ed.* 5. *p.* 28. *Suppl. Pl. f.* 2 *A.*" *Sowerby, Ferns of Gt. Brit. p.* 84. *t.* 49. *Moore, Brit. Ferns, Nat. Print. t.* 6*. *Hook. and Arn. Br. Fl. ed.* 8. *p.* 581.

PHEGOPTERIS alpestris. *Mettten. Fil. Hort. Lips. p.* 83; *Phegopt. p.* 10.

ASPIDIUM alpestre. *Sw. Syn. Fil. pp.* 42, 59. *Willd. Sp. Plant. v.* 5. *p.* 280. *Schk. Fil. p.* 58. *t.* 60 (A. umbrosum *on the Plate*), *excellent (excl. syn. Linn.*).

ASPIDIUM rhæticum. *Sw. in Schrad. Journ.* 1800. *v.* 2. *p.* 41. *Syn. Fil. p.* 59. *Willd. Sp. Pl. v.* 5. *p.* 280 (*excl. syn. Linn.*).

POLYPODIUM rhæticum. *Villars. Pallas, It.* "2. *p.* 28." *Ledeb. Fl. Ross. v.* 4. *p.* 510. *Fries, Summa Veget. p.* 82.

ATHYRIUM rhæticum. *Roth, Tent. Germ. v.* 3. *t.* 67.

PSEUDATHYRIUM alpestre. *Newm.*

ASPLENIUM alpestre. *Mettten. Asplen. p.* 198.

Var. *flexile,* Moore, Brit. Ferns, l. c.; stipes scarcely any, pinnæ short, ovato-lanceolate, spreading or deflexed, pinnules distant. (TAB. NOSTR. Fig. 5.)

POLYPODIUM flexile. *Moore, Handb. of Brit. Ferns, p.* 225.

PSEUDATHYRIUM flexile. *Newm.*

Hab. Moist rocky glens, in the mountains of Forfarshire. I possess fine specimens from *Mr. Jas. Backhouse, Jun.,* gathered in Clova; and of var. β, from Glen Prosen, Ben-y-Mac-Dhui, and other places in Braemar, *Mr. Croall.*

This is a very distinct and well-marked species of *Polypodium*, and cannot easily be confounded with any other of the *Phegopteris* group, whether British or exotic. Indeed there is more danger of its being mistaken for *Asplenium (Athyrium) Filix-fœmina*, and we have reason to believe that before it was recognized among us as a species, it had been gathered or heedlessly passed by for that plant. Schkuhr represents a rather broad, brown, convex involucre, such as might belong to an *Athyrium* rather than an *Aspidium* or *Lastrea;* but no author has since recognized such an involucre; and certainly the sori are globose, not oblong. Mettenius, in his work on *Phegopteris*, places it there, as he had done previously in his Fil. Hort. Lips.; but in his monograph on *Asplenium* he refers it to that genus, and remarks, "J. Duval-Jouve (Études sur le Pétiole des Fougères) indusium tenerrimum, soros juveniles obtegens, propriis observationibus confirmans, *A. alpestre*, crescendi modo, vernatione, petiolorum basi fasciculisque vasorum, nec minus palcis omnino cum *A. Filix-fœmina* congruere exponit, ergoque formam *A. Filicis-fœminæ* 'soris subrotundis, indusiis aut nullis aut rudimentariis insignem' sistere putat." The figures however of these supposed indusia given by Mettenius (Asplen. t. 6. f. 1–6), are very unlike any true indusium known to us, and no two seem to be alike; nor have I been able to see such upon any of my specimens.

On the continent of Europe, *P. alpestre* seems to be found chiefly in the north, Norway, Lapland, Russia, Germany; and on the Alps in the south. It probably passes from Russia into Siberia; for it again appears in North-west America, at Sitka, whence I possess the plant from Barclay. It is singular that from the same respective persons and localities I have received true *Asplenium (Athyrium) Filix-fœmina*, and more recently from the Cascade Mountains, British Columbia, 49° N. lat., gathered by Dr. Lyall, R.N., of the Oregon Boundary Commission.

PLATE 6. Fig. 1. Portion of a stipes, with scales, etc. 2. Portion of a frond of *Polypodium* (Phegopteris) *alpestre*, Hoppe,—*nat. size*. 3. Portion of a pinnule, with sori,—*magnified*. 4. Single sorus,—*more magnified*. 5. Small portion of a frond of var. *flexile*,—*natural size*.

Plate 7.

WOODSIA HYPERBOREA, *Br.*

Round-leaved Woodsia.

Gen. Char. Sori scattered, roundish, having *beneath* an *involucre*, which is cut at the edge into many, often capillary segments.—Fronds *small, annual, separating at a joint above the base of the stipes, at least in the British species.*

WOODSIA *hyperborea;* caudex short, thick, ascending or subrepent, densely rooting, and bearing exceedingly compact, rather flaccid, cæspitose, lanceolate, pinnated fronds, from two to six inches long, which are generally sparingly hirsute and ciliate; pinnæ oval or bluntly triangular, pinnatifid, with about five to seven, obtuse, rounded, nearly entire lobes; sori distinct, three to five upon the lobes; stipites castaneous, glossy, and, as well as the rachis, partially, and costa beneath more or less setaceo-paleaceous.

WOODSIA hyperborea. *Br. Trans. Linn. Soc. v.* 11. *p.* 173. *t.* 11. *Sm. Engl. Fl. v.* 4. *p.* 323. *Hook. and Arn. Brit. Fl. ed.* 8. *p.* 581. *Moore, Handb. of Brit. Ferns, ed.* 2. *p.* 68.

POLYPODIUM hyperboreum. *Sm. Syn. Fil. p.* 39. *Willd. Sp. Pl. v.* 5. *p.* 197. *Engl. Bot. t.* 2023.

POLYPODIUM Arvonicum. *Sm. Fl. Brit. p.* 1115.

POLYPODIUM Ilvense. *With. Bot. p.* 774.

ACROSTICHUM alpinum. *Bolton, Fil. Brit. p.* 76. *t.* 42.

CETERACH alpinum. *De Cand. Fl. Fr. ed.* 2. *p.* 567.

WOODSIA alpina. *Gray, Brit. Pl. v.* 2. *p.* 17. *Moore, Brit. Ferns, Nat. Print. t.* 47 *B.*

WOODSIA Ilvensis (including W. hyperborea). *Benth. Handb. of the Brit. Fl. p.* 637. *Bab. Man. of Brit. Bot. ed.* 4. *p.* 420 (β and γ).

Hab. Alpine exposed rocks, chiefly in the Perthshire and Breadalbane mountains, at an elevation of two to three thousand feet above the sea-level. Mountains of Carnarvonshire.

This rare northern Fern does not appear to have been found anywhere in Britain except in the counties above given, and even elsewhere seems to be of much less common occurrence than the following species, *Woodsia Ilvensis.* Our Continental specimens are from Sweden, Lapland, and Norway (in the latter country Mr. Backhouse finds a narrow perfectly glabrous form, quite corresponding with *Woodsia glabella* of Arctic America), from the Sudetian and Carinthian Alps, from Switzerland, from the Spanish Pyrenees, on the Col de l'Hôpital de Viella, *Bourgeau*; in northern Asia, Ircut; Punjaub, on "rocks on the summit of the Rotang Pass," Kulu (*Edgeworth*); in British North America, Norway House (*Sir J. Richardson*); in the Rocky Mountains (*Drummond*); westward, on the Dalles of the Columbia River, *Major Kaines*, United States Army (communicated by *D. C. Eaton, Esq.*), but this almost passes into *W. glabella* (Asa Gray gives "Rocks, Little Falls, New York; Dr. Vasey," as a station for *W. glabella*, Br.). Dr. Hooker reports it from Port Kennedy; and from Greenland, on the authority of *Dr. Walker*.

Such differences as we may distinguish between this and *Woodsia Ilvensis* we shall give under the latter species. The present is mainly characterized by its tender texture, green colour, more or less hairy, very moderately paleaceous fronds, and the scales almost setaceous and pale-coloured, by the shorter, much less divided pinnæ, and the rounded form of the lobes.

PLATE 7. Fertile specimens of *Woodsia hyperborea*, Br., with narrow and with broader fronds,—*natural size*. Fig. 1. Pinna,—*magnified*. 2. Sorus, with involucre,—*highly magnified*.

PLATE 8.

WOODSIA ILVENSIS, *Br.*

Oblong Woodsia.

WOODSIA *Ilvensis;* caudex short, thick, ascending, subrepent, densely rooting and bearing exceedingly compact, firm and subrigid, cæspitose, lanceolate, pinnated fronds, 2–6 inches long; pinnæ oblong, palenceo-hirsute, deeply pinnatifid or almost again pinnate; segments numerous, oblong or oval-oblong, sinuated at the somewhat reflexed margin; stipites castaneous, glossy, and as well as the rachises (especially when young), clothed with slender, paleaceous, ferruginous, setaceous scales, mixed with broader lanceolate ones with long points; sori marginal, at length confluent.

WOODSIA Ilvensis. *Br. Trans. Linn. Soc. v.* 11. *p.* 173. *Sm. Engl. Fl. v.* 4. *p.* 322; *Engl. Bot. Suppl. t.* 2616. *Hook. and Arn. Brit. Fl. ed.* 8. *p.* 582. *Bab. Man. of Brit. Bot. ed.* 4. *p.* 420; *and Benth. Handb. Brit. Fl. p.* 637 (*including* W. hyperborea). *Moore, Brit. Ferns, Nat. Print. t.* 47. *Asa Gray, Bot. N. U. St. p.* 669.

ACROSTICHUM Ilvense.* *Linn. Sp. Pl. p.* 1528. Bolton, *Fil. Brit. p.* 14. *t.* 9.

POLYPODIUM Ilvense. *Sw. Syn. Fil. p.* 39. *Sch. Fil. t.* 19. *Willd. Sp. Pl. v.* 5. *p.* 198.

NEPHRODIUM rufidulum. *Mich. Fl. Bor. Am. v.* 2. *t.* 269.

LASTREA rufidula. *Pr. Tent. Pterid. p.* 76.

POLYPODIUM Arvonicum. *With. Br. Pl. v.* 2. *p.* 774 (*not Sm.*).

WOODSIA Rajana. *Newm.*

Hab. Elevated mountains in the north of England. First detected near the top of Snowdon by *Dr. Llwyd,* and by *Dr. Richardson* in other parts of Wales Westmoreland, *Mr. Clowes,* and Cumberland, Teesdale, Durham, *Mr. Hailstone.* Breadalbane and Clova Mountains, Scotland.

This species, in Europe at least, generally inhabits the same northern or high alpine regions along with *W. hyperborea,* and, judging by the numerous specimens I have received, it is much more plentiful; by way of Siberia, Songaria, the Amur, and Manchouria, extending to the northern islands of Japan, Hakodadi (*Wilford*); indeed our finest specimens are from this latter country. In North America, although it attains a very high

---

* *Ilva,* from whence this name is derived, is the classical name for the island of Elba, so named, Sir Jas. Smith correctly observes, because Linnæus believed this Fern to be the same as one figured by old Dalechamp, in an execrable figure, named "Lonchitis aspera Ilvensis," with which indeed our plant has little affinity. Use has rendered the name familiar to us; and sanctioned as it further is by the authority of Linnæus, so incorrect a name has never been attempted to be altered by any succeeding author.

latitude, Fiskaerness in Greenland (*Dr. Sutherland*); it continues south as far as New York and Wisconsin, and is stated by Dr. Asa Gray to be frequent in exposed rocks in the middle United States, far from any mountains, and further south to the Alleghanies, but there in the mountains (*Chapman*).

In general, with well-developed specimens, there is no difficulty in distinguishing this species from *W. hyperborea;* it is more erect, more firm and rigid, much more paleaceous, and the scales, more or less broad, are ferruginous and often so copious as to give a reddish tinge to the whole frond, whence Michaux's appropriate name, *Nephrodium rufidulum;* the pinnæ are more elongated, more deeply pinnatifid (so as to be almost again pinnate) with much narrower and more oblong segments. Still I have many specimens so intermediate that myself and others have found it difficult to pronounce satisfactorily upon them. I have wavered in my opinion as to their distinctness; but my late examinations incline me to lean to their validity. Our figure well represents perfect specimens of the two.

PLATE 8. *Woodsia Ilvensis*, Br., fertile specimens,—*nat. size.* Fig. 1. Segment of a pinna, with the scaly portion of the rachis, and with sori,—*magnified.* 2. Involucre and portion of a sorus,—*more magnified.*

W. Fitch del et lith.

PLATE 9.

ASPIDIUM (§ POLYSTICHUM) LONCHITIS, *Sw.*

Alpine Shield-Fern, or Holly-Fern.

*Gen. Char.** *Sori* dorsal, subglobose. *Involucre* orbicular, peltate (fixed by the centre). *Veins* simple or forked, in all the British species.

Obs. Of the genus *Aspidium*, as here defined, we have, in Britain, only one subgenus or division, which corresponds with the genus *Polystichum*, Presl; a very natural group upon the whole, distinguished by the free venation and a peculiarly firm and rigid habit, generally having spinulose teeth to the margins of the pinnules of the pinnate or more compound fronds. I fear we cannot reckon on more than two species, natives of Great Britain.

ASPIDIUM (Polystichum) *Lonchitis*, Sw.; caudex stout, oblique, densely paleaceous, as are the usually short stipites and base of the rachis, with very large, ovato-lanceolate, ferruginous scales; fronds 6–18 inches long, densely tufted, erect, rigid, lanceolate, pinnated; pinnæ numerous, approximate, from a broad, nearly sessile, obliquely cuneated base, ovate or lanceolate, falcate, very acute, spinuloso-serrate, the superior base truncated and auriculate; sori confined to the upper half of the frond, in two or more series upon the pinnæ.

ASPIDIUM Lonchitis. *Sw. Syn. Fil. p.* 43. *Willd. Sp. Pl. v.* 5. *p.* 224. *Sm. Fl. Brit. p.* 1118. *Engl. Fl. v.* 4. *p.* 284. *Schk. Fil. p.* 29. *f.* 29. *Hook. and Arn. Brit. Fl. ed.* 8. *p.* 582.

POLYPODIUM Lonchitis. *Linn. Sp. Pl. p.* 1548. *Engl. Bot. t.* 796. *Bolt. Brit. Ferns, p.* 34. *t.* 19.

POLYSTICHUM Lonchitis. *Roth, Germ. v.* 3. *p.* 71. *Bab. Man. of Brit. Bot. p.* 411. *Presl, Tent. Pterid. p.* 82. *Asa Gray, Man. of Bot. of the U. States, p.* 632. *Moore's Brit. Ferns, Nat. Print. t.* 9.

Hab. Patterdale, Ulleswater (*Rev. W. H. Hawker*). Lofty mountains, clefts,

---

* The subject of the limits of the genera of Ferns is notoriously one of great difficulty; and while one party is disposed to consider every diversity of structure, whether in the fructification, or venation, or the composition of the frond, singly or in combination, as constituting generic distinctions, others, seeing the manifest inconvenience arising from such a course, in the immense multiplication of the genera (186, according to Mr. Moore's 'Index Filicum'), are disposed to go to the opposite extreme, and to return as much as possible to the Linnæan and Swartzian system of deriving the generic characters *mainly* from the fructification. This appears to me a good rule, if exercised with judgment, and with certain modifications. Thus the extensive Swartzian genus *Aspidium* is conveniently divided into *Aspidium*, Br. (*verum*), "involucres orbicular and peltate;" and *Nephrodium*, Mich., Br., "involucres reniform, attached by the sinus, and these again divided and subdivided, according to venation, etc., into subgenera." It is true these characters are sometimes difficult to be distinguished, but where are unexceptionable characters among Ferns to be found?

rocks, and among loose stones, in the north of England, Yorkshire and Wales; much more abundant in Scotland, especially in the Breadalbane and Clova districts; rare in Ireland.

It would be a comparatively easy task to describe the Ferns if all were as distinct and well marked as the present species. It belongs indeed to a small section of the *Polystichum* group, which has simply pinnated fronds, and is the smallest species of that group, with the shortest pinnæ. It has probably an extensive range in the northern hemisphere, from Greenland (Disco, *Dr. Lyall*) in the north, south throughout Europe, to Switzerland, Spain and Portugal, and Italy, Greece (Mount Olympus, *Aucher-Eloi*). Eastward we possess it from Davuria (*Turczaninow*), and we have a well-marked specimen from the Paris Museum, gathered by Jacquemont in north-western India, among woods of Birch, "a Castres ad cacumina quæ Pye Pundo." In British North America it was gathered in the Rocky Mountains by *Drummond*, where it is apparently rare; and in the United States, Michigan, "probably in cold woods, near the northern lakes," is the only locality recorded by Dr. Asa Gray.

PLATE 9. *Aspidium* (Polystichum) *Lonchitis*, Sw., fertile plant,—*natural size*. Fig. 1. Pinna, with sori,—*magnified*. 2. Sorus, with involucre,—*more highly magnified*.

Plate 10.

ASPIDIUM (Polystichum) aculeatum, *L.*

Prickly Shield-Fern.

Var. a. LOBATUM.

Aspidium (Polystichum) *aculeatum;* caudex short, erect, stout, knotted, densely paleaceous with rusty-coloured ferruginous scales, often half an inch and more long, ovate, with finely acuminated points, and these extend up the stipes for some way, and gradually on the rachises and under sides of the costæ become smaller and subulate; stipites short, stout; fronds one to two feet and more long, oblong-lanceolate, acuminate, bipinnate, rigid coriaceous; primary pinnæ approximate from a broadish subpetiolated base, very acuminate, subfalcate; pinnules close, ovate, spinulose-acuminate, free and subpetiolulate, or more or less decurrent and united to the adjacent ones, the margins sharply and strongly spinulosely or setosely serrated, the superior basal one generally larger than the rest and more or less auricled; veinlets once or twice forked; sori in two rows, nearer the costa than the margin.

Polypodium aculeatum. *Linn. Sp. Pl. p.* 1552.
Aspidium aculeatum. *Benth. Handb. Brit. Flora, p.* 628.
Aspidium lobatum. *Metten. Aspid. p.* 48.
Var. a. *lobatum;* pinnules very rigid, sessile, decurrent, and more or less confluent at the base, superior basal pinnule the longest, and that pinnule chiefly auricled. (Our Plate 10.)
Aspidium lobatum. *Sw. in Schrad. Journ.* 1800. *v.* 2. *p.* 37.
Var. β. *intermedium;* less coriaceous, pinnules subpetiolulate, with spinulose points to the serratures. (See Plate 11.)
Aspidium aculeatum. *Sw. in Schrad. Journ.* 1800. *v.* 2. *p.* 37.
Var. γ. *angulare;* submembranaceous, pinnules small, petiolulate, lax, teeth of the serratures large, long bristle-pointed rather than spinulose. (See Plate 12.)
Aspidium angulare. *Willd. Sp. Pl. v.* 5. *p.* 257.
Hab. (*Var. β.* lobatum.) Abundant in England, Scotland, and Ireland, in shady banks and lanes.

Linnæus is the original authority for the *Polypodium* (now *Aspidium*) *aculeatum*, "native of Europe," a plant now well known to scientific botanists, under modified forms and often under very different names, to be an inhabitant of almost every part of the globe. Our present object, however, is only with British forms or conditions of the species, and the majority of the botanists of our country have preserved three forms as specifically distinct, viz. *A. aculeatum*, *A. lobatum*, and *A. angulare*. The most laborious of our pteridologists, Mr. Moore, in his 'British Ferns, Nature-printed,' maintains two, namely, *A. aculeatum* and *A. angulare*; making, however, five varieties of the former (*A. lobatum*) and no less than seventeen of the latter (*A. angulare*). His concluding remarks, however, in the last edition of his 'Handbook of British Ferns,' throws great doubt on the propriety of keeping the latter distinct, where, after enumerating its localities in different parts of the world, in Europe, Asia, Africa, and America, he observes that " the tropical forms render it almost impossible to distinguish *angulare* from *aculeatum*, though the British forms of these plants appear sufficiently distinct." In the correctness of this last sentence I cannot at all agree. My own herbarium, of British samples alone, exhibits all intermediate grades between the two; and it is shown by Mr. Moore that Asa Gray, Fée, Kunze, Sir James Smith, Braun, and Hudson have called *angulare* by the name of *aculeatum*. The able and accurate Mettenius unites all the three, but under the name of *A. lobatum*. Mr. Bentham unites them more properly under the more appropriate and older name of *aculeatum*.

Of the three usually accepted species, the opposite extremes are doubtless what have been called *A. lobatum* and *A. angulare*. The former, now under consideration, is chiefly characterized by the more coriaceous frond, and the pinnules being decurrent at the base. Numerous synonyms might be added to the few above given, but we prefer giving those only that can be pretty safely identified, by means of authentic specimens or figures, as belonging to the respective forms. Others must determine how far they think our views here expressed are correct. Each form will be represented in this number.

PLATE 10. Fig. 1, 2. Frond of *Aspidium* (Polystichum) *aculeatum*, L., var. *lobatum*,—*nat. size*. 3. Fertile pinnule, seen from beneath,—*magnified*. 4. Portion of a pinnule, with a single sorus,—*more magnified*.

PLATE 11.

ASPIDIUM (POLYSTICHUM) ACULEATUM, *L.*

Prickly Shield-Fern.

Var. β. INTERMEDIUM.

ASPIDIUM (Polystichum) *aculeatum;* caudex short, erect, stout, knotted, densely paleaceous with rusty-coloured ferruginous scales often half an inch and more long, ovate, with finely acuminated points, and these extend up the stipes for some way, and gradually on the rachises and under sides of the costæ become smaller and subulate; stipites short, stout; fronds one to two feet and more long, oblong-lanceolate, acuminate, bipinnate, rigid coriaceous; primary pinnæ approximate from a broadish subpetiolated base, very acuminate, subfalcate; pinnules close, ovate, spinuloso-acuminate, free and subpetiolulate, or more or less decurrent and united to the adjacent ones, the margins sharply and strongly spinulosely or setosely serrated, the superior basal ones generally larger than the rest, and more or less auricled; veinlets once or twice forked; sori in two rows, nearer the costa than the margin.

Var. *β. intermedium;* frond rigid, submembranaceous, pinnules distant, subsessile, several of the lower ones auricled, serratures spinulose. (Our PLATE 11.)

ASPIDIUM aculeatum. *Sw. Syn. in Schrad. Journ.* 1800. *v.* 2. *p.* 37. *Willd. Sp. Pl. v.* 5. *p.* 258. *Sm. Fl. Brit. p.* 1122. *Engl. Fl. v.* 4. *p.* 277. *Engl. Bot. t.* 1562. *Hook. and Arn. Brit. Fl. ed.* 8. *p.* 582.

POLYPODIUM aculeatum. *Huds. Angl. p.* 459.

POLYSTICHUM aculeatum. *Roth, Fl. Germ. v.* 3. *p.* 79. *Moore, Brit. Ferns, Nat. Print. t.* 10.

HAB. (*Var. β.* intermedium.) Equally common in Great Britain with the preceding form of *A. aculeatum,* var. *lobatum,* given in our last Plate, and inhabiting similar localities.

Although this is by many thought more closely united to the var. *lobatum* than to var. *angulare,* so much so that some who unite it with *A. lobatum* keep *angulare* distinct, yet it is more difficult to express the difference in words from the latter. *Lobatum* has the pinnules mostly sessile, and decurrent with the pinnule next below, so that when the plant is held up between the eye and the light, the pinnæ are seen to be rather pinnatifid than pinnate. In our present plant, in the same point of view, the pinnules are seen to be subpetiolulate, or at most sessile. Its distinction from *angulare* depends mainly on the larger size of the pinnules and on the presence of auricles on more than one of the inferior pinnules.

PLATE 11. Fig. 1, 2. Frond of *Aspidium* (Polystichum) *aculeatum,* var. *β, intermedium:—natural size.* 3. Pinnule, with a small portion of the rachis. 4. Single sorus:—*more magnified.*

PLATE 12.

ASPIDIUM (POLYSTICHUM) ACULEATUM, *L.*

Prickly Shield-Fern.

Var. γ. ANGULARE.

ASPIDIUM (Polystichum) *aculeatum* ; caudex short, erect, stout, knotted, densely paleaceous with rusty-coloured ferruginous scales often half an inch and more long, ovate, with finely acuminated points, and these extend up the stipes for some way, and gradually on the rachises and under sides of the costæ become smaller and subulate ; stipites short, stout ; fronds one to two feet and more long, oblong-lanceolate, acuminate, bipinnate, rigid coriaceous ; primary pinnæ approximate from a broadish subpetiolated base, very acuminate, subfalcate ; pinnules close, ovate, spinulose-acuminate, free and subpetiolulate or more or less decurrent and united to the adjacent ones, the margins sharply and strongly spinulosely or setosely serrated, the superior basal ones generally larger than the rest, and more or less auricled ; veinlets once or twice forked ; sori in two rows, nearer the costa than the margin.

Var. γ. *angulare* ; more membranaceous, and stipes and rachises more chaffy, pinnules small, orbicular-rhomboid, mostly auriculate, the deep serratures setiferous rather than spinulose. (Our PLATE 12.)

ASPIDIUM angulare. *Willd. Sp. Pl. v. 5. p.* 257. *Smith, Engl. Fl. v.* 4. *p.* 278. *Eng. Bot. Suppl. t.* 276. *Hook. and Arn. Brit. Fl. ed.* 8, *p.* 583.

ASPIDIUM aculeatum, β. *Sm. Fl. Brit. p.* 1122.

POLYSTICHUM angulare. *Presl, Tent. Pterid. p.* 83. *Moore, Brit. Ferns, Nat. Print. t.* 11 *and* 12.

ASPIDIUM aculeatum, *b.* angulare. *Braun. Mett. Fil. Hort. Lips. p.* 88 ; *Aspid. p.* 48.

Hab. (Var. γ. angulare.) Common in the south and middle of England, on shady banks and in moist woods, said to be more rare in the north and in Scotland and Ireland. But it has been so often looked upon as a form of *aculeatum*, that it has probably been passed by as such.

Although *Aspidium angulare* was published as a Hungarian plant by Willdenow more than half a century ago, it was not till the appearance of the last volume of the 'English Flora,' in 1828, that it was recognized as a British plant. It was then that Sir James Smith judged, from Willdenow's description, that his own *A. aculeatum* β of Fl. Brit. p. 1122, must be the same. This has been generally assented to, and it has kept its place as a distinct species in our Flora almost ever since. Sir James Smith's remarks on the plant are most excellent :—"It is

softer and more delicate in texture, as well as more shaggy, than
A. aculeatum. The leaflets are smaller, more numerous, blunter,
and rounded at the extremity, though with a soft" (and *long*, he
might have added) "bristly point, and each of them, even the
smallest, has a broad conspicuous lobe at the base of the upper
margin; the lowest of all at the upper edge of each main leaf,
is half as long again as its next neighbour, more strongly serrated, and in its lower part generally *pinnatifid.* All the lobes
and serratures end in long bristly points. Stalk and principal
rib densely covered with scales, which are narrower in proportion as they are higher up, those on the partial ribs or on the
leaflets being almost capillary. The outline of the whole frond
is rather broader than *A. aculeatum*, and the more copious, distinct, rounded, auricled leaflets give the whole a rich and elegant
aspect."

The above description, excellent as it is, is but one of the
seventeen forms described by Moore. Mr. Moore's var. *proli-
ferum* (Brit. Ferns, Nature-printed, t. 13 C.) could not be recognized by it. It has the pinnules quite narrow and elongated,
and so deeply pinnatifid that the frond might almost be said to
be tripinnate. The plant we have figured here, which may be
looked upon as the normal state of *angulare*, does so gradually
pass into our var. *intermedium*, that no clear line of distinction
can possibly be drawn.

PLATE 12. Fig. 1, 2. Frond of *Aspidium* (Polystichum) *aculeatum*, var. γ. *angulare,—nat. size.* 3. Fertile pinnule, seen from beneath,—*magnified.* 4. Single sorus :—*more magnified.*

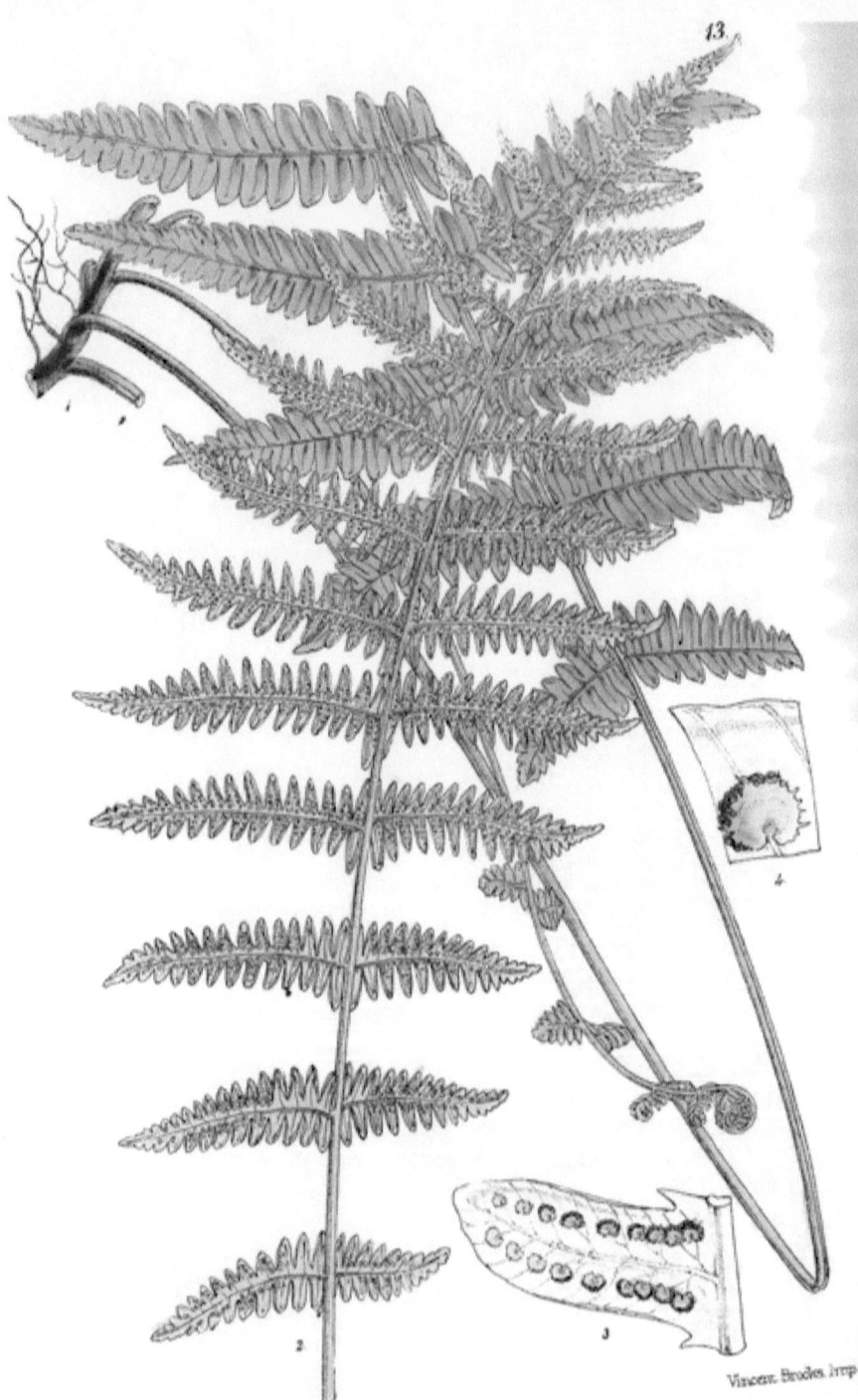

PLATE 13.

NEPHRODIUM (LASTREA) THELYPTERIS, *Desv.*

Marsh Buckler-Fern.

Gen. Char. Sori dorsal, subglobose. *Involucres* reniform or cordate, fixed by the sinus. *Veins* free, simple or forked in all the British species.

Obs.—It will be here seen, as well from a note under Plate 9 as from the above character, that I adopt the views of Robert Brown and Desvaux in regard to the genera *Aspidium* and *Nephrodium*, making the chief character to depend upon the shape of the involucre, *orbicular* and *peltate* in *Aspidium* (from ασπις, ιδος, *a round shield;* see our Plates 9, 10, 11, and 12); *reniform* or *cordate* in *Nephrodium* (from νεφρος, *a kidney*), as in the present and species that follow. Of this genus we have only one group natives of our country, having the veins free (not anastomosing), corresponding with *Lastrea* of Presl.

NEPHRODIUM (Lastrea) *Thelypteris;* caudex long, creeping, branched, black, scarcely scaly; stipites distant, very long; fronds oblong-lanceolate, scarcely tapering at the base, one to two to three feet long, membranaceous, pinnated; pinnæ sessile, horizontal, from a broad base oblong or linear-oblong, tapering towards the rather obtuse apex, deeply (almost to the rachis) pinnatifid; segments ovato-oblong, moderately acute, the margins in the old fertile plants more or less revolute, glabrous, or with a few white, spreading hairs on the costa and veins beneath; veins rather distant, very generally once or twice forked; sori between the costa and the margin; involucres cordato-reniform, rather small, membranaceous, more or less glandulosely toothed at the margin.

NEPHRODIUM Thelypteris. *Desv. Mém. Soc. Linn. v.* 6. *p.* 257.
ASPIDIUM Thelypteris. *Sw. in Schrad. Journ.* 1803, *v.* 2. *p.* 280; *Syn. Fil. p.* 57. *Willd. Sp. Pl. v.* 5. *p.* 249. *Schk. Fil. p.* 51. *t.* 52. *Sm. Engl. Bot. t.* 400; *Engl. Fl. v.* 4. *p.* 272. *Metten. Fil. Hort. Lips. p.* 92; *Aspid. p.* 112. *Hook. and Arn. Brit. Fl. ed.* 8. *p.* 583.
LASTREA Thelypteris. *Pr. Tent. Pterid. p.* 76. *Hook. Gen. Fil. t.* 45 A 2. *Moore, Brit. Ferns, Nat. Print. t.* 29.
DRYOPTERIS Thelypteris. *Asa Gray, Bot. of the N. U. St. p.* 630.
HEMESTHEUM. *Newm.*
POLYSTICHUM. *Roth.*
THELYPTERIS palustris. *Schott.*

(In the southern hemisphere, at the Cape of Good Hope and in New Zealand, is a remarkable state of this plant, with very conspicuous, nearly orbicular, membranaceous scales on the rachis of the pinnæ, at the insertion of the costule of the segments. This is *Aspid. squamulosum*, Klfs.; *A. Thelypteris*, β *squamosum*, Schlecht. Fil. Cap. p. 23. t. 11; *A. Thelypteris*, Pappe and Rawson; and *Nephrodium squamulosum*, Hook. fil. Fl. N. Zeal. v. 2. p. 39; and according to Ecklon, *Aspid. rivulorum*, Thunb.)

Hab. Marshy and boggy places in various parts of England and Ireland; rare in Scotland, where it is said to be peculiar to Forfarshire; Bog of Restenet, *Croall, in Herb. Nostr.*

This is one of the most easily recognized of all our British Aspidiaceous Ferns, especially if the very long, black, creeping and branching caudex be observed, and the very black base of the stipes, and then the general configuration of the frond and pinnæ and segments; but I have not been able satisfactorily to make up my mind as to distinctness from the *Aspidium Noveboracense* of Swartz (*Nephrodium thelypteroides*, Mich.), of North America. The caudex, the shape of the frond, and form of pinnæ and segments, differ in no respect. The main differences recorded by the American botanists are:—1. The different outline of the frond; in *A. Noveboracense* "tapering below, from the lower pinnæ (two to several pairs) being gradually shorter and deflexed; the lobes flat. 2. The veins all simple, except in the lowest pairs. 3. Fruit-dots never confluent, near the margin." Now various specimens exhibit no difference in the outline of the frond, nor in the deflexion of the pinnæ; the lobes are only flat in the young state, but certainly they have recurved margins in age, when also the fruit-dots become confluent, exactly as in *Thelypteris*. I do however find the veins almost universally simple, and very straight, or with a slight curvature (never flexuose); the sori are perhaps generally nearer the margin than in *A. Thelypteris*, but a little variable in both; it is moreover common for the fronds to be hairy, especially beneath, with white, spreading hairs (which occur but rarely in *Thelypteris*), and even the involucres are villous. I ought therefore not to have said, as I have done in the Flora Bor. Am. v. 2. p. 110, that the two are *quite* identical.

Both *N. Noveboracense* and *N. Thelypteris* inhabit North America, from the extreme south, New Orleans and Florida, to Canada (*Drummond, Chapman, Cleghorn*) in the north.

N. Thelypteris is also found by Bourgeau at Lake Winipeg, in the Hudson's Bay Territories, but I am not sure it has been detected further west in that latitude. It is common throughout Europe, in Germany and Sweden, Songaria; in Asia we have the ordinary form from Khasya, *Dr. Hooker* (n. 246*); from Kashmir, *Jacquemont*, n. 35; from Manchouria, *Wilford;* from the Amur, at Usuri, *Maximovicz;* and I have already alluded to the squamulose form at the Cape and in New Zealand. All these have the exact venation of *N. Thelypteris*.

PLATE 13. Fig. 1. Portion of a caudex, a stipes, and lower portion of a frond of *Nephrodium* (Lastrea) *Thelypteris*, Desv. 2. Fertile frond:—*natural size*. 3. Segment of a fertile pinna, showing the venation and sori. 4. Single sorus :—*more or less magnified*.

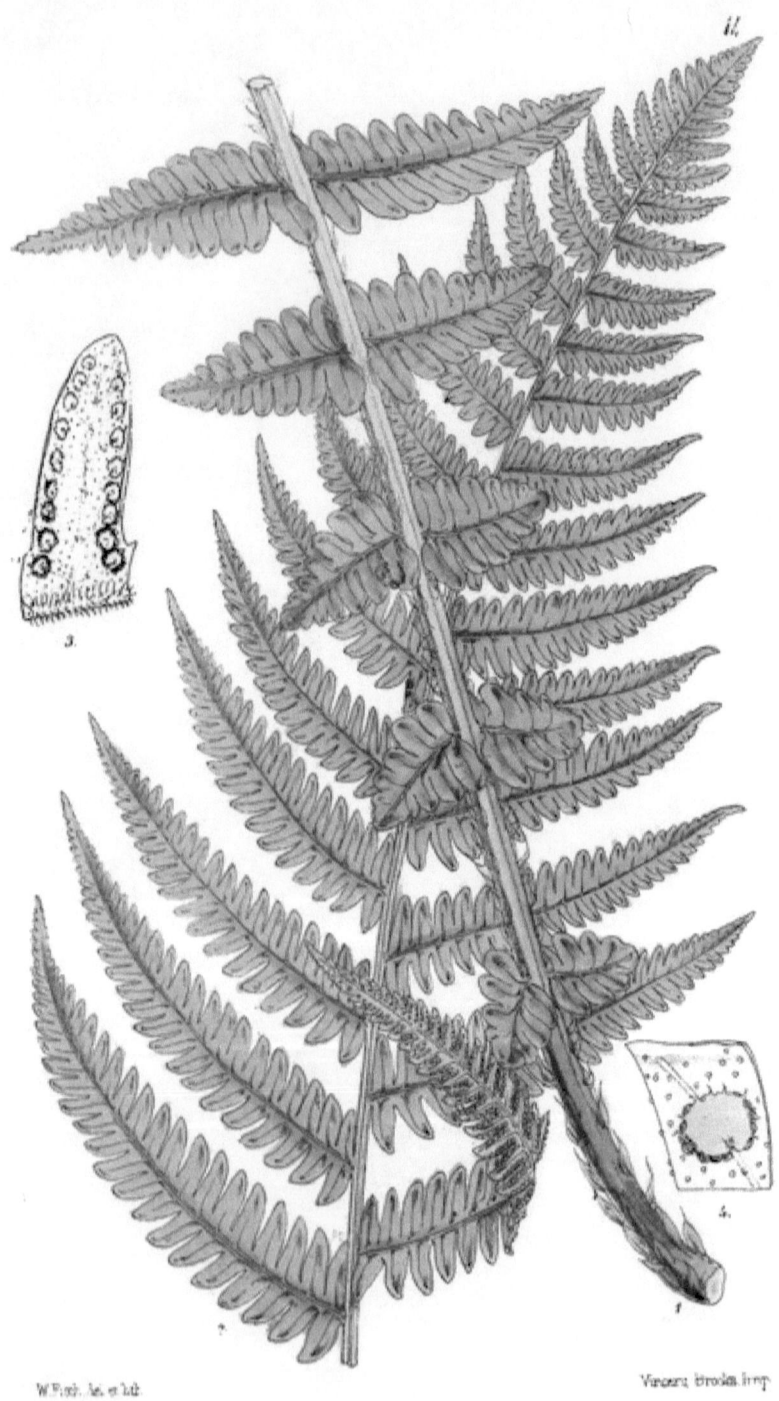

W. Fitch del. et lith.　　　　　　　　　　　　Vincent Brooks Imp.

PLATE 14.

NEPHRODIUM (LASTREA) OREOPTERIS, *Desv.*

Mountain Buckler-Fern.

NEPHRODIUM (Lastrea) *Oreopteris;* caudex short, erect or decumbent, copiously scaly; stipites short, tufted, scaly below; fronds 1½-2 feet long, firm-membranaceous, broad-lanceolate, gradually tapering and attenuated below, glandular; pinnæ two to three inches long, patent, sessile, from a broad base lanceolato-acuminate, deeply (more than halfway down) pinnatifid, from near the middle of the frond gradually becoming shorter downward, more distant and deltoid, the lowest less than an inch long; segments plane, nearly entire, oblong, very obtuse; veins simple or forked; sori quite marginal; involucres very delicate, membranaceous, more or less toothed at the margin, soon obsolete; rachis often subulato-squamose; costæ pubescent.

NEPHRODIUM Oreopteris. *Desv. Mém. Soc. Linn. v.* 6, *p.* 588.

ASPIDIUM Oreopteris. *Sw. in Schrad. Journ.* 1803, *v.* 2, *p.* 279; *Syn. Fil. p.* 50. *Willd. Sp. Pl. p.* 247. *Schk. Fil. p.* 37. *t.* 35, 36. *Sm. Engl. Fl. v.* 4. *p.* 273. *Hook. and Arn. Brit. Fl. ed.* 8. *p.* 583. *Metten. Fil. Hort. Lips. p.* 92. *Aspid. p.* 111.

LASTREA Oreopteris. *Pr. Tent. Pterid. p.* 76. *Moore, Brit. Ferns, Nat. Print. t.* 28.

POLYPODIUM Oreopteris. *Ehrh. Smith, E. Bot. t.* 1019.

POLYSTICHUM. *De Cand.*—Polyst. montanum, *Roth.*

HEMESTHEUM montanum. *Newm.*

POLYPODIUM Thelypteris. *Huds. Bolt. Brit. Ferns, p.* 40. *t.* 22.

HAB. Frequent in exposed situations in hilly and mountain regions, in England, Scotland, and Ireland; yielding a balsamic fragrance when handled, from the copious glands of the frond.

This well-marked species is common on the continent of Europe as far north as Norway. It appears in the middle of Russia, Lithuania, Volhynia, Moscow; and we have specimens from as far south as Asturias in Spain, *Durieu, in Herb. Nostr.* As this is marked from "Pico de Arras and Pico de Tozaque," it is, I have no doubt, the locality alluded to by Mr. Moore, when he says, "We have a memorandum of its occurrence at Pico, —one of the Azorean islands being probably intended." The North American specimen in the Hookerian herbarium, also mentioned by Mr. Moore, is there marked from "Herb. Turner," and bears no stamp of authority whatever, and, being incorrectly named *Aspid. marginale,* was on that account probably *believed* to have been American.

PLATE 14. Fig. 1, 2. *Nephrodium* (Lastrea) *Oreopteris,* DESV.,—*natural size.* 3. Fertile segment of a pinna,—*magnified.* 4. Sorus,—*more magnified.*

Plate 15.

NEPHRODIUM (Lastrea) Filix-mas, *Rich.*

Male Buckler-Fern.

Nephrodium (Lastrea) *Filix-mas:* caudex short, stout, erect, densely paleaceous with ovato-lanceolate, finely acuminated, generally tawny scales; stipites tufted, scaly; fronds 1½ to two and three feet or more long, broadly oblong-lanceolate, acuminate, firm-membranaceous, subbipinnate, approximate, from a broad sessile base oblong-lanceolate, acuminate, deeply (nearly to the rachis) pinnatifid, or more or less, especially the inferior ones, again pinnate; segments or pinnules oblong-obtuse, sometimes forming a parallelogram, crenato-serrate towards the apex, or sometimes inciso-serrate; veins simple or forked; sori few on each segment, arranged in two series between the costa and the margin; involucres convex, firm, orbiculari-reniform, with a deep sinus, quite smooth; rachises more or less setaceo-paleaceous.

Nephrodium Filix-mas. *Rich. Desv. Mem. Soc. Linn. v.* 6. *p.* 260. *Hook. Fil. Exot. t.* 98.

Aspidium Filix-mas. *Sw. Syn. Fil. p.* 55. *Schk. Fil. p.* 45. *t.* 44. *Willd. Sp. Pl.* 5. *p.* 259. *Sm. Engl. Bot. t.* 1458 *and t.* 1949 (*Asp. cristatum.*) *Engl. Flora, v.* 4. *p.* 275. *Hook. and Arn. Brit. Fl. ed. v.* 8. *p.* 584.

Lastrea Filix-mas. *Pr. Tent. Pterid. p.* 76. *Moore, Brit. Ferns, Nat. Print. t.* 14, 15, 16, 17.

Polypodium Filix-mas. *Linn. Sp. Pl. p.* 1551. *Bolton, Brit. Ferns. p.* 44. *t.* 24.

Polystichum. *Roth. De Cand.*—Dryopteris, *Schott, Newman.*—Lophodium, *Newm.*

Var. *incisum.* Moore, Metten.; nearly bipinnate; segments or pinnules inciso-serrate (see our Plate 15, f. 3). *Moore, l. c. t.* 15.

Aspidium depastum. *Schk. Fil. p.* 50. *t.* 51.

Var. *paleaceum.* Moore, Metten.; caudex and base of the stipes copiously paleaceous, with very large scales, and generally of rich tawny or almost golden colour. *Moore, l. c. t.* 17.

Aspidium paleaceum. *Don, Prodr. Nep. p.* 4.

Hab. One of the most common of Ferns, and at the same time one of the most beautiful, not only in the shape of the fronds, but in their mode of growth, forming a circle or crown at the summit of the stout, scaly caudex, thus adorning our woods, copses, and hedge-banks in almost every part of England, Scotland, and Ireland; ascending to a great height upon our mountains, and then become very dwarfish.

It is no wonder that a plant of such very common occurrence as this is throughout Europe, growing at such different elevations, in such different soils and exposures, should present variations:

but the importance given to these differences, even of the slightest and most insignificant character, at the present day, is something almost absurd. A *dwarf-growing form* makes one of these varieties; and a *permanently small dwarf* constitutes another. The consequence of such hair-splitting is, that if this small dwarf should happen not to be permanent, it will add another to the list of varieties. I have not thought it needful to particularize more than two British forms, neither of them perhaps of rare occurrence; both of these have been made species by authors, viz. the var. *incisum*, which is the *Aspid. depastum* of Schk., and probably the *Aspidium erosum* of the same author (though that is referred by Mettenius and others to *Nephrod. dilatatum*), and the var. *paleacea*. The type of this latter is Don's *Aspidium paleaceum* of Nepal, common enough in other parts of India and elsewhere; and the main characters depend upon having "truncatedly obtuse pinnules, and stipes and rachis shaggy with long tapering scales, usually of a lustrous golden-brown colour." Now the plant I have figured here, I believe is the British state of this variety, from Braemar (*Mr. Croall*), and the so-called *Dryopteris Borreri* of Mr. Newman (of which he says that "*certainly* many, and possibly *most* of the synonyms cited for *Filix-mas*, belong to this plant"). Indeed, I am disposed to consider it a good representative of the normal or most perfect condition of the species. There is also a remarkable state of our present species which Mr. Moore has called *cristatum*, and of which he has given excellent representations, *l. c. t.* 16. The pinnæ are contracted and proliferous in a crested manner at the apex, and it is much prized in ferneries; but it has more the appearance of a diseased plant than what is ordinarily deemed a variety. A pinna is given at our Fig. 4.

I have not space to enumerate the many exotic localities of what I believe to be specifically identical with this wide-spread Fern, in the tropics as well as in temperate climates, some of which indeed have very marked peculiarities, and have even given rise to two new genera, *Dichasium*, Braun and Fée, and *Artobotrys* of Wallich (see our remarks under *N. Filix-mas*, var. *paleacea*, in Fil. Exot. t. 98).

PLATE 15. Fig. 1, 2. *Nephrodium* (Lastrea) *Filix-mas*, Rich.,—*natural size*. 3. Segment from a fertile pinna, showing the venation and sori,—*magnified*. 4. Single sorus,—*more magnified*. 5. Var. *incisum*, portion of pinna,—*natural size*. 6. Pinna of a peculiar cristate form (a monstrosity),—*natural size*.

Plate 16.

NEPHRODIUM (Lastrea) rigidum, *Desv.*

Rigid Buckler-Fern.

Nephrodium (Lastrea) *rigidum* ; caudex short, stout, erect, densely paleaceous, as are the tufted stipites, which are 4-5 inches long ; fronds a span to nearly a foot in length, oblong-acuminate, obtuse (not tapering) at the base, firm-membranaceous, erect and rigid, glandular beneath (and fragrant) bipinnate ; pinnæ horizontal, lower primary ones remote, the rest approximate, about two inches long, from a broad sessile base, sometimes an inch broad, gradually tapering to a point ; pinnules sessile, subdecurrent, oblong, strongly inciso-serrate, the serratures very sharp, scarcely spinulose, those of the lowest pinnæ pinnatifid (not very deeply), the segments serrated ; veins mostly forked, sori in two rows between the costule and the margin, at length confluent ; involucres exactly reniform, convex, firm, glandular and fringed with glandular hairs ; main rachis chaffy.

Nephrodium rigidum. *Desv. Mém. Soc. Linn. v. 6. p. 261.*
Aspidium rigidum. *Sw. Syn. Fil. p. 53. Schk. Fil. p. 40. t. 38. Willd. Sp. Pl. v. 5. p. 265. Hook. Suppl. Engl. Bot. t. 2724. Hook. and Arn. Fl. ed. 8. p. 585. Metten. Fil. Hort. Lips. p. 93. Aspid. p. 56.*
Lastrea rigida. *Pr. Tent. Pterid. p. 77. Moore, Brit. Ferns, Nat. Print. t. 18.*
Polypodium rigidum, *Hoffm.*—Polystichum rigidum, *De Cand.*—Polystichum strigosum, *Roth.*—Lophodium rigidum, *Newm.*—Polypodium fragrans, *Vill.*

Var. *pallidum* ; fronds generally longer, pale green.

Aspidium pallidum. *Link, Fil. Hort. Berol. p. 107.*
Nephrodium pallidum. *Bory, Fl. de la Péloponn. p. 67. t. 38 (good).*

? Var. *Americanum* ; fronds twice or thrice larger, scarcely at all glandular.

Aspidium argutum. *Kaulf. En. Fil. p. 242. Hook. and Arn. Bot. of Beech. Voy. p. 162.*

Hab. Rare in Britain, said to be confined to limestone districts in Westmoreland, Lancaster, and York, often at considerable elevations above the level of the sea. Ireland, county of Lowth, "on a wall of clay slate," *Mr. Darby.*—I fear forms of *N. dilatatum* have often been mistaken for this. My own herbarium exhibits native specimens from Ingleborough, *Rev. W. T. Bree*, and Whernside, Yorkshire, *Mr. Wilson* (one specimen has the frond twenty inches long). Settle, Yorkshire, at an elevation of 1550 feet above the level of the sea, *Mr. J. Tathom, Jun.* I have specimens marked "Cornwall," but as there is no name of the finder, the locality is probably an error. Yet if we are correct in considering *Nephrodium pallidum*, Bory, a Mediterranean plant, and *N. argutum*, a Californian species, synonymous with these, there is no reason why it should not be found in the south of England, and in much milder regions than our northern hills.

With the two first species of *Nephrodium* described in this work, viz. *N. Thelypteris* and *N. Oreopteris*, there were few critical remarks required : their limits are almost universally acknowledged. It is otherwise with our third species, *N. Filix-mas* (the last described); and, easily as our usual British forms of that are to be recognized, if it had been our duty to have introduced the varied forms of the *exotic* kinds from different parts of Asia, Africa, and America, we should have incurred a great amount of difficulty, happily here avoided or deferred. But we now come to another form of Fern in the *Nephrodium rigidum*, which holds a sort of intermediate place between certain states of *N. Filix-mas*, and what may be called the *dilatatum-* or *spinulosum*-group (which we shall have soon to consider). The present is certainly a rare British plant, and our native specimens have great uniformity with each other and with the Continental specimens, chiefly from the Alps of Switzerland and Savoy. It is indeed said, but *doubtfully*, to be a native of Altaic Siberia (*Ledebour*), and I have *identically* the same from Mount Sypilus, in Asia Minor (*Aucher-Eloi*). All of them, too, correspond exactly with the *Polypodium fragrans* of Villars: these are usually of small size, the stipites rather short and very chaffy; the fronds a span or more high; with a stout rachis which gives a stiff and rigid character; and the pinules are small, and nearly uniform throughout. Mettenius, as far as I know, was the first to unite with it specifically the *Aspid. pallidum*, Link (*Nephrodium*, Bory, whose accurate figure I have quoted above), and some of my specimens of this scarcely differ but in their paler colour, from *N. rigidum*. Those in my herbarium are from Taygetus, in the Morea, *Heldreich*, Asia Minor, *Professor Forbes;* one specimen precisely the usual form, another almost exactly resembling *Nephr.* (Lastrea) *remotum*, Braun; Dalmatia, *Dr. Alexander Prior;* Sicily, *Huet du Pavillon*, and Messina, *Churchill Babington;* Taurian Alps, Cilicia, elevation 4000 feet, *Kotschy* (frond two feet high, pinnules large, more acuminate); and Djebel Yarghouan, *Kralik*, "Plantæ Tunetanæ, n. 343:" there is however one specimen approaching the simple-fronded state of *N. dilatatum*. Mr. Moore, I believe, first referred the Californian *Aspid. argutum*, Kaulf., to the European *rigidum*, and I think correctly so, for though some of our original specimens are much larger, and have rather a different aspect, yet one from Whipple's Exploring Expedition for a railway route through California, sent by Dr. J. M. Bigelow, is quite identical, whilst another from the same source (both marked *Aspid. argutum*) is so large as very much to resemble the var. *incisum* of *Nephr. Filix-mas*. Mr. Moore further brings as a synonym to *N. rigidum*, *Aspid. Boottii*, Tuck., on the authority of Asa Gray, in Bot. of North Am. U. S.;" but in a subsequent edition Dr. Gray pronounces this to have been an error, and I shall have to allude to *Aspid. Boottii* in an early number, when treating of a plant that has created much discussion of late, namely, *Aspid. remotum* of A. Braun.

PLATE 16. Fertile plant of *Nephrodium* (*Lastrea*) *rigidum*, Desv.,—*nat. size*. Fig. 1. Pinnule, with sori,—*magnified*. 2. Single sorus,—*more magnified*.

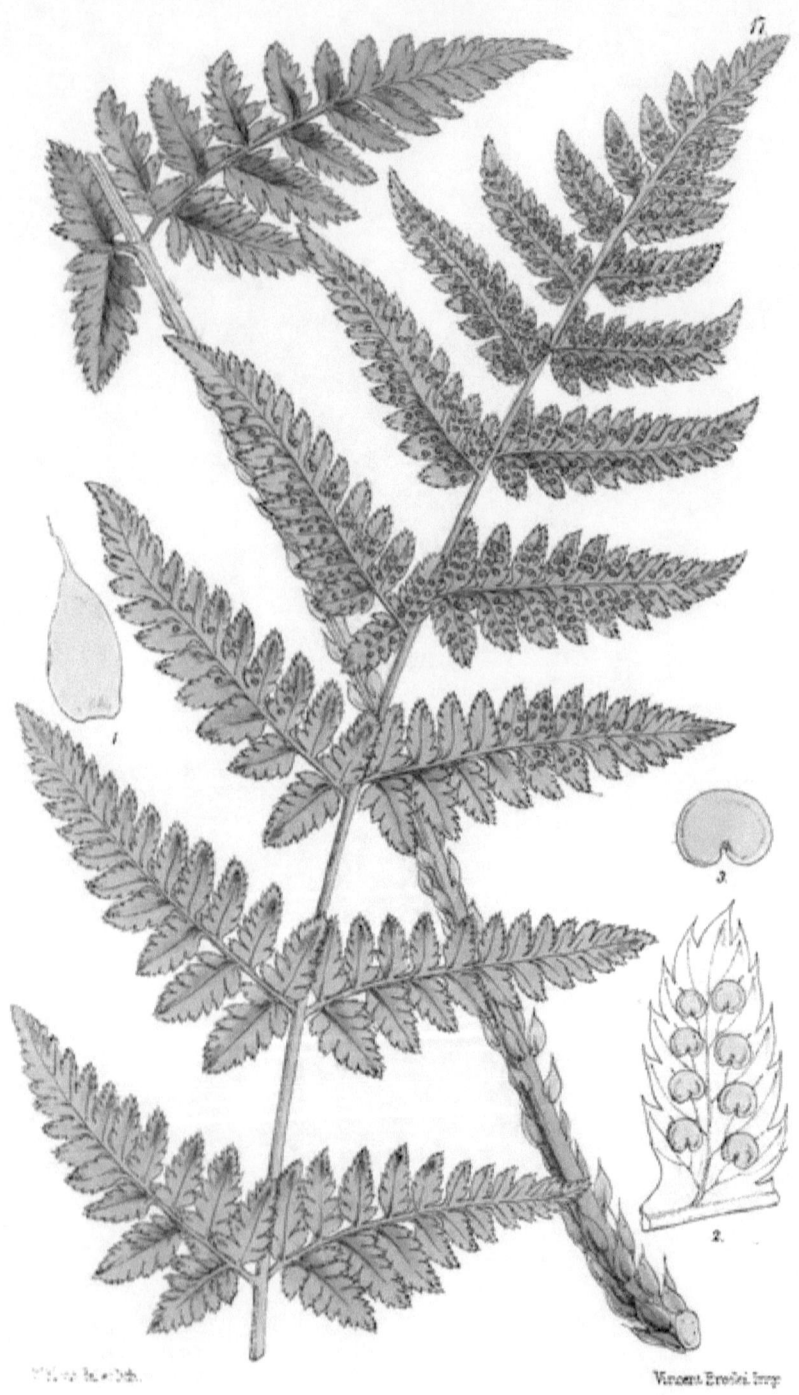

Plate 17.

NEPHRODIUM (Lastrea) cristatum, *Mich.*

Crested Buckler-Fern.

NEPHRODIUM (Lastrea) *cristatum*; caudex short, stout, erect or oblique, densely paleaceous; stipites tufted, stramineous, rather stout, paleaceous with ovate acuminate scales; fronds erect, glabrous, oblong-lanceolate, one to one and a half foot high, pinnate; pinnæ shortly petiolate, from the almost truncated base, oblong, obtusely acuminate, deeply pinnatifid, the lowermost ones distant, deltoideo-acuminate, rarely again pinnate; pinnules or segments of the pinnæ ovate or oblongo-ovate, subspinuloso-serrate; sori chiefly on the upper half of the frond, copious, in two rows upon each segment; involucres slightly convex, the margins entire.

NEPHRODIUM cristatum. *Mich. Fl. Bor. Am. v.* 2. *p.* 269. *Desv. Mém. Soc. Linn. v.* 6. *p.* 260.

POLYPODIUM cristatum. *Linn. Sp. Pl. p.* 1551.

ASPIDIUM cristatum. *Sw. in Schrad. Journ.* 1803, *v.* 2. *p.* 276. *Syn. Fil. p.* 52. *Willd. Sp. Pl. v.* 5. *p.* 253. *Schk. Fil. p.* 39. *t.* 37 (*good*). *Engl. Bot. t.* 2125 (*very indifferent*), not *t.* 1949, *which is probably* Nephrod. F.-mas), *Hook. in Flora Londinensis, ed.* 2. *t.* 113 (*very accurate*). *Metten. Fil. Hort. Lips. p.* 93. *Aspid. p.* 56. *Hook. and Arn. Brit. Fl. ed.* 8. *p.* 585. (*excl.* β *and* γ). *Asa Gray, Manual of Bot. Illustr. p.* 598.

LASTREA cristata. *Presl, Tent. Pterid. p.* 77. *Moore, Brit. Ferns, Nat. Print. pl.* 19 (*scarcely pl.* 20, *and not the right hand figure there*). *Newm. Brit. Ferns, p.* 203.

ASPIDIUM lancastriense. *Sw.*

LOPHODIUM Callipteris. *Newm. Brit. Ferns, ed.* 3. *p.* 169 (*with very accurate reduced figure*) *and* 170.

POLYSTICHUM cristatum. *Roth, Tent. v.* 3. *t.* 84. *Koch, Syn. Fl. Germ. p.* 978.

Hab. Rare in England, in boggy heaths, chiefly in Norfolk, Holt, Lynn, near Burnley Hall, *A. O. Black*; near Norwich; all places whence we possess specimens, as well as from Fritton and Westleton; said also to be found near Ipswich; at Hoxton bogs and Hulwell marshes, Notts; Madely and Newcastle-under-Lyne, Staffordshire; and Wybunbury bog, Cheshire.

I have long been familiar with this plant in its native bogs in Norfolk, and long considered it a truly distinct and well marked species, continental European specimens and specimens from North America quite corresponding with it. Of late years, however, doubts have been expressed as to its distinctness from some forms of the *spinulosum*-group, especially that form which has been called *Lastrea uliginosa*, and at length a still more compound state of *spinulosa*, more resembling the var. *dilatata*, was united with it by Mr. Moore. (See plate 20, the right figure, in his 'British Ferns, Nature-Printed.') To this view I cannot readily subscribe, and I only cautiously assented to such a union in the last (the eighth) edition of 'British Flora.' Immature plants of *L. uliginosa* (especially the middle figure of Mr. Moore, Nat. Print., plate 20), do indeed a good deal resemble our *N. cristatum*; but I still think the perfect condition of this plant is more allied to our *Nephrod. spinulosum* than to *N. cristatum*. It would take more space than we can give to notice the various views of modern authors on the subject of this and the following species of the British *Nephrodia*, and could not be very profitable. Every one must form his own judgment in regard to the limits of the species, which all must acknowledge to vary extremely (less so in regard to the present species) and to be pre-eminently difficult of satisfactory determination.

PLATE 17. Fertile frond and stipes of *Nephrodium* (Lastrea) *cristatum*, Mich.,— *natural size*. Fig. 1. Scale from the stipes. 2. Fertile segment of a pinna. 3. Involucre :—*all more or less magnified*.

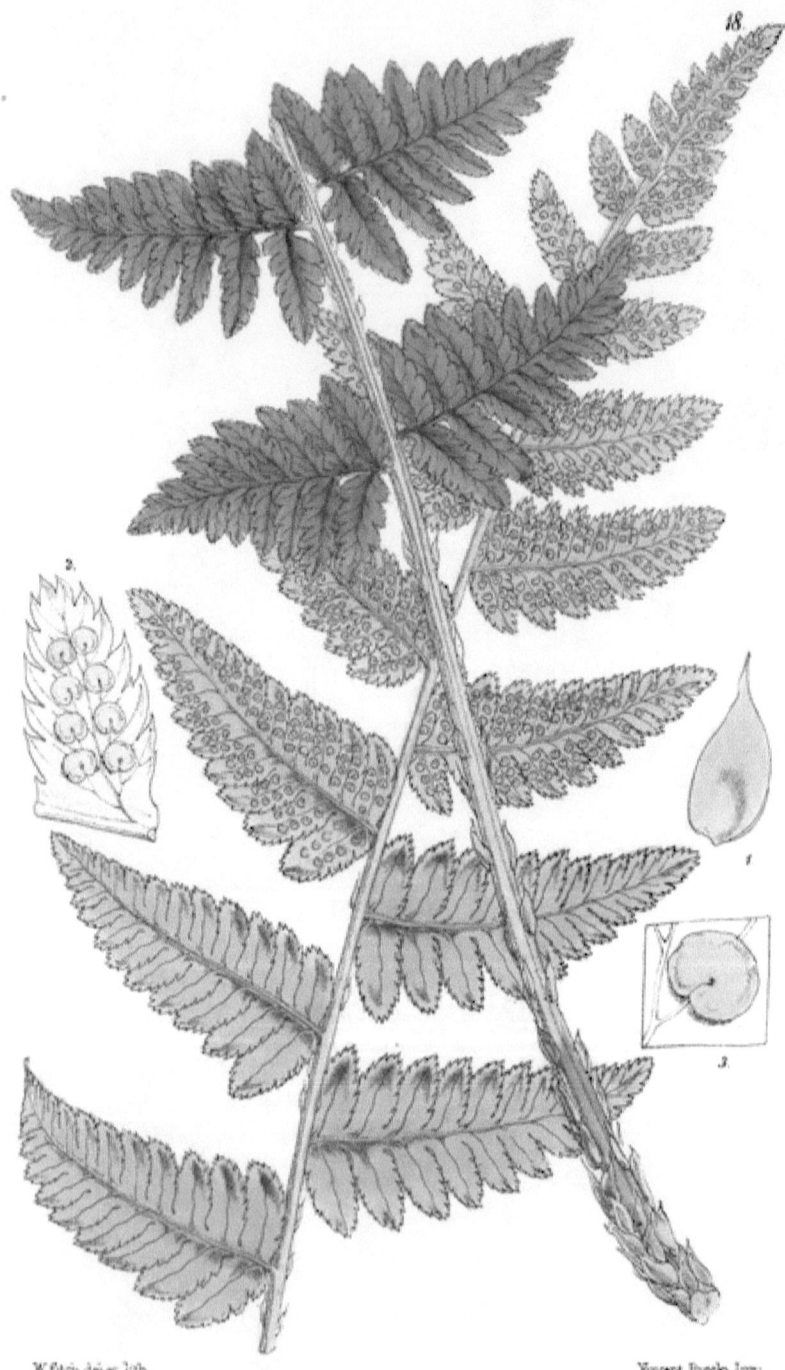

Plate 18.

NEPHRODIUM (Lastrea) spinulosum, *Sw.*,
a. BIPINNATUM.

Prickly Buckler-Fern; bipinnate var.

NEPHRODIUM (Lastrea) *spinulosum*; caudex short, stout, suberect, paleaceous; stipites tufted, stramineous, brown at the base, scaly; fronds ovate or oblong-ovate, one to two feet and more long, bi-tripinnate; primary pinnæ rather distant, upper ones from a broad subtruncate base, oblong, inferior ones ovate, both gradually acuminate, secondary ones and pinnules close-placed, ovate or oblong, sessile, more or less coarsely spinuloso-serrate, or pinnatifido-serrate; sori chiefly on the upper half of the frond, in two rows upon each pinnule, involucres entire or fringed with glandular hairs.

a. *bipinnatum*; scales of the stipes ovato-acuminate, brown, pale towards the margin; fronds glabrous, bipinnate; involucres entire at the margin. (PLATE 18.)

ASPIDIUM spinulosum. *Sw. Syn. Fil. p.* 420. *Schk. Fil. p.* 48. *t.* 48 *b and c: very good. Willd. Sp. Pl. v.* 5. *p.* 252. *Sm. Fl. Brit. p.* 1121; *Engl. Bot. p.* 1460; *Engl. Fl. v.* 4. *p.* 292. *Hook. and Arn. Brit. Fl. ed.* 7. *p.* 586. (*var. a*). *Asa Gray, Manual of Bot. Illustr. p.* 597. *Chapm. Fl. of Southern United States*, p. 595.

LASTREA spinulosa. *Pr. Tent. Pterid. p.* 76. *Moore, Brit. Ferns, Nat. Print. pl.* 21 (*but with no creeping caudex, as in the description*).

LASTREA cristata, γ spinulosa. *Moore, Handb. of Brit. Ferns, p.* 115 (*this is also quoted under* Lastrea cristata *as var.* uliginosa *of it*), *ed.* 3. *p.* 122.

POLYSTICHUM spinosum. *Roth, Fl. Germ. v.* 3. *p.* 91.

LOPHODIUM spinosum. *Newm. in Phytol. v.* 4. *p.* 371. *Brit. Ferns, ed.* 3. *p.* 157.

LOPHODIUM glandulosum *and* uliginosum. *Newm. ?*

Hab. Boggy places and moist heaths in various parts of England; but by some confounded with *N. cristatum*, by others with the var. *dilatatum* of *A. spinulosum*.

Viewing, as I am disposed to do, this and the three following subjects of this work, as varieties of one and the same species, I consider this among the least divided (or compound) forms of them, as its chief distinguishing character. The broader scales of the stipes and paler colour, and the entire absence of fringe to the margin of the involucres, are considered by some as further entitling this plant to specific distinction; but if I am correct in referring Mr. Newman's *Lophodium glandulosum* here, the presence or absence of minute glands is not much to be depended upon: and I possess all kinds of intermediate forms between this and var. *dilatatum*. Our specimen, from which the present figure is taken, is marked in our herbarium "true *Lastrea spinulosa*," by Mr. Moore.

PLATE 18. Fertile frond and stipes of *Nephrodium* (Lastrea) var. *spinulosum*, Hook.,—*natural size*. Fig. 1. Scale from the stipes. 2. Fertile pinnule,—*magnified*. 3. Involucre,—*more magnified*.

Plate 19.

NEPHRODIUM (Lastrea) spinulosum, *Sw.*,
var. DILATATUM.

Prickly Buckler-Fern; broader tripinnate var.

Nephrodium (Lastrea) *spinulosum*; caudex short, stout, suberect, paleaceous; stipites tufted, stramineous, brown at the base, scaly; fronds ovate or oblong-ovate, one to two feet and more long, bi-tripinnate; primary pinnæ rather distant, upper ones from a broad and subtruncated base, oblong, inferior ones ovate, both gradually acuminate, secondary ones and pinnules close-placed, ovate or oblong, sessile, more or less coarsely spinuloso-serrate or pinnatifido-serrate; sori chiefly on the frond, in two rows upon each pinnule; involucres entire or fringed with glandular hairs.

β. *dilatatum*; scales of the stipes ovato-lanceolate, frequently firm, dark-brown, with a pale margin; fronds generally broad-ovate or subdeltoid, tripinnate; involucres often with glandular hairs at the margin. (Plate 19.)

Aspidium dilatatum. *Willd. Sp. Pl. v.* 5. *p.* 263. *Sm. Fl. Brit. p.* 1125; *Engl. Bot. t.* 1461. *Sw. Syn. Fil. Add. p.* 421. *Hook. and Arn. Brit. Fl. ed.* 8. *p.* 586.

Lastrea dilatata. *Pr. Tent. Pterid. p.* 77. *Moore, Brit. Ferns, Nat. Print. pl.* 22–26 *inclusive; Handb. of Brit. Ferns, p.* 124.

Polypodium dilatatum. *Hoffm. Germ. v.* 2. *p.* 7.

Dryopteris dilatata. *Asa Gray, Bot. of N. U. S. p.* 631.

Polypodium cristatum. *Bolt. Fil. v.* 42. *t.* 23.

Aspidium drepanum. *Schk. Fil. p.* 43. *t.* 47.

Aspidium erosum. *Schk. Fil. p.* 46. *t.* 45 (*a very indifferent figure*).

Aspidium spinulosum, *var.* dilatatum. *Hook. and Arn. Brit. Fl. ed.* 7. *p.* 586. *Asa Gray, Manual of Bot. Illust. p.* 597. *Chapm. Flora of Southern U. S. p.* 595.

Aspidium campylopterum. *Kze.*

Lastrea multiflora. *Newm. Brit. Ferns, ed.* 2. *p.* 216.

Polypodium tanacetifolium. *Hoffm. Deutschl. Fl. v.* 2. *p.* 8 (*large and very compound var.*).

Hab. Swampy grounds and marshy places, often in woods; abundant throughout England, Scotland, and Ireland.

It would be vain to attempt to verify, except in few cases, the numerous synonyms that have been supposed by different authors to belong to this species, *Nephr. dilatatum,* or, as we believe it to be, this form of *N. spinulosum.* Those who have a desire to know more of its history may consult the labours of Mr. Moore, in the 'British Ferns, Nature-Printed,' and the varieties he records. After five imperial folio pages devoted to this matter, he is obliged to confess that "besides the varieties already mentioned, which we consider the most distinct and important, there are many other, indeed almost endless, modifications:—the following is a brief summary of the various forms which have come under our observation." These forms are eighteen in number! The plates, too, 22–26 inclusive, may be consulted; which, being Nature's printing, must give a faithful representation of the specimens from which they are taken, but which hardly throw any light on the permanency of the species. With us the plant is a more compound form of *N. spinulosum*.

PLATE 19. Fertile frond, with stipes of *Nephrodium* (Lastrea) *spinulosum*, β *dilatatum*, Hook.,—*natural size*. Fig. 1. Scales from the stipes,—*magnified*. 2. Fertile pinnule. 3. Involucre :—*more magnified*.

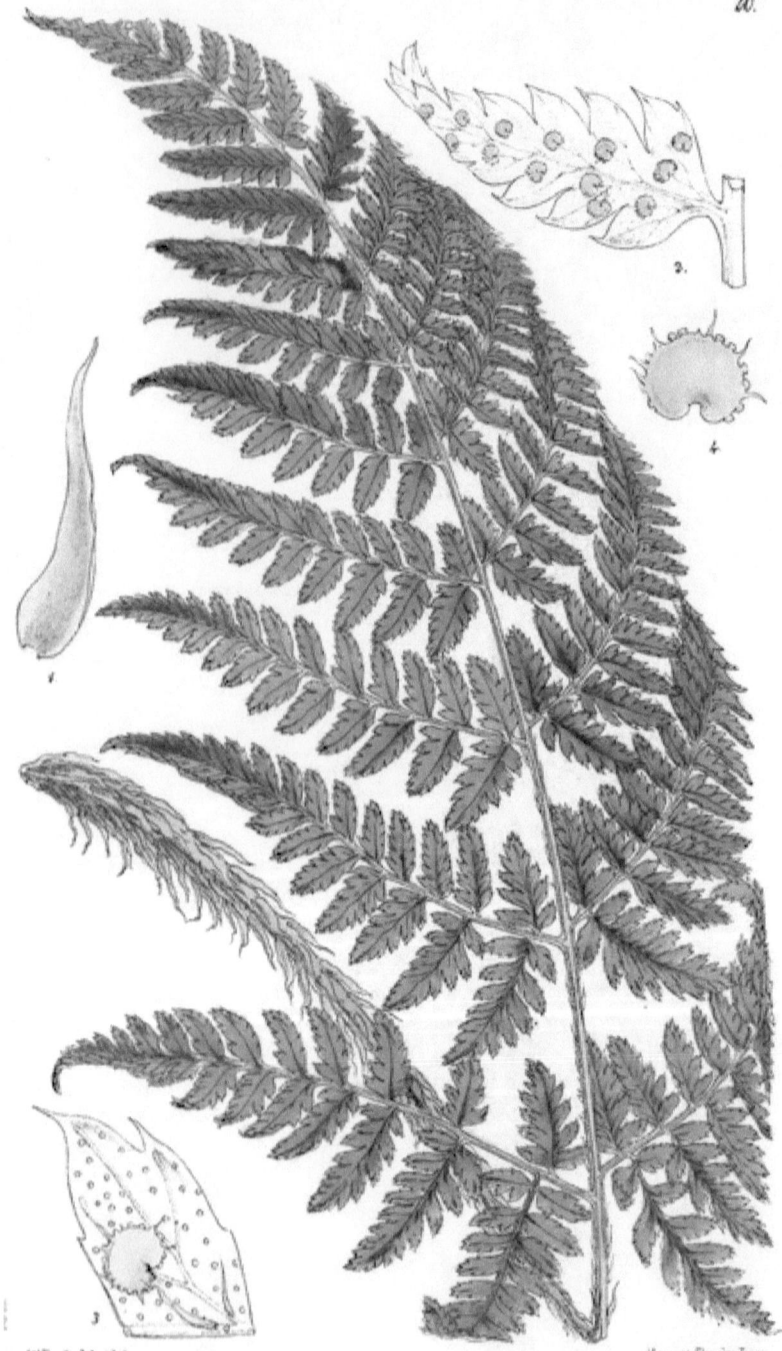

Plate 20.

NEPHRODIUM (Lastrea) spinulosum, *Willd.*,

γ. ÆMULUM.

Prickly Buckler-Fern; var. *æmulum.*

NEPHRODIUM (Lastrea) *spinulosum;* caudex short, stout, suberect, paleaceous; stipites tufted, stramineous, brown at the base, scaly; fronds ovate or oblong-ovate, one to two feet and more long, bi-tripinnate; primary pinnæ rather distant, upper ones from a broad truncated base, oblong, inferior ones ovate, both gradually acuminate, secondary ones and pinnules close-placed, ovate or oblong, sessile, more or less coarsely spinuloso-serrate or pinnatifido-serrate; sori chiefly on the upper half of the frond, in two rows upon each pinnule; involucres entire or fringed with glandular hairs.

γ. *æmulum;* "fronds triangular or triangular-ovate, spreading, tripinnate; *pinnules concave;* pinnulets pinnatifid, the mucronately serrated lobes *curved upwards;* scales of the stipes concolorous, narrow-lanceolate, *laciniate or fimbriate contorted;* indusium margined with minute sessile glands." *Moore.* (PLATE 20.)

POLYPODIUM æmulum.* *Solander in Ait. Hort. Kew. ed. 1. v. 3. p. 466.* ("Fronde quadripinnatifida glabra, pinnis oblongo-linearibus incisis, laciniis apice denticulatis.")

ASPIDIUM æmulum. *Sw. Syn. Fil. p. 60. Willd. Sp. Fil. v. 5. p. 283. Ait. Hort. Kew. ed. 2. v. 5. p. 513. Metten. Aspid. p. 58.*

LASTREA æmula. *Brack. Fil. U. S. Expl. Exp. p. 200. J. Sm. Cat. Kew Ferns, p. 58. Moore, Handb. of Brit. Ferns, ed. 3. p. 139.*

NEPHRODIUM Fœnisecii. *Lowe, Prim. Faunæ et Floræ Maderæ, p. 7.† Seubert, Fl. Azor. p. 16.*

LASTREA Fœnisecii. *Wats. in Phytol. v. 2. p. 568. Bab. Man. of Brit. Bot. ed. 4. p. 422. Moore, Brit. Ferns, Nat. Print. t. 27.*

LOPHODIUM Fœnisecii, L. recurvum, *and* Lastrea concava. *Newm.*

ASPIDIUM recurvum. *Bree, in Phytol. v. 1. p. 173.*

ASPIDIUM dilatatum, var. recurvum. *Bree, in Mag. of Nat. Hist. v. 4. p. 162. Hook. and Arn. Brit. Fl. ed. 8. p. 586.*

ASPIDIUM dilatatum. *Höll, Fl. of Mad. in Hook. Journ. of Bot. 1834, v. 1. p. 16.*

* I believe it was Mr. James Yates Johnson, who was the first to determine (in 1856), by comparison in the Banksian Herbarium, that the *Aspidium Fœnisecii* of Lowe is identical with the *Polypodium æmulum* of Dr. Solander, as related in Hook. Kew Garden Misc. v. 9. p. 163.

† "Fronde triangulari v. ovata, 3-4-pinnatifida, utrinque glabra: laciniis (tertii quartique ordinis) oblongis, obtusis; ultimis incisis, mucronato-serratis; omnium inferioribus exterioribus internis oppositis majoribus: soris numerosis distinctis: indusiis primo semiovatis vel reniformibus, demum orbiculatis emarginatis: stipite breviusculo, basi sparsim subpaleaceo, fusco, superne rachique pallidis." "Species *Aspidio dilatato* et *spinuloso* auct. certe proxima; sed distingui posse credo, figura frondis abbreviata, deltoidea; stipite breviore, minus (sc. basi tantum) paleaceo" (not so in our Madeira specimens), "pinnis angustioribus, odore. His adde frondem magis decompositam." *Lowe, l.c.*

ASPIDIUM spinulosum, γ. *Hook. and Arn. Brit. Fl. ed.* 7. *p.* 586.

Hab. This, which I have never had the good fortune to recognize in its native locality, is described by Mr. Hewett Watson, in his valuable 'Cybele Britannica,' as "rupestral and sylvestral," and was first detected in Cornwall, where it is said to be abundant, by the Rev. W. T. Bree. The Rev. W. S. Hore has found it in Devon; the Rev. W. H. Coleman in Somerset; Sir W. C. Trevelyan at Tunbridge Wells; Mr. Anderson on Hoy Hill, Orkney. Other, but less certain, localities are Hastings, Sussex; in Yorkshire and Durham; Cumberland; Northumberland; in Arran; in Forfarshire; and even in the outer Hebrides, in North Uist.

It was the Rev. W. T. Bree that first called public attention to this Fern by its discovery in Cornwall, and respecting which Mr. Watson justly observes, "much ink has been shed and much paper has been printed over, and considerable diversity and collision of opinion have been shown, on its specific distinctions, correct nomenclature, and localization." It is equally true, too, as that gentleman further remarks, that it "is now generally" (but not universally) "admitted for a true species by British botanists;" and not by British botanists only, but by botanists who have treated of exotic plants. It is undoubtedly the *Nephrodium Fœnisecii* of Lowe, and acknowledged as such by him and appears to be equally certainly the *Polypodium æmulum* of Dr. Solander, as above stated; but, till very recently, no figure has appeared of it, and it is the misfortune of this plant, that the descriptions which have been published do not give any tangible characters by which the specimens can be readily recognized. If we look at what must be considered the most accurate figures of it (because nature-printed), those of Mr. Moore,* I candidly confess I can see nothing to distinguish it from our *Nephrodium spinulosum*, var. *dilatatum*, and there is but little in the same author's specific character which I have quoted above. The chief mark is the *upward curvature of the lobes of the pinnules*, which indeed is not observable in a dry state; yet no such character is noticed by the authors of *N. Fœnisecii* or of *Polypodium æmulum*, though we know that the former studied the plant attentively from living specimens. It is remarkable, too, that though so widely dispersed over England and Scotland, it is nowhere recorded as a native of the continent of Europe. Madeira and the Azores, and the Cape de Verd Islands (according to Newman), are the only other countries known to afford the plant. From the two former countries I possess specimens; and it is further singular that its near ally, *Nephrodium dilatatum*, is

* Singularly enough, Mr. Newman denies that these figures belong to the species. He quotes the description, "excluding the figures."

not noted as inhabiting those countries, except that, as shown by Mr. Lowe, his *Fœnisecii* was taken by Dr. Höll for it, and given in his list of Madeira plants. Mr. Newman includes the Canaries as possessing *Polypodium Fœnisecii*, but Mr. Webb takes no notice of it in his Flora, and I think the statement must have arisen in error. Certain it is, that wherever found, the close affinity of the species with the *Nephrodium* (or *Lastrea*) *dilatatum* has been invariably acknowledged; and a renewed study of the subject has led me to the conclusion, that there are as good reasons for looking upon it as a form of that variable plant as a distinct species, respecting the distinctive characters of which no two writers agree. The fragrance of the plant no doubt depends upon the presence of an essential oil in the glands of the frond; but these glands do not appear to be constant. The "evergreen" nature of the fronds, described by Dr. Allchin, requires confirmation. They are certainly not so in the Royal Gardens of Kew, and Mr. Newman says, expressly (l. c. p. 142), that "this character fails in the fertile fronds."

PLATE 20. Fertile frond of *Nephrodium* (*Lastrea*) *spinulosum*, Sw., var. *œmulum*, seen from above,—*nat. size*. Fig. 1. Scale from the stipes. 2. Fertile pinnule,—*magnified*. 3. Portion of a fertile pinnule, with sorus and glands. 4. Involucre:—*more highly magnified*.

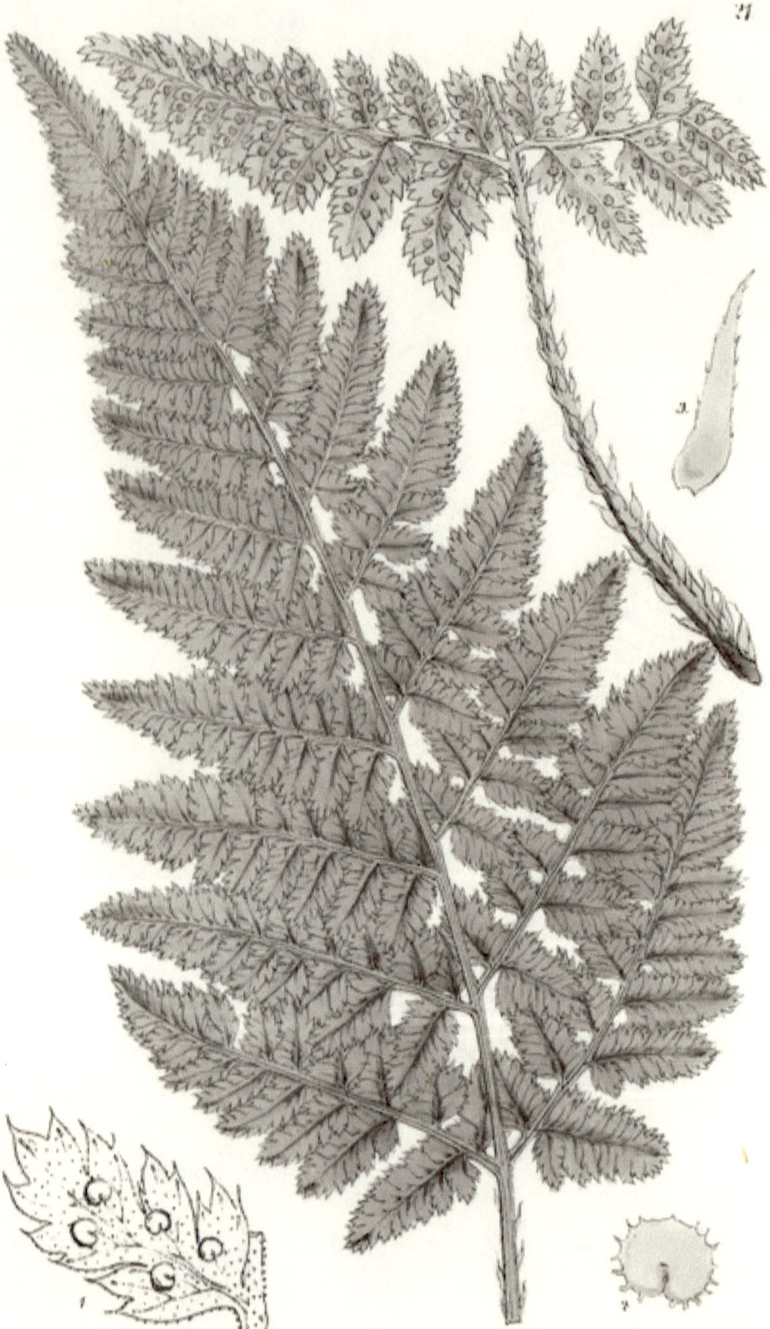

W Fitch del et lith.

Vincent Brooks Imp.

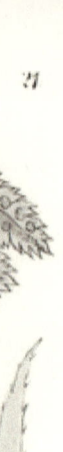

Plate 21.

NEPHRODIUM (Lastrea) SPINULOSUM, *Sw.*,
δ. DUMETORUM.

Prickly Buckler-Fern; var. *dumetorum.*

Nephrodium (Lastrea) *spinulosum;* caudex short, stout, suberect, paleaceous; stipites tufted, stramineous, brown at the base, scaly; fronds ovate or oblong-ovate, one or two feet and more long, bi-tripinnate; primary pinnæ rather distant, upper ones from a broad truncated base, oblong, inferior ones ovate, both gradually acuminate; secondary ones and pinnules close-placed, ovate or oblong, sessile, more or less coarsely spinuloso-serrate or pinnatifido-serrate; sori chiefly on the upper half of the frond, in two rows upon each pinnule; involucres entire or fringed with glandular hairs.

δ. *dumetorum;* "frond doubly pinnate, pinnules pinnatifid, lobes with terminal sharp prickly teeth, common stalk scaly, involucres flat, orbicular, with a deep notch," *Sm. under* Aspid. dumetorum.—(Plate 21.)

Aspidium dumetorum. *Sm. Eng. Fl. v.* 4. *p.* 281.

Lastrea dumetorum. "*T. Moore, MS. in Herb. (not L. dilatata, var. dumetorum, ib. Handb. of Brit. Ferns, p.* 124)," *according to Moore, in Brit. Ferns, Nat. Print.* 1855; *but the same reference is retained in Moore, Handb. of Brit. Ferns, ed.* 3, 1857.

Lastrea dilatata, *var.* dumetorum. *Moore, Brit. Ferns, Nat. Print. t.* 25.

Aspidium spinulosum, β. *Hook. and Arn. Brit. Fl. ed.* 7. *p.* 586 (*in ed.* 8 *it is given as a synonym of* A. dilatatum).

Lastrea dilatata, *var.* collina. "*Moore, Handb. of Brit. Ferns, in part.*"

Lastrea dilatata, *var.* maculata. *Moore, Hand. of Brit. Ferns, ed.* 2. *p.* 123, *in part.*

Lastrea multiflora, *var.* collina. *Newm. Brit. Ferns, ed.* 2. *p.* 222, "*in part.*"

Lastrea collina. *Newm. Brit. Ferns, ed.* 2. *p.* 224.

Lastrea maculata. *Deakin, Florigr. Brit. v.* 4. *p.* 110.

Lophodium collinum. *Newm.* "*App. to Phytol.* 1851. xviii. (*in part*). *Brit. Ferns, ed.* 3. *p.* 144 (*in part*)," (*certainly not the figure at p.* 145).

Polypodium cristatum, β. *Huds. Angl. ed.* 1. *p.* 391 (*Sm.*).

Filix montana ramosa, minor, argute denticulata. *Raii Syn. p.* 124 (*fide Sm.*).

Filix alpina, myrrhidis facie, Cambrobritannica. *Pluk. Almag. p.* 155. *Phyt. t.* 89. *f.* 4. *good* (*Sm.*).

Hab. "Wales, summit of Mount Glyder, *Mr. Llwyd;* near Phanion Vellor, *Dr. Richardson;* Westmoreland, Scotland, near Edinburgh, and among bushes in Derbyshire (*J. E. Smith*).

It would be hardly doing justice to the labours of Sir James Smith among British Ferns, if we did not introduce a fourth state of *Nephrodium spinulosum*, which he and others have been disposed to consider a distinct species (but, in my view of the subject, with no more title to distinction than the other forms we have particularized), and, as is to be expected in such a case, with very different ideas of specific distinctions. I have adopted Sir J. Smith's character, as best showing what he intended by the plant. Mr. Moore's latest definition (Handb. ed. 3) is thus expressed: "Fronds dwarf or dwarfish, oblong-ovate or triangular-ovate; stipes, rachides, and veins beneath clothed with glands; pinnules convex, oblong; scales broad-lanceolate, usually pale, indistinctly two-coloured, fimbriate; sori large, with gland-fringed indusia." I can, indeed, conceive all these characters to exist also in Smith's plant, all showing a tendency to pass into other forms of what we venture to consider one and the same species. The small size, rarely exceeding a foot in height, including the stipes, deltoideo-ovate form, compact habit, scarcely more than bipinnate fronds, are perhaps the most leading features. Mr. Moore's plate 25, above quoted, is very characteristic, and his diagnosis quite accords with the specimen here figured.

PLATE 21. Fertile frond of *Nephrodium* (Lastrea) *spinulosum*, Sw., var. *dumetorum*,—*natural size*. Fig. 1. Pinnule with sorus. 3. Scale from the stipes:—*magnified*.

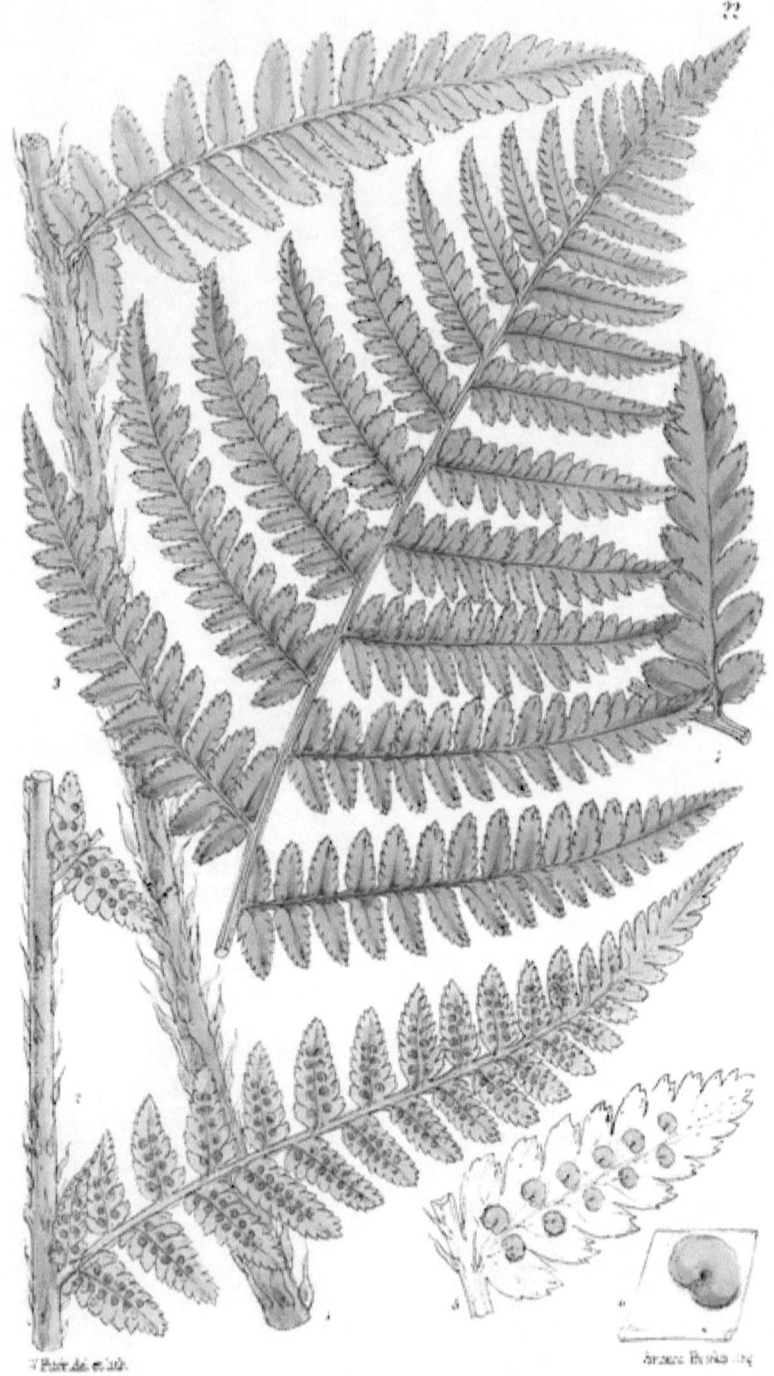

Plate 22.

NEPHRODIUM (Lastrea) remotum, *Hook.*

Distant-leaved Buckler-Fern.

Nephrodium (Lastrea) *remotum;* caudex "erect," stipites tufted, stout, a span or more long, paleaceous, with rather large, long-lanceolate, membranaceous, pale-brown scales; fronds 3–4 feet long, oblong-lanceolate submembranaceous, glabrous, without glands, bipinnate; lower pinnæ remote, from a broad petiolate base, oblong-acuminate, the rest oblongo-lanceolate; uppermost ones sessile, the longest of them 6 inches long; pinnules $\frac{1}{4}$–$\frac{3}{4}$ of an inch long, ovate-oblong, adnato-sessile, horizontal, moderately distant, very uniform, those of the inferior pinnæ pinnatifid nearly halfway down, the segments short, ovate, with 2–4 sharp terminal serratures; those of the upper pinnæ coarsely and sharply but scarcely spinulosely serrated; sori copious on all except the inferior pinnæ, arranged in two lines, one on each side near the costule; involucre orbicular-cordate, membranous, pale, concave, entire.

Aspidium remotum. *A. Braun. Kze. in Linnæa*, xxiii. p. 230. *Metten. Fil. Hort. Lips. p.* 93. *Aspid. p.* 57. *Fée, Gen. Fil. p.* 229. *Hook. and Arn. Brit. Fl. ed.* 8. *p.* 584.

Lastrea remota. *Moore, Ind. Fil. p.* 102; *in Proceed. of Lin. Soc. v.* 4. *p.* 103, *and in Phytol. for March,* 1860, *p.* 83 (*excl. the syn. of* Polystichum remotum, *Koch, Syn. ed.* 2. *p.* 969 (*where such a name does not appear*). *Clowes, in Phytol. for Aug.* 1860. *p.* 227.

Aspidium rigidum, β. remotum. *A. Braun,* "*Doell. Fl. d. Rheinl. p.* 16."

Dryopteris rigida. *Asa Gray, Man. of Bot. of N. U. St.* 1848, *p.* 631 (*but not* Aspid. rigidum, *Sw.*).

Aspidium dilatatum, *var.* Boottii. *Asa Gray, Man. of Bot. of N. U. St. ed.* 2. *p.* 598.

Aspidium Boottii. *Tuckerman.*

Hab. Windermere, Westmoreland, *Mr. Isaac Huddart.*

The Fern here characterized and for the first time figured, has been, within these few years, detected, first, in Germany, although I do not find the exact locality recorded; secondly, in United States of America, Massachusetts, by *Mr. Wm. Boott,* and in Connecticut, by *Mr. D. C. Eaton;* and thirdly, at Windermere, in Westmoreland, by *Mr. Isaac Huddart,* as recorded by *Mr. Clowes* (to whom I am indebted for cultivated specimens); and it would appear to be rare in these localities.

To Mr. T. Moore is due the credit of referring it to the

Aspidium remotum of A. Braun, a name adopted by Mettenius; but Braun afterwards considered it a variety of *Aspidium* (our *Nephrodium*) *rigidum* of Swartz. Of this German plant I have received authentic, but cultivated specimens, through the kindness of Dr. Mettenius. Of the American native plant I have specimens also, from a valued correspondent, D. C. Eaton, Esq., of New York, and this is, I think, identical with our plant.

The different views of botanists who have studied this Fern, prove how difficult it is to come to a satisfactory conclusion as to its specific identity, and yet nearly all agree as to its nearest affinities. I have already mentioned the changes of opinion in Braun, in now considering it a form of *Aspidium rigidum*.[*] Professor Koch does not, that I can find anywhere, call it "*Polystichum remotum*," but says, under his *Polystichum rigidum* (Syn. Fl. Germ. ed. 2. p. 979), that it is perhaps rather to be considered as a very vigorous and submuticous state of *Aspid. spinulosum*, than as referable to *rigidum*. Mr. Moore, though preserving it as a species, says that "its structure agrees more closely with that of *Filix-mas* than with *spinulosum* or *rigidum*." Mr. Clowes, in the 'Phytologist,' above quoted, has some very interesting remarks on the affinities of this plant (which he has cultivated for several years), but which are too long to be here introduced *in extenso*. Both Mr. Huddart and himself (and it would seem it was detected by them in concert) considered it a luxuriant specimen of *Lastrea cristata*, var. *spinulosa*, "but in the garden it gradually became more like *Filix-mas*, indeed it was found growing with *Filix-mas*, var. *incisa*, and *abbreviata*, with *L. spinulosa* and *L. dilatata*, and about five miles from Limestone Rocks, where *L. rigida* is abundant;" and he concludes, "as this Fern appears to connect the two forms *L. spinulosa* and *Filix-mas*, we have now, it would seem, a continuous series from typical *Filix-mas* to *L. dilatata*, as the *latter* and *spinulosa* are apparently united by *glandulosa*."

The American botanists have experienced the same difficulty on this subject with their plant. Not having access probably to the German authors, it was considered by Mr. Tuckerman a new species, which he described under the name of its discoverer in the United States, *Aspid. Boottii*. Dr. Asa Gray, in the first edition of his 'Flora of the Northern United States,' looked upon it to be a luxuriant form of *Aspid. rigidum*, Sw., yet allied to *spinulosum*. In his second edition of that valuable Flora, he makes it var. *Boottii* of *Aspidium spinulosum*, Sw.; "the least dissected form, intermediate in appearance between

---

[*] Mr. Moore indeed says, "it appears from specimens lately received from Braun, that he now considers it a variety of *Aspidium Filix-mas*."

A. spinulosum and *A. cristatum:*" and in this view he is followed by Mr. D. C. Eaton. For my own part I am far from satisfied respecting its being a good species, and I only make it so provisionally, until more numerous and native specimens shall, as I trust they will ere long, be placed at my disposal. Of the American specimens the nearest affinity is with *spinulosum*, perhaps with var. *dumetorum* (in structure, not in size); while Mettenius's German specimen, and our Windermere one, rather from the more rigid habit than any well-marked character, more resembles a gigantic *A. rigidum*; it approaches still nearer perhaps a specimen of *Asp. pallidum*, Bory et Chamb., in my Herbarium, from Lycia.

PLATE 22. Fig. 1, 2, 3. Portions of a fertile frond of *Nephrodium* (Lastrea) *remotum*, Hook., from a cultivated Windermere specimen, derived from Mr. Clowes. 4. Primary pinna of a small sterile frond, from the same source:—*natural size.* 5. Fertile pinnule,—*magnified.* 6. Sorus,—*more highly magnified.*

Plate 23.

CYSTOPTERIS fragilis, *Bernh.*

Brittle Bladder-Fern.

Gen. Char. Sori subglobose. *Involucre* ovate, cucullate at the base, having its origin beneath the sorus, generally acuminate at its extremity.

- Cystopteris *fragilis;* caudex creeping, elongated, very paleaceous towards the apex, with pale-brown, lanceolate, copious, very membranaceous scales; stipites copious, approximate, slender, brittle, scaly near the base; fronds lanceolate, very membranaceous, bipinnate (rarely pinnate, with the pinnæ deeply pinnatifid); pinnæ deltoideo-ovate, acuminate; pinnules ovate or ovate-lanceolate, variously toothed or laciniate or pinnatifid, the segments entire or sharply lobato-serrate; rachis winged.
- *α. vulgaris;* fronds broad-lanceolate; pinnules subpetiolate, ovate, obovate or lanceolate, somewhat cuneate at the base, incise or pinnatifid; segments toothed; sori generally crowded, at a distance from the margin.

Cystopteris fragilis. *Bernh. N. Journ. Bot. v.* 1. *part* 2. *p.* 27. *t.* 2. *f.* 9. *Hook. and Arn. Brit. Fl. ed.* 8. *p.* 197. *Hook. Gen. Fil. t.* 52 *B; Sp. Fil. v.* 1. *p.* 197. *Presl, Tent. Pterid. p.* 93. *t.* 3. *f.* 1. *Moore, Brit. Ferns, Nat. Print. pl.* 46 *A.*

Polypodium fragile. *Linn. Sp. Pl. p.* 1558. *Bolt. Fil. p.* 50. *t.* 27 *and* 46.

Aspidium fragile. *Sw. in Schrad. Journ.* 1800, *v.* 2. *p.* 40. *Syn. Fil. p.* 58. *Willd. Sp. Pl. v.* 5. *p.* 280. *Schk. Fil. p.* 53. *t.* 54–56 (*very good, including several forms*).

Cyathea fragilis. *Sm. Engl. Bot.* 5417; *Fl. Brit. p.* 1139; *Engl. Bot. t.* 1587.

Cystea fragilis. *Sm. Engl. Fl. v.* 4. *p.* 298.

(Subvar. *angustata.*)

Cystea angustata. *Sm. Engl. Fl. v.* 4. *p.* 301. *Forst. in E. Bot. Suppl. t.* 2790.

Cystopteris dentata, β. *Hook. Brit. Fl. ed.* 2. *p.* 443.

Cyathea fragilis, β. *Sm. Fl. Brit. p.* 1139.

Polypodium rhæticum. *Dicks. H. Sicc. Fasc.* 1. *p.* 17.

β. *dentata;* fronds subbipinnate, pinnæ ovato-lanceolate, pinnules sessile, ovate or oblong, obtuse, bluntly and unequally toothed, rarely pinnatifid, sori submarginal; (intermediate between the common form and var. γ).

Cyathea dentata. *Sm. Engl. Bot. t.* 1558.

Cystea dentata. *Sm. Engl. Fl. v.* 4. *p.* 300.

Cystopteris dentata. *Hook. Brit. Fl. ed.* 5. *p.* 441.

Polypodium dentatum. *Dicks. Crypt. Fasc.* 3. *p.* 1. *t.* 7.

Aspidium dentatum. *Sw. Syn. Fil. p.* 59.

Aspidium Pontederæ. *Willd. Sp. Pl. v.* 5. *p.* 278.

γ. *Dickieana*, Moore; fronds ovate-oblong, obtuse, very delicate, pinnate or subbipinnate; pinnæ ovate, obtuse, subdeflexed; segments broad, obovate or ovate, obtuse, crenate, crowded, often overlapping each other.

CYSTOPTERIS Dickieana. *Sim in Gardeners' Journ.* 1848, *p.* 308. *Newm. Brit. Ferns*, ed. 3. *p.* 93.

CYSTOPTERIS fragilis, Dickieana, *Moore, Brit. Ferns, Nat. Print. t.* 46. *f.* 5.

Hab. Rocks and walls, throughout hilly and mountainous regions, especially in the west of England, and generally throughout Scotland and Ireland.

How very variable is this species, any one can testify who has felt it his duty to examine the individuals from different localities in our own country, and from the different parts of the world which this plant is now known to inhabit. See too the numerous and various synonyms of authors, especially the careful list drawn up by Mr. Thomas Moore, and given in his 'British Ferns, Nature-Printed,' the different names alone amounting to fifty-seven, and this exclusive of the older authors. Eight varieties are there enumerated. We have contented ourselves with noting three of them: but the two first gradually pass into each other; and the third, though bearing copious fructification, owes probably much of its abnormal character to growing in a very wet shady place, as where it was first found by Professor Dickie, on dripping rocks " in a cave at Cove, near Aberdeen."

In regard to exotic localities, there would not be space here to enumerate them. I must refer to my 'Species Filicum,' where they are given as Europe and Northern Asia, and in various parts of North and South America, to which may now be added South Africa and New Zealand (in the latter country recently found by Dr. Sinclair and W. J. Locke Travers, Esq.).

I trust our figures, showing the extremes of the British forms, will now remove all difficulty in determining this species.

PLATE 23. Fig. 1. Plant of *Cystopteris fragilis*, Bernh.,—*natural size*. 2. Fertile pinna,—*magnified*. 3. Sorus and involucre,—*more magnified*. 4. Fertile frond of *Cystopteris fragilis*, Bernh., var. *Dickieana*, seen from above,—*natural size*. 5. Pinnule, with sori,—*magnified*.

Vincent Brooks Imp

PLATE 24.

CYSTOPTERIS alpina, *Desv.*

Alpine Bladder-Fern.

CYSTOPTERIS *alpina;* caudex creeping or ascending, scaly towards the apex; stipites tufted, slender, brittle, moderately scaly at the base; fronds oblong-lanceolate, tripinnate; ultimate pinnules ovate, obtuse, deeply pinnatifid, oblong or linear-cuneate, very obtusely bi-trifid, rarely entire; rachis compresso-alate.

CYSTOPTERIS alpina. *Desv. Mém. Soc. Linn. v.* 6. *p.* 264. *Hook. Sp. Fil. v.* 1. *p.* 199. *Hook. and Arn. Brit. Fl. ed.* 8. *p.* 199.

POLYPODIUM alpinum. *Wulf. in Jacq. Collect. v.* 2. *p.* 17. *Jacq. Ic. Plant. Rar. v.* 3. *t.* 642 (*excellent*).

ASPIDIUM alpinum. *Sw. in Schrad. Journ. Bot.* 1800, *v.* 2. *p.* 41. *Syn. Fil. p.* 60. *Willd. Sp. Pl. v.* 5. *p.* 281. *Schk. Fil. p* 60. *t.* 62 and 62 *b.*

CYATHEA alpina. *Sm. Mém. de l'Acad. Roy. Tur. v.* 5. *p.* 417.

POLYPODIUM regium. *Linn. Sp. Pl. p.* 1553.

CYSTOPTERIS regia. *Presl, Tent. Pterid. p.* 93. *Moore, Brit. Ferns, Nat. Print. t.* 46 *B.*

ASPIDIUM regium. *Sw. in Schrad. Journ. Bot.* 1800, *v.* 2. *p.* 41. *Syn. Fil. p.* 58. *Willd. Sp. Pl. v.* 5. *p.* 281.

CYATHEA regia. *Forst. in Sym. Syn. p.* 194. *Sm. Fl. Brit. p.* 1140.

CYATHEA incisa. *Sm. Engl. Bot. t.* 163 (*good*).

CYSTEA regia. *Sm. Engl. Fl. p.* 4. *p.* 302 (*excl. all the localities, except that of Low Leyton*).

ASPIDIUM Taygetense, *Bory and Chamb. Fl. Péloponn. p.* 67.

Hab. On a wall at Low Leyton, Essex ("plentifully," *Smith*).—I remember being taken to the locality by Mr. Edward Forster, more than half a century ago. It was not plentiful then, and there is too much reason to suspect that it had been planted. The wall is now removed or repaired, so that the Fern no longer exists.

A species undoubtedly nearly allied to the preceding one, *Cystopteris alpina;* but I think truly distinct, in the more deeply pinnatifid and more finely cut pinnules, the segments being oblong-linear or cuneate entire, obtusely toothed. There is no question of its having been found, *apparently* wild, on a wall at Leyton, in the flattest part of Essex; but nowhere else in Britain, for the Welsh and Scotch habitats have proved to be *C. fragilis;* while all the localities upon the Continent indicate the plant to be peculiar to the Alps of southern Europe, and at elevations of from six to eight thousand feet. I possess specimens from Switzerland (Canton de Vaud, *Miss Hay*) and Savoy, Carinthia and Styria; in Greece, Mount Taygetes, *Bory, Heldreich*; Taurus, *Kotschy*; and it is said to be found in the Pyrénées.

PLATE 24. Fertile plant of *Cystopteris alpina*, Desv., from the wall at Leyton, —*natural size*. Fig. 1. Pinnule with sori,—*magnified*. 2. Segment, with a single sorus,—*magnified*.

Plate 25.

Cystopteris montana, *Bernh.*

Mountain Bladder-Fern.

Cystopteris *montana*; caudex slender, long, creeping, scaly in the younger portions; stipites distant, slender, scaly chiefly below, with lax, ovate, acuminated scales; fronds four to five inches long, triangular, membranaceous, flaccid, tripinnate; pinnæ and pinnules spreading; ultimate pinnules ovate or oblong, inciso-dentate or generally deeply pinnatifid; lobes or segments toothed chiefly at the apex; rachises with a very narrow wing; involucres thin, membranaceous, broad ovate, cucullate, more or less incised at the margin, towards the apex.

Cystopteris montana. *Bernh. in Schrad. Neu. Journ. Bot. v.* 1. *P. II. p.* 26. *Link, Hort. Reg. Berol. v.* 2. *p.* 231. *Presl, Tent. Pterid. p.* 93. *Hook. Sp. Fil. v.* 1. *p.* 200. *Hook. and Arn. Brit. Fl. ed.* 8. *p.* 588. *Moore, Brit. Ferns, Nat. Print. t,* 46 C. *Hook. Fl. Bor. Am. v.* 2. *p.* 260. *Ledeb. Fl. Ross. v.* 4. *p.* 517.

Aspidium montanum. *Sw. in Schrad. Journ. Bot.* 1800, *v.* 2. *p.* 42. *Syn. Fil. p.* 61. *Schkh. Fil. t.* 63. *Willd. Sp. Pl. v.* 5. *p.* 286.

Cyathea montana. *Sm. Act. Taur. v.* 5. *p.* 417.

Polypodium montanum. *Lam. Fl. Fr. v.* 1. *p.* 23.

Cystopteris myrrhidifolia. *Newm. Brit. Ferns, ed.* 3. *p.* 97.

Polypodium myrrhidifolium. *Vill. Delph. v.* 3. *p.* 851. *t.* 53.

Cystopteris Allionii. *Newm. in App. to Phytol.* 1851, *p.* xxv.

Hab. Scotland; discovered in 1836, on Ben Lawers, by *Mr. W. Wilson.* We have specimens from *Mr. Borrer,* gathered in the mountains of Glen Lochay, still in the Breadalbane range, where it was detected by *Messrs. Gourlie and Adamson;* Glen Islay, Clova, Forfarshire, *Jas. Backhouse.* Mr. Moore mentions it as having been found in Banffshire, on the authority of 'The Naturalist,' but with no station or name of author, or any particular locality. Dr. Dickie, in his 'Botanist's Guide to Aberdeen and Kincardine' (1860), gives as a new station, "Rocks at the head of Glen Callater, *Mr. Croall:*" this is in Aberdeenshire.

This is a very elegant Fern, and may be reckoned among the rarest of the British species, only four particular stations having been recorded for it. The form of the frond, its triangular outline or circumscription, together with the creeping filiform caudex, and the distantly placed stipites, at once distinguish it from the two preceding, *C. fragilis* and *alpina.* On the continent of Europe it seems much more abundant, extending from Lapland and Norway in the north, to the Alps of the south of

Europe. In the Russian dominions, the only station known is Kamtschatka (*Mertens*). We possess five specimens from the east side of the Rocky Mountains, gathered by *Drummond*.

PLATE 25. Fertile plant of *Cystopteris montana*, Bernh.,—*natural size*. Fig. 1. Fertile pinnule,—*magnified*. 2. Single sorus, with involucre,—*magnified*. 3. Involucres,—*magnified*.

PLATE 26.

ASPLENIUM SEPTENTRIONALE, *Hoffm.*

Forked Spleenwort.

Gen. Char. Asplenium, *Linn.* Sori dorsal, linear or oblong, rarely curved or somewhat horse-shoe-shaped, attached to a vein and opening on one side towards the disk (rarely almost obsolete).—Ferns *of very varied habit and aspect, chiefly inhabiting tropical and temperate climates.* Caudex *short and erect, or more or less creeping.* Venation *extremely variable, free or anastomosing; of the latter we only possess one species in* Aspl. Ceterach (*Ceterach officinarum,* auct.) *and in this the involucre is so small and indistinct as to have escaped the notice of many authors.*

N.B. In this genus we include, besides many exotic genera, *Athyrium* of Presl, *Acropteris* of Link, and the *Ceterach* of Willdenow.

ASPLENIUM *septentrionale,* Hoffm.; small; caudex short, thick, scarcely scaly, copiously rooting, with branched fibres; stipites numerous, tufted, three to six inches high, erect, flexuose, green, brown at the base; fronds one to two inches long, coriaceous, glabrous, once or twice forked, rarely simple; pinnæ or segments three-quarters to two inches long, petiolate, erect, linear or linear-lanceolate, often very acute or acuminate, subunguiculate, nearly entire or subpinnatifid with sharp, erect, subulate teeth or segments; veins forked, parallel (no distinct costa); sori very long, linear, placed near to, and parallel with, the margin, solitary, or from two to four upon a pinna, entire at the margin.

ASPLENIUM septentrionale. *Hoffm. Deutschl. Fl. v.* 2. *p.* 12. *Hull, Brit. Flora,* p. 241. *Sw. Syn. Fil. p.* 75. *Schk. Fil. p.* 62. *t.* 65. *Willd. Sp. Pl. v.* 5. p. 307. *Pr. Tent. Pterid.* p. 106. *t.* 3. *f.* 8. *Engl. Bot. t.* 1017. *Sm. Engl. Fl. v.* 4. *p.* 308. *Hook. Fl. Lond. N. S. v.* 5. *t.* 162. *Hook. and Arn. Brit. Fl. ed.* 8. *p.* 588. *Moore, Brit. Ferns, Nat. Print. t.* 41 C. *Hook. Sp. Fil. v.* 3. *p.* 174. *Metten. Asplen. p.* 141.

ACROSTICHUM septentrionale. *Linn. Sp. Pl. p.* 1524. *Bolt. Brit. Ferns, p.* 12. *t.* 8.

ACROPTERIS septentrionalis. *Link, Hort. Ber. v.* 2. *p.* 56. *Fée, Gen. Fil. p.* 77. *t.* 6 *A. f.* 1.

ANESIUM septentrionale. *Newm. Brit. Ferns, ed.* 3. *p.* 265.

Hab. Clefts of rocks and walls in the mountain districts: on the borders of Devon and Somerset; Ingleborough, Yorkshire; Kyloe Crags, Northumberland; Ambleside, Westmoreland; in various parts of Cumberland, and in Caernarvonshire. In Scotland, near Kelso, on Minto Crags, Roxburghshire; Arthur's Seat and Blackford Hill, near Edinburgh; Stenton Rock, near Dunkeld; Pass of Ballater, Aberdeenshire (*Dr. Patterson,* 1855). Not known as a native of Ireland.

Widely as this plant is dispersed throughout England, it seems in none of the localities to be very abundant; and, judging from our own herbarium, and the comparative paucity of samples there, such appears to be the case also on the Continent; yet stations are recorded in almost every country of Europe, from Norway in the west to Siberia and Altai in the east; and south to Spain, Portugal, and Italy. Still further east, I possess excellent specimens from Kashmir, *Dr. T. Thomson*; from Kunawar, in deep clefts of rocks, at an elevation of 9000 feet, *Jacquemont* (Aspl. furcatum, *Jacquem. MS.*); from Gurhwál, elevation 11,000 feet; on the Himalaya, *Strachey and Winterbottom*. I have also been gratified in receiving it from *Mr. C. Wright* (n. 2122), gathered on a journey to New Mexico in 1851 and 1852.

PLATE 26. Fertile plants of *Asplenium septentrionale*, Hoffm.,—*natural size*. Fig. 1. Fertile pinna,—*magnified*.

PLATE 27.

ASPLENIUM GERMANICUM, *Weiss.*

Alternate-leaved Spleenwort.

ASPLENIUM *Germanicum*, Weiss; small; caudex short, subrepent, rooting; stipites tufted, two to three inches long, green, brown below, scaleless; fronds about three inches long, subcoriaceous, narrow-oblong or sublanceolate in circumscription, pinnate, rarely and only in the lowest pair again pinnate; pinnæ alternate, erecto-patent, from seven to nine in number, alternate, cuneato-lanceolate, occasionally subfalcate, simple or bifid, toothed or subtrifid at the apex; veins several times forked; sori linear more or less elongated, two to four on each pinnule or large segment, entire at the margin.

ASPLENIUM Germanicum. *Weiss, Plantæ Crypt.* p. 299. *Newm. Brit. Ferns, ed.* 2. p. 265. *Willd. Sp. Pl.* p. 330. *Hook. and Arn. Brit. Fl. ed.* 8. p. 589. *Hook. Sp. Fil.* v. 3. p. 175. *Moore, Brit. Ferns, Nat. Print.* t. 41 B. *Presl, Tent. Pterid.* p. 108.

ASPLENIUM alternifolium. *Wulf. in Jacq. Misc. Austr.* v. 2. p. 51. t. 5. f. 2. *Engl. Bot.* t. 2558. *Hook. Scot.* v. 2. p. 156. *Smith, Engl. Fl.* v. 4. p. 296.

ASPLENIUM Breynii, *Retz, Obs. Bot. fasc.* 1. p. 32. *Schk. Fil.* p. 77. f. 81. *Metten. Asplen.* p. 142.

SCOLOPENDRIUM alternifolium. *Roth, Fl. Germ.* v. 3. p. 53.

ANESIUM Germanicum. *Newm. Brit. Ferns. ed.* 3. p. 258.

Hab. Mountains of North Wales, *Mr. Williams, Mr. H. Wilson.* On Helvellyn, *Rev. W. H. Hawker.* Borrowdale, *Miss Wright.* Kyloe Crags, Northumberland, *Mrs. Tate.* Lowlands of Scotland, Minto Crags, *Mr. W. Nichol;* Dunfermline, Fifeshire, *Dr. Dewar;* near Dunkeld, Perthshire (*Mr. Moore*).

On the continent of Europe, this Spleenwort inhabits generally the same countries as our preceding species, *Asplenium septentrionale*, with the exception of Russia, where it is not recorded, except in Finland, near Helsingfors (*Dr. Nylander*); but it is not a native of India nor of America. It is generally considered to hold an intermediate place between *Aspl. alternifolium* and our next species, *Aspl. Ruta-muraria*, much nearer the latter than the former. The fronds are more compound than the first, and the shape of the pinnæ is very different, and the sori very much shorter, and it is less compound than the latter, of which some of the varieties with narrow pinnæ, called "*cuneatum*" by Moore, have been confounded in herbaria, and according to Mettenius, both *Germanicum* and *Ruta-muraria* are included under the name of *Aspl. murale*, by Bernhardi, in

Schrad. Journ. v. i. p. 311 (not so at that page in my copy of the Journal). Breynius, in his Cent. Plant. p. 189. t. 97, calls our present plant, "Adiantum novum germanicum Rutæ-murariæ facie." Newman indeed expresses an opinion that *A. septentrionale*, *Germanicum*, and *Ruta-muraria*, are forms of one and the same species.

PLATE 27. Tuft of *Asplenium Germanicum*, Hoffm., with fertile fronds,—*natural size*. Fig. 1. Represents a frond a little more divided than usual,—*natural size*. 2. Pinna, with sori,—*magnified*.

PLATE 28.

ASPLENIUM Ruta-muraria, *L.*

Wall-Rue.

ASPLENIUM *Ruta-muraria*, L.; small, caudex short, subrepent, rooting; stipites thickly tufted, two to four inches long, green, brown below and scaleless; fronds one to two, rarely three inches long, ovate in circumscription, bipinnate (very rarely subtripinnate); primary pinnæ few, subcoriaceous, three to seven; pinnules and superior pinnæ (which are often undivided) rhomboid or obovato-cuneate, tapering below into a rather long winged petiole, very obtuse or even truncated at the apex, and three-toothed, often bifid or trifid; veins several times forked, subflabellate; sori linear-oblong, two to four or five on a pinnule, entire or more frequently erose at the margin.

ASPLENIUM Ruta-muraria. *Linn. Sp. Pl. p.* 1541. *Sw. Syn. Fil. p.* 85. *Schk. Fil. p.* 75. *t.* 80 *B. Willd. Sp. Pl. v.* 5. *p.* 341. *Engl. Bot. t.* 850. *Bolton Fil. p.* 28. *t.* 16. *Hook. Gen. Fil. t.* 30. *Sm. Engl. Fl. v.* 4. *p.* 309. *Hook. and Arn. Brit. Fil. ed.* 8. *p.* 589. *Moore, Brit. Ferns, Nat. Print. t.* 41 *A.*

ASPLENIUM murorum. *Lam. Fl. Fr. v.* 1. *p.* 28.

ACROSTICHUM Ruta-muraria. *Lam. Ill. t.* 865. *f.* 1.

ANESIUM Ruta-muraria. *Newm. Brit. Ferns, ed.* 3. *p.* 263.

SCOLOPENDRIUM. *Roth.*

TARACHIA, *Pr.*

Hab. Common on rocks and old walls and buildings throughout Great Britain and Ireland; less frequent in the extreme north.

I have already alluded to the close affinity between this and the much rarer *Asplenium Germanicum*, the subject of our last Plate. This is by far the most abundant, and affects dry walls as well as the clefts of rocks, often on their perpendicular faces, the roots and even the caudex or rhizomes so tightly imbedded as to render it frequently very difficult to obtain good specimens. It seems to be widely distributed in other countries, from the north of Sweden, throughout all Europe and temperate Asia. Altai (*Ledebour*); North and South Africa (*the Hon. Rawson W. Rawson*); northern India, Kashmir (*Dr. Thomas Thomson*); Karabagh, in Georgia (*herb. nostr.*); Tibet (*Hooker fil. and Thomson*); and I possess fine specimens from the United States, Pennsylvania, Kentucky (where it grows in fissures of limestone rocks, *Dr. Short*), and Virginia (*B. D. Greene, Esq.*). Like our preceding species it does not appear to have been found anywhere in British North America.

PLATE 28. Fig. 1 and 2. Fertile specimens of *Asplenium Ruta-muraria*, L., —*natural size*. 3. Fertile pinnæ from Fig. 1. 4. Fertile pinna from Fig. 3:—*magnified*.

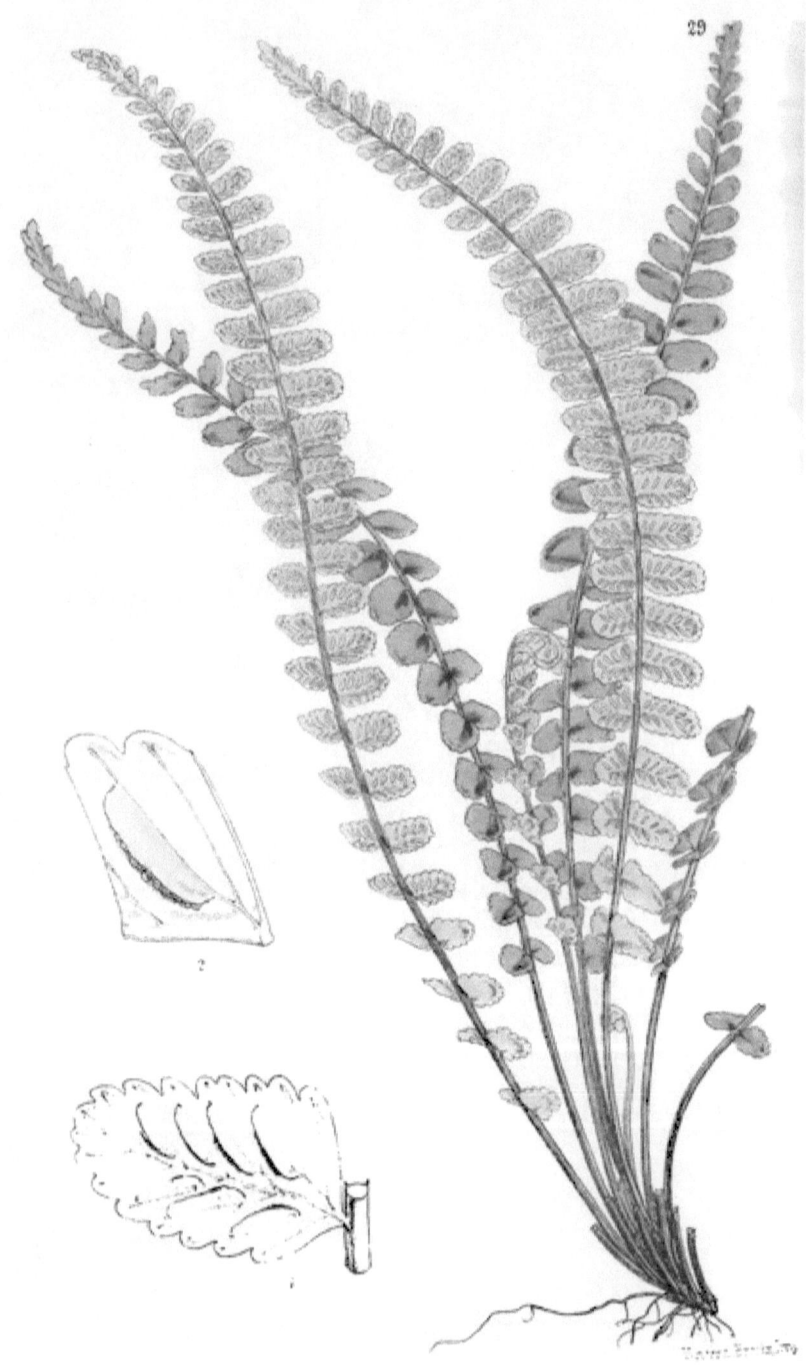

Plate 29.

ASPLENIUM Trichomanes, *L.*

Common or Maidenhair Spleenwort.

Asplenium *Trichomanes*; small; caudex short, thick, densely fibrous; stipites one to four or five inches long, numerous, tufted, dark-castaneous or black-ebeneous, glossy, margined; fronds four to six or more inches long, linear-lanceolate, coriaceo-membranaceous, dark dull-green, paler beneath, pinnated; pinnæ numerous, horizontal, scarcely petiolate, lower ones distant and smaller, oval or obovate or oval-oblong, obliquely cuneate at the base, superior base rounded, sometimes truncated and even auriculated, sometimes excised at the inferior base, the margin entire or irregularly crenato-serrate or rarely incised (β *incisum*, Moore); costa subcentral; veins few, distant, oblique, generally forked above the middle; sori oblique, in two equal series; involucres pale brown, membranaceous, entire or jagged at the margin.

Asplenium Trichomanes. *Linn. Sp. Pl.* p. 1540, *in part. Huds. Angl.* p. 452. *Sm. Eng. Bot. t.* 567. *Sw. Syn. Fil.* p. 80. *Schk. Fil.* p. 69. *t.* 74. *Bolt. Fil. Brit.* p. 22. *t.* 13. *Mich. Fl. Bor. Am. v.* 2. p. 264. *Sm. Eng. Fl.* p. 305. *Hook. Fl. Lond. v.* 5. *t.* 166. *Hook. and Arn. Brit. Fl. ed.* 8. p. 589. *Hook. Gen. et Sp. Fil. v.* 3. p. 136. *Hook. Fl. Tasm. v.* 2. p. 145. *Asa Gray, Man. Bot. N. U. States,* p. 594. *Pappe and Raws. Syn. Fil. Afr. Austr.* p. 19. *Metten. Asplen.* p. 138. *Moore, Brit. Ferns, Nat. Print.* *t.* 39.

Asplenium trichomanoides. *Cav. Demonstr.* p. 257. *n.* 635 (*not Mich.*).

Asplenium melanocaulon. *Willd. Sp. Pl. v.* 5. p. 332. *Mart. et Gal. Fil. Mex.* p. 59.

Asplenium densum. *Brack. Fil. U. S. Expl. Exp.* p. 151. *t.* 20.

Asplenium dichroum. *Kze. in Herb. Nostr. Pr. Tent. Pterid.* p. 108; *and* Aspl. heterochroum, *Kze. in Linnæa, v.* 9. p. 67.

(A large form of this species is found in Madeira, Teneriffe, and the Azores, which is the *Aspl. anceps,* Sol. MS. and Hook. and Grev. Ic. Fil. t. 195. In Mexico and New Granada is a still larger form, the *Aspl. castaneum,* Schlecht.)

Hab. A very frequent inhabitant of Great Britain, from the south of Devon and Cornwall to the extreme north in the Orkneys, usually growing from the crevices of walls and rocks.

This well-known *Spleenwort* seems to have been confounded by Linnæus and some of the older botanists with the far more local *Asplenium viride*. The two are, however, I believe, quite distinct, and the present is readily distinguished by its darker coloured fronds, far more rigid habit, and the ebeneous stipites and rachises; to which may be added, more rhomboid pinnæ, never auriculated at the superior base. Mr. Hewett Watson indeed has the following remark, which, coming from such a seeker of truth, deserves recording here:—" A rupestral species, seldom found above the agrarian region, gradually giving place to its very near ally *A. viride* on the acclivities of the mountains. A specimen is in my herbarium of *A. Trichomanes* from Fullarton, Forfarshire, which approximates to the larger and more austral species, *A. anceps*. Indeed, if *A. viride* and *A. anceps* had been the commoner species, well known and named before *A. Trichomanes* was discovered, this last would have stood a good chance of being pronounced an intermediate and perhaps uniting variety." *Cybele Brit.* v. 3. p. 277.

Abroad, the geographical range of this species is very considerable, in warm countries probably (for the elevations in such are seldom faithfully recorded) peculiar to mountain regions, so as probably pretty nearly to correspond with the range of mean temperature accorded to it by Mr. Watson in Britain, viz. 52°–42°, and to an elevation with us from the level of the sea to 650–700 yards in North Wales. Such laws, however, are not so much to be depended upon in the case of Ferns and cryptogamic as to the phænogamic plants.

Our recently-published volume of 'Species Filicum' (vol. iii.) gives, as countries inhabited by this almost ubiquitous species, " Throughout Europe, Caucasus, and the Tauria, Greece; South Africa; New South Wales, Bathurst, Paramatta, Victoria, etc.; Tasmania; Persia (Ghilan, *Aucher-Eloi*); East Indies, Kashmir, Ladak, Mussoorie, and Afghanistan in the west, through the range of Himalaya to Bootan in the east, at elevations between 6–12,000 feet; North America, Canada, United States, Rocky Mountains, and west to the coasts of the Pacific; Mexico and New Mexico, Andes of Peru, New Granada, Andes of Ecuador, Guatemala; Sandwich Islands (*A. densum*, Brack.); West Indies, Cuba and Jamaica:" to which countries has since been added New Zealand, mountains in the Middle Island, *Sinclair, Travers*.

PLATE 29. Fertile fronds of *Asplenium Trichomanes*, Linn.,—*natural size*. Fig. 1. Fertile pinna, seen from beneath,—*magnified*. 2. Single sorus,—*more magnified*.

PLATE 30.

ASPLENIUM VIRIDE, *Huds.*

Green Spleenwort.

ASPLENIUM *viride;* caudex short, creeping, clothed with black subulate scales, forming a closely compacted rooting mass; stipites densely cæspitose, two to four inches long, slender, glossy-black below, then castaneous or stramineous, green in the rachis; fronds three to five, rarely six inches long, linear-lanceolate, submembranaceous, bright-green, glabrous, scarcely acuminated, pinnated; pinnæ two to three lines long, rather distant, all petiolate, rhombeo-ovate, obtuse, more or less obliquely cuneate at the base, deeply but rather irregularly crenate, scarcely lobed; veins subflabellate; sori two to four near the disk, remote from the margin, oblong, oblique, at length confluent; involucres very thin-membranaceous, soon obliterated.

ASPLENIUM viride. *Huds. Angl.* p. 453. *Sw. Syn. Fil.* p. 80. *Schk. Fil.* p. 68. *t.* 73. *Willd. Sp. Pl. v.* 5. *p.* 332. *Engl. Bot. t.* 2257. *Sm. Engl. Fl. v.* 4. *p.* 306. *Hook. Sp. Fil. v.* 3. *p.* 104. *Hook. and Arn. Brit. Fil. ed.* 8. *p.* 589. *Moore, Brit. Ferns, Nat. Print. t.* 40. *Metten. Aspl. p.* 139.

ASPLENIUM Trichomanes ramosum. *Bauhin, Hist. v.* 3. *p.* 745. *Linn. Sp. Pl.* p. 1541 (*a branched state*). *Bolton, Fil. Brit.* p. 25. *t.* 2. *f.* 3.

ASPLENIUM intermedium. *Pr. Del. Prag. v.* 1. *p.* 233. *Tent. Pterid. t.* 3. *f.* 22.

ASPLENIUM umbrosum. *Vill. Delph. p.* 281.

Hab. Rocks in mountain districts of England, Wales, and Ireland; especially abundant in Scotland.—Upon the continent of Europe this species appears more universally distributed than in Britain; from the extreme north, Norway to Italy, Spain and Dalmatia in the south. In Northern India it is found in the western districts of Himalaya (12,000 feet elevation, *Strachey and Winterbottom*); in Russia and Siberia. In North America it appears in the Rocky Mountains (*Drummond, Bourgeau*).

This is one of the most delicate and elegant of our Ferns, and was supposed by myself and others to have been confounded by Linnæus with *Asplenium Trichomanes*, from the fact of his calling it "*A. Trichomanes ramosum;*" but he seems merely to have adopted Bauhin's brief character for his specific name, for which, as observed by Sir James Smith, Hudson's "*A. viride*" is now universally substituted. Linnæus's plant had the frond in an abnormal branched state, as represented by Bolton. The distinguishing characters between this and *A. Trichomanes* are given under the latter species.

PLATE 30. Fertile plant of *Asplenium viride*, Huds.,—*natural size*. Fig. 1. Fertile pinna, seen from beneath,—*magnified*. 2. Sori,—*more magnified*.

PLATE 31.

ASPLENIUM MARINUM, *Linn.*

Sea Spleenwort.

ASPLENIUM *marinum*; caudex short, thick, woody, crowned with long, dense, glossy, purple-brown, subulate scales; stipites tufted, and as well as the greater part of the rachis ebeneous-brown; fronds three inches to a span and more in length, oblong or broad-lanceolate, coriaceo-membranaceous, pinnate; pinnæ one to two inches long, oblong or lanceolate, subrhomboid, obtuse, sinuato-lobate or serrate, the obliquely cuneate base entire; in oblong, often confluent; involucres subcoriaceous; veins obscure, forked; inferior base slightly excised, the superior base truncate or subauriculate; uppermost pinnæ decurrent, the extreme lobe pinnatifid; sori large, oblique rachis winged, green above.

ASPLENIUM marinum. *Linn. Sp. Pl.* p. 1540. *Sw. Syn. Fil.* p. 79. *Schk. Fil.* t. 68. *Willd. Sp. Pl.* v. 5. p. 318. *Engl. Bot.* t. 392. *Sm. Engl. Fl.* v. 4. p. 307. *Hook. and Arn. Brit. Fl.* ed. 8. p. 589. *Metten. Fil. Hort. Lips.* p. 73. *Asplen.* p. 135. *Moore, Fil. Brit. Nat. Print.* t. 38. *Bolt. Fil. Brit.* p. 26. t. 15. *Hook. Fl. Lond.* t. 60.

ASPLENIUM trapeziforme. *Huds. Angl.* p. 385.

Hab. Clefts and caves of the rocky coasts of Great Britain and Ireland, from the extreme south to the Orkneys; far more general on the west than on the east coasts, and in Ireland. Rarely seen inland.

This seems almost peculiarly a maritime species, growing even on old walls, if but within the influence of the sea, as on the ruins of Icolmkill, where, in the dry and exposed parts especially, it penetrates with its fibrous roots so deep into the crevices of the buildings that it is difficult to remove a tuft of the fronds without leaving the caudex or rhizome in the wall. In Lancashire and Berwickshire it is recorded by Mr. Hewett Watson, to be found some miles inland. On the continent, however, of Europe, it nowhere appears in Germany or Scandinavia, but it extends along the coasts of France and Spain to the Canary Isles; also in Tangiers and in the western islands of the Mediterranean. I possess specimens from New Brunswick, Nova Scotia, in British North America, and from Rio Grande do Sul, in South Brazil, and a solitary specimen from St. Vincent, in the West Indies (sent by the Rev. Lansdown Guilding). Some of our specimens from Madeira have the fronds a foot long, independent of the stipites. Though variable in size, and even in the form of the fronds and of the pinnæ (sometimes elongated and pinnatifid), yet it is a species easily recognized by the large size among our pinnated *Asplenia*, and the stout ebeneous stipites.

PLATE 31. Fertile fronds of *Asplenium marinum*, Linn.,—*natural size*. Fig. 1 and 2. Pinnæ,—*magnified*. 3. Sorus,—*more magnified*.

PLATE 32.

ASPLENIUM LANCEOLATUM, *Huds.*

Lanceolate Spleenwort.

ASPLENIUM *lanceolatum;* caudex short, thick, woody, palcaceous, with dark-brown, long, setaceo-subulate scales; stipites tufted, three to four inches to a span long, dark castaneous; fronds broad-lanceolate, membranaceous, bright green, pale beneath, and there having small, scattered, deciduous scales, bipinnate; primary pinnæ lanceolate, sessile or nearly so, obtuse or acuminate, one to two inches long, inferior ones remote; pinnules crowded (often confluent, especially towards the apices), broad-ovate or obovate, serrato-dentate, the teeth sharp and apiculate; veins forked, moderately patent; sori submarginal, at first small, at length large and confluent; involucres small, whitish, membranaceous, oblong, patent, entire, rarely horseshoe-shaped.

ASPLENIUM lanceolatum. *Huds. Aug. v.* 2. *p.* 454. *Sm. Syn. Fil. p.* 83. *Willd. Sp. Pl. v.* 5. *p.* 346. *Engl. Bot. t.* 240. *Moore, Brit. Ferns, Nat. Print. t.* 35 *B. Hook. and Arn. Brit. Fl. ed.* 8. *p.* 590. *Hook. Sp. Fil. v.* 3. *p.* 190. *Metten. Asplen. p.* 140.

ATHYRIUM lanceolatum. *Heufl. Aspl. Europ. p.* 111.

TARACHIA lanceolata. *Pr. Epim. Bot. p.* 82.

ASPLENIUM rotundatum. *Kfs. Presl, Tent. Pterid. p.* 108.

ASPLENIUM cuneatum *and* Aspl. Bellottii. *Schultz.*

ASPLENIUM marinum, *var.* microdon. *Moore, Brit. Ferns, Nat. Print. under t.* 38 (*fide Moore*).

ASPLENIUM lanceolatum, *var.* microdon. *Moore, Handbook Brit. Ferns, ed.* 3. *p.* 166, *with figure.*

ASPLENIUM obovatum. *Viv. Fl. Lib. Specim. p.* 68. *Hook. and Grev. Ic. Fil. t.* 147. A. Forsteri, *Sadl.,* Athyrium, *Fée,* Tarachia, *Pr., are now generally acknowledged to be southern forms of this species.*

Hab. Rocks; south of England, Wales, and Ireland, as Jersey (frequent), Devon, Cornwall (abundant), Kent, Sussex, Somerset, Gloucestershire, Pembroke, Glamorgan, and other parts of Wales, Kinsale, Cork. (I have generally seen it in the greatest abundance within the influence of the sea atmosphere.)

In Britain this is a very local species, almost peculiar to the south and west of England and Wales; nor does it appear to be found anywhere north of the latitude of England on the Continent. It finds no place in Ledebour's 'Flora Rossica,' but is a native of France, Spain, and Portugal, Algeria, and islands of the Mediterranean, Madeira, Azores, St. Helena (*Dr. Hooker*) etc. The *Asplenium obovatum* of Viviani is a slightly abnormal southern form.

PLATE 32. Fertile fronds of *Asplenium lanceolatum*, Huds.,—*natural size*. Fig. 1. Pinnule,—*magnified*. 2. Sorus,—*more magnified*.

Plate 33.

ASPLENIUM Adiantum-nigrum, *L.*

Black Spleenwort.

ASPLENIUM *Adiantum-nigrum*; caudex stout (when old thickly clothed with the remains of former stipites), horizontal or ascending; stipites densely tufted, castaneous, generally ebeneous at the base, often a span and more long; fronds a span to a foot and more long, ovate or ovate-oblong, acuminate, firm, membranaceo-coriaceous, glossy, bi-tripinnate; primary pinnæ petiolate, ovato-acuminate; secondary also petiolate; tertiary usually sessile, from a cuneate base ovate or oblong or lanceolate or even linear, more or less acuminate, but not sharply, rarely very obtuse, inciso-pinnatifid, the lobes coarsely and subspinulosely serrated; veins pinnated, erecto-patent; sori copious, approximate, linear-oblong, at length confluent; involucres firm, membranaceous, pale-brown, entire; rachises alate.

ASPLENIUM Adiantum-nigrum. *Linn. Sp. Pl. p.* 1541. *Sw. Syn. Fil. p.* 84. *Willd. Sp. Pl. v.* 5. *p.* 346. *Schk. Fil. p.* 74. *t.* 80 *a*. *Eng. Bot. t.* 1950. *Sm. Eng. Fl. v.* 4. *p.* 310. *Hook. and Arn. Brit. Fl. ed.* 8. *p.* 590. *Metten. Asplen. p.* 144. *Moore, Brit. Ferns, Nat. Print. t.* 36. *Hook. Sp. Fil. v.* 3. *p.* 187.

ASPLENIUM Oreopteris. *Linn. Sp. Pl. ed.* 1. *p.* 1081 (*according to Moore, but Mettenius refers this to the var.* acutum).

ASPLENIUM argutum. *Kfs. En. Fil. p.* 176.

ASPLENIUM humile. *Bl. En. Fil. Jav. p.* 185 (*according to Presl and Moore, while Blume compares it with* Aspl. pumilum, *a West Indian species*).

ASPLENIUM Silesiacum, *Milde.* A. nigrum, *Beruh.*, A. luridum, *Salisb.*, and A. Capense, *L.*, are generally referred hither.

β. *acutum*, Pollin; pinnæ, pinnules, and segments narrower, often linear, acute or acuminate. *Moore, Brit. Ferns. Nat. Print. t.* 37.

ASPLENIUM acutum. *Bory in Willd. Sp. Pl. v.* 5. *p.* 347.

ASPLENIUM productum. *Lowe, Trans. Cambr. Phil. Soc. v.* 6. *p.* 524.

γ. *obtusum*, Moore; pinnules and lobes very broad, more acutely dentate.

ASPLENIUM obtusum. *Kit. in Willd. Sp. Pl. v.* 5. *p.* 341.

ASPLENIUM Adiantum-nigrum, *var.* Capense, *Schlecht. Adumbr. Fil. Cap. p.* 31. *t.* 18 (*excellent*).

ASPLENIUM cuneifolium. *Vis. Fl. Ital. Fragm. p.* 16. *t.* 18.

ASPLENIUM Serpentini. *Tausch and Heufl. Aspl. Europ. p.* 1. *t.* 1. 2.

(To this form Mr. Moore refers *A. fissum*, Weinm., *A. Forsteri*, and *A. novum*, Sadl., *A. incisum*, Opitz, *A. multicaule*, Scholtz, and *A. tabulare*, Schrad.—There is enumerated in our 'Species Filicum,' the var. δ *Gaudichaudianum*, Hook., which is the *Aspl. patens* of Gaudich. in Freyc. Voy. Bot. p. 320, *A. Adiantum-nigrum* of Brackenr. and of Metten.).

Hab. The normal form from which γ *obtusum* is very little distinct, is very common on shady banks, walls, and fissures of rocks, throughout Great Britain. β is more local, and is, I believe, in the British dominions, confined to Ireland: Killarney, county Kerry, near Tralee, Cork, and the island of Jersey: it may therefore be considered a southern form.

Besides being a very common Fern, this is certainly a very variable one, and it is no wonder that pseudo-botanists have made several species of it. Regarding its geographical distribution I may quote the following from our 'Species Filicum:'—"Of the vars. α (or normal state), β, and γ, they are found throughout Europe, in Greece and Northern Asia, Turkey, the shores and islands of the Mediterranean, North and South Africa, Madeira, the Canaries, Azores, Cape de Verd Islands, St. Helena, Abyssinia, *Schimper, n.* 669 and 1356. Northern India, Affghanistan, Mussoorie (*Bacon*), Kashmire and Simla, *Griffith, Edgworth, Hook. fil. et Thomson*; Mascaren Islands, *Bory*; Java?, *Blume*. In the New World Virginia is given on the authority of a specimen in the Herbarium of the British Museum (Moore), but it is nowhere recorded in the Floras of the United States (except where the *A. montanum*, Willd., has been mistaken for it, and Portorico, *Herb. Willd., Moore*). Var. δ is found in Mouna Roa and other mountains in the Sandwich Islands, *Gaudichaud, Douglas, n.* 55, *Breckenridge*, elev. 8–10,000 feet. Extended as is the geographical distribution of this well-known species, I have never seen any specimens from either North or South America. These two localities rest entirely on the authority of the Banksian and Willdenovian Herbaria: nor have I seen any specimens from Java or the Mascaren Islands. I cannot join Mettenius in wishing to record the numerous varieties and subvarieties "ab Heufler expositæ." Those I adopt from Moore satisfactorily embrace the forms found in England, including the narrow-segmented state of Bory's *A. acutum*, and the broad variety denominated *A. obtusum* by Kitaibel. The broadest and most peculiar form is gathered by Mr. Milne on Table Mountain, at the Cape, in which country, indeed, the several European forms are also found.

PLATE 33. Fertile plant of *Asplenium Adiantum-nigrum*, L.,—*natural size*. Fig. 1. Portion of var. *acutum*. 2. Portion of the obtuse form. 3. Fertile segment:—*more or less magnified*.

Plate 34.

ASPLENIUM FONTANUM, *Bernh.*

Smooth Rock Spleenwort.

ASPLENIUM *fontanum*; small; caudex short, thick, subtuberous, densely rooting; stipites one to three inches in length, slender, pale brownish-green, densely tufted; fronds three to six inches long, linear- or broad-lanceolate, attenuated below, membranaceous, bright-green, bipinnate; pinnæ approximate, a quarter to half an inch long, patent or sometimes reflexed, sessile, ovate, obtuse, lowest ones dwarfed, tripartite; pinnules obovate or cuneate, minute, half a line long, the base entire, the rest coarsely and spinuloso-dentate; sori few on each pinnule or lobe, at length confluent; involucres very small, athyroid, white, thin, membranaceous.

ASPLENIUM fontanum. *Bernh. in Schrad. New. Journ.* 1806. *v.* 1. *pt.* 2. *p.* 26. *Sm. Eng. Fl. v.* 4. *p.* 312. *Hook. et Arn. Brit. Fl. ed.* 8. *p.* 500. *Metten. Asplen. p.* 140. *Moore, Brit. Ferns, Nat. Print. t.* 35 *A. Hook. Sp. Fil. v.* 3. *p.* 193.

ASPLENIUM Halleri (*fronds narrow-lanceolate*), *Willd. Spr. Syst. Veget. v.* 4. *p.* 88.

ATHYRIUM fontanum. *Roth, Fl. Germ. v.* 3. *p.* 59.

ATHYRIUM Halleri. *Roth, Fil. Germ. v.* 3. *p.* 60. *Fée, Gen. Fil. p.* 180.

ASPLENIUM fontanum. *Sw. in Schrad. Journal, v.* 2. *p.* 40. *Syn. Fil. p.* 57. *Schk. Fil. p.* 52. *t.* 53. *Willd. Sp. Pl. v.* 5. *p.* 272. *Engl. Bot. t.* 2024.

POLYPODIUM fontanum. *Linn. Sp. Pl. p.* 1550. *Bolton, Fil. p.* 38. *t.* 21. *Sw. Syn. Fil. p.* 67.

Hab. Walls and rocks; very rare, and indeed, as the accurate Mr. Hewett Watson considers it, a very dubious native. Tooting, Surrey; Matlock, Derbyshire; Swanage, Dorsetshire; Petersfield, Hants, and in Merionethshire, are given as stations, and indeed some other localities: but all need confirmation. Consult, on this subject, H. Watson's 'Cybele,' v. 3. p. 275; our own observations in 'Kew Garden Miscellany,' v. 7. p. 340, and Mr. Moore's notes at p. 25 of vol. 8 of the same Miscellany.

This is a very beautiful and well-marked species in all the specimens (including Mr. Hawker's, from a wall in Hampshire) which we have seen; small, with very finely cut pinnæ and pinnules, the lower pinnæ dwarfed and remote, the rest approximate and often compact. But Mr. Moore has under this species (in Brit. Ferns, Nat. Print. sub t. 35) introduced a cultivated plant of unknown origin, under the name of *Asplenium refractum*, and which I have, in my 'Species Filicum,' provisionally placed as var. *refractum*, "larger, pinnæ broad, pinnatifid, very crowded; stipes and rachis beneath castaneous:" but I know too little about it to offer further remarks.

The localities of this Fern, on the Continent, are usually, if not entirely, south of the parallel of England, central European; France, Italy, Spain, Germany, etc.

PLATE 34. Fertile plant of *Asplenium fontanum*, Bernh.,—*natural size*. Fig. 1. Fertile pinnule. 2. Fertile segment:—*magnified*.

PLATE 35.

ASPLENIUM FILIX-FŒMINA, *Bernh.*

Short-fruited Spleenwort, or Lady-Fern.

ASPLENIUM (Athyrium) *Filix-fœmina*; caudex ascending, palenceous, with broad ferruginous scales; stipites tufted, a span to a foot or more long, stramineous-brown; fronds one and a half to three feet long, oblong, rather suddenly acuminate, submembranaceous, bi- rarely tri-pinnate; primary pinnæ numerous, patent, from a moderately broad, nearly sessile base, oblong-lanceolate, acuminate, four to six inches long; pinnules numerous, approximate, horizontally patent, sessile, half to three-quarters of an inch long, oblong, rather obtuse, lower ones deeply pinnatifid, the segments ovate, with two to three strong and sharp serratures, superior ones more entire, coarsely serrated, uppermost ones confluent into a pinnatifid or serrated apex; sori copious, one to each segment of the pinnule, near the rachis, oblong; involucres very convex, straight or variously curved, and horseshoe-shaped, membranaceous, more or less fringed or erose at the margin.

ASPLENIUM Filix-fœmina. *Bernh. in Schrad. N. Journ. Bot.* 1806, v. 1. pt. 2. p. 26. t. 2. f. 7 (*sori*). *Hook. and Arn. Brit. Fl. ed.* 8. p. 591. *Metten. Fil. Hort. Lips.* p. 79. t. 13. f. 15–16. *Asplen.* p. 199 (*pinnæ and sori excellent*). *Asa Gray, Man. Bot. N. U. St. Illustr.* p. 595. *Hook. Sp. Fil.* p. 217.

NEPHRODIUM Filix-fœmina. *Mich. Fl. Bor. Am.* v. 2. p. 268.

ATHYRIUM Filix-fœmina. *Desv. Pr. Tent. Pterid.* p. 98. t. 3. f. 5 (*involucres straight*). *Moore, Brit. Ferns, Nat. Print.* t. 30–34.

ASPIDIUM Filix-fœmina. *Sw. Syn. Fil.* p. 59. *Schk. Fil.* p. 56. t. 48–59. *Willd. Sp. Pl.* v. 5. p. 276. *Engl. Bot.* t. 1459. *Sm. Eng. Fl.* v. 4. p. 295.

POLYPODIUM Filix-fœmina. *Linn. Sp. Pl.* p. 1551, *and Pol. rhæticum, Linn. Herb.*

ASPIDIUM asplenioides. *Sw. Syn. Fil.* p. 60. *Willd. Sp. Pl.* v. 5. p. 276. *Pursh, Fl. Am.* v. 2. p. 664.

NEPHRODIUM asplenioides. *Mich. Fl. Bor. Am.* v. 2. p. 268.

ASPIDIUM angustum. *Willd. Sp. Pl.* p. 277. *Pursh, Fl. Am.* v. 2. p. 661.

ATHYRIUM angustum. *Pr.*

ATHYRIUM Michauxii. *Spr. Kze.*

ATHYRIUM asplenioides. *Desv. Fée, Gen. Fil.* p. 186. *Moore, Ind. Fil.* p. 179.

ASPLENIUM elatius. *Link, Fil. Sp.* p. 94 (*fide Moore*).

POLYPODIUM dentigerum. *Wall. Cat.* n. 334.

ATHYRIUM tripinnatum. *Rupr.* (*fide Moore in Herb. Nostr.*): var. broader and tripinnate.

Var. *latifolium*; pinnules broader elliptical. *Hook. Sp. Fil.* v. 3. p. 218.

ATHYRIUM ovatum. *Newm.*

Hab. Moist shady places, and damp woods; abundant in England, Scotland, and Ireland; *var.* latifolium, Keswick, Cumberland, *Miss Wright.*

Perhaps no species of Fern has given rise to more difference of opinion, as to specific limits, than the present one. Like all Ferns of extended geographical distribution, it is liable to considerable variation, and no two botanists can agree as to the amount of importance which should be given to these variations: the consequence is that we find given by the careful Mr. Moore, such an amount of synonyms as happily falls to the lot of few Ferns. Eighteen different specific names are noticed in Mr. Moore's 'British Ferns, Nature-Printed,' and thirty-one varieties are recorded. In his 'Index Filicum,' where the synonyms are worked out with greater care, the number is "legion,"—these, however, include the freaks of Nature. We are content here to introduce one variety, namely the *latifolium*, and even that passes by insensible degrees into the more common form. The involucre is singularly variable, from a straight line, and closely resembling that of true *Asplenium*, to hippocrepiform or horseshoe-shaped, which again comes so near the reniform, that not a few botanists have referred the species to *Aspidium* and *Nephrodium*.

Asplenium Filix-fœmina is widely distributed throughout the Continent of Europe and Northern Asia. Himalaya, from the extreme north-west to Bhotan, *Wallich, Edgworth, Hook. fil. and Thomson*, elev. 10–12,000 feet, according to *Strachey* and *Winterbottom*; Kamtschatka, *Beechey*; Japan and Manchuria and Amur, *C. Wright, Wilford*. Crete, small specimens almost passing into *Asplenium Hohenackerianum*; and the same form is sent by *Schimper*, n. 1270 and 740, from Abyssinia. Madeira, *Lowe and others* (a deeply incised form); Canaries, *Webb*; Algeria, *Boué*; North America, quite identical with the European plant; Canada (*Goldie*) to New Orleans, and westward to the Rocky Mountains, and to Oregon and British Columbia (where it is often tripinnate). South America; Venezuela, *Fendler*, n. 405; Caracas, *Linden*, n. 518; Cuba, *Pœppig*; Mexico, *Galeotti*, n. 6425?

PLATE 35. Fig. 1 and 2. Fertile plant of *Asplenium Filix-fœmina*, Bernh.,—*natural size*. 3. Fertile pinna of var. *latifolium*,—*natural size*. 4. Fertile pinna. 5. Sorus:—*magnified*.

Plate 36.

ASPLENIUM (HEMIDICTYUM) CETERACH, *L.*

Common Ceterach, or Scaly Spleenwort.

ASPLENIUM (Hemidictyum) *Ceterach*; caudex short, thick, densely rooting; fronds six to eight or ten inches long, cæspitose, lanceolate, subcoriaceous, opaque, deeply pinnatifid, green above and scaleless, beneath densely clothed with imbricated, tawny, entire or toothed scales, the base tapering into a paleaceous slender stipes; segments broad-ovate or oblong, horizontal, obtuse, lowest ones (sometimes free) much abbreviated; veins united and anastomosing towards the margin; sori short, oblong; involucre very narrow, sometimes obsolete.

ASPLENIUM Ceterach. *Linn. Sp. Pl. p.* 1538. *Bolton, Fil. Brit. p.* 20. *t.* 12. *Hook. Sp. Fil. v.* 3. *p.* 273.

GRAMMITIS Ceterach. *Sw. Syn. Fil. p.* 23. *Schk. Fil. p.* 186. *t.* 7.

GYMNOGRAMME Ceterach. *Sp. Syst. Veg. v.* 4. *p.* 38. *Pr. Tent. Pterid. p.* 219. *t.* 9. *f.* 10.

GYMNOPTERIS Ceterach. *Bernh. in Schrad. Journ. Bot.* 1806, *v.* 1. *pt.* 2. *p.* 22.

SCOLOPENDRIUM Ceterach. *Symons. Engl. Bot. t.* 1244. *Sm. Engl. Fl. v.* 4. *p.* 302.

CETERACH officinarum. *Desv. Willd. Sp. Pl. v.* 5. *p.* 136. *Hook. Gen. Fil. t.* 113 *A. Hook. et Arn. Brit. Fl. ed.* 8. *p.* 579. *t.* 9. *f.* 1. *Fée, Gen. Fil. p.* 206. *t.* 30 *A. f.* 2. *Metten. Fil. Hort. Lips. p.* 80. *t.* 13. *f.* 13.

CETERACH, *and* NOTOPLEURUM Ceterach. *Newn.*

(A splendid var. of this plant is found in Teneriffe, β *aureum*; larger, segments much elongated, scales of the frond generally strongly toothed:— Ceterach aureum, *Link, in Von Buch, Canar. Ins. p.* 138. *Webb, Fl. Canar. v.* 3. *p.* 433. Acrostichum aureum, "*Cav. Anal. de Cienc. Nat. v.* 4. *p.* 104." Grammitis aurea, *Sw. Syn. Fil. pp.* 33 *and* 45. Ceterach Canariense, *Willd. Sp. Pl. v.* 5. *p.* 137. Asplenium latifolium, *Bory, Iles Fort. p.* 311. *t.* 6. Ceterach latifolium, *Fée, Gen. Fil. p.* 206. *t.* 30. *f.* 1 (*excellent*).

Hab. Rocks and old walls, but local; chiefly in limestone districts in England and Ireland; rare in Scotland. Our finest specimens are from Fred. J. Foot, Esq., gathered in Ireland; intermediate between our common form and the very fine state found in the Canary Islands.

On the continent of Europe this is found as far north as the islands of Gothland: eastward it extends to Uralian Siberia, and through southern Europe to the Caucasus, Asia Minor to Kurdistan (*Major Garden*); to North-western Persia, province of Karebagh, Afghan, Kashmir, and Thibet, *Edgworth, Griffith, Hooker fil. and Thomson.* It does not appear to inhabit the New World. On the African continent it is found in the extreme north, Algeria, *Hochstetter;* and the extreme south, at Bavian's River, Cape of Good Hope, *Krebs.*

I have stated my reasons in my 'Species Filicum' for restoring the old Linnæan name to this Fern. Too many naturalists have seen and figured the *involucre* to question its existence, however small and indistinct; and then we have only the venation to separate it from true *Asplenium.*

PLATE 36. Fertile plant of *Asplenium (Hemidictyum) Ceterach,* L.,—*natural size.* Fig. 1. Underside of fertile lobe, with its covering of scales. 2. The same, with the scales removed. 3. Sorus with most of the capsules removed, showing the involucre and the anastomosing venation. 4. Scale from the back of the frond ;—*all more or less magnified.*

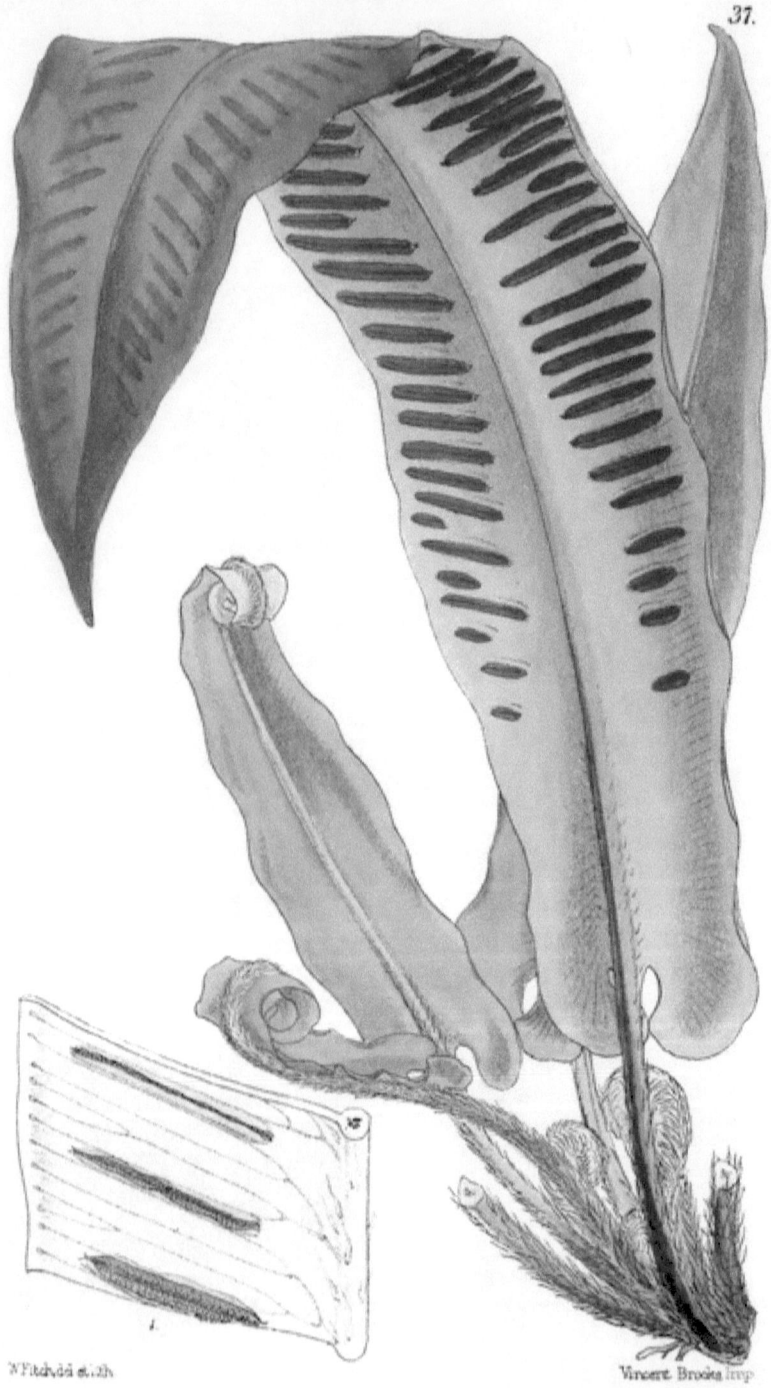

Plate 37.

SCOLOPENDRIUM VULGARE, *Sm.*

Common Hart's-tongue.

Gen. Char. Sori dorsal, linear, transverse, approximate in opposite pairs, opening face to face, often giving the appearance of one sorus bursting in the middle longitudinally. *Veins* free, parallel, simple or forked: occasionally anastomosing towards the margin of the frond.

Scolopendrium *vulgare*; caudex short, erect, stout, scaly as well as the tufted stipites; fronds oblong strap-shaped, moderately acute, deeply auriculato-cordate at the base.

Scolopendrium vulgare. *Sm. Mém. Acad. Roy. des Sc. Turin, v. 5. p. 421. t. 9. f. 2. Sm. Engl. Bot. t. 1150. Engl. Fl. v. 4. p. 301. Hook. and Arn. Brit. Fl. ed. 8. p. 591.*

Scolopendrium officinarum. *Sw. in Schrad. Journ. Bot. 1800. v. 2. p. 61. Syn. Fil. p. 80. Schkh. Fil. p. 78. t. 83. Willd. Sp. Pl. v. 5. p. 348. Pr. Tent. Pterid. p. 119. t. 4. f. 15.*

Scolopendrium Phyllitis. *Roth.*

Asplenium scolopendrium. *Linn. Sp. Pl. p. 1537. Bolton, Fil. Brit. v. 18. t. 11.*

Phyllitis Scolopendrium. *Newman.*

Hab. Woods and shady lanes, sheltered hedge-banks; frequent in England, Scotland, and Ireland.

The common Hart's-tongue, formerly used in rustic medicine on account of its astringent properties, is one of the greatest ornaments to many of our moist shady banks and deep dells, especially near the sea. Mr. Moore observes of it that "it is one of the most prolific in varieties and *monstrous* forms among known Ferns." Curious these are undoubtedly in a physiological point of view, as are the abnormal forms in the animal creation: but one cannot but regret to see such a passion for these deformities among cultivators. To such, however, the sixty-six aberrant forms carefully described by Mr. Moore, in his 'British Ferns, Nature-Printed,' and the plate of deformities there given, will be very acceptable. Amongst the most remarkable of them is Moore's var. *marginatum*; it is found in a wild state, and a garden specimen from the younger Linnæus is in the herbarium of the late Sir J. E. Smith. "The fronds are linear strap-shaped, truncate at the base, the margin incisolobate, the epidermis of the under surface near the margin developed into a lobed excurrent membrane, which as well as the frond itself bears sori." We have native specimens from Nettlecombe, Somerset, communicated by Sir Walter C. Trevelyan, Bart. From the Rev. Mr. Berkeley, too, we possess a specimen gathered in Devonshire, with lobed fronds, having short (but quite perfect) sori on both superficies of the frond. On the upper side they originate invariably at the margin, which forms the narrow sinuses of the lobes, while on the under side they commence (if I may so say) where those of the upper side terminate. In other words, the sori of both sides may be considered one and the same, as a pin forced halfway through the frond transversely at a distance from the margin and applied flat to the two surfaces would be. In this specimen the sori are more numerous on the upper than on the under side.

In the remarkable *Polypodium anomalum*, from Ceylon, described by us in Lond. Journ. of Bot. v. 8. p. 360. t. 11, the normal state of the plant is to have the sori *all* on the superior face of the frond.

Scolopendrium vulgare grows as far north as Scandinavia, " ubi rarissima filix," and south to Greece, Italy, Spain, Madeira, and the Azores : in the Caucasus, in Asia Minor (Nicomedia), *Aucher-Eloi*. I possess it from the State of New York, *Dr. Torrey* (very rare), and from *Pursh*, gathered at Lake Onondaga. From Chiapas, Mexico, I have a specimen gathered by *Linden*, and lately I have received fine specimens gathered at Hakodadi, Japan, *Wilford*.

PLATE 37. A fertile plant of *Scolopendrium vulgare*, Sm.,—*natural size*. Fig. 1. Portion of a frond, with sori :—*magnified*.

Plate 38.

PTERIS (§ Ornithopteris) aquilina, *Linn.*

Common Brake or Bracken.

Gen. Char. Sori continuous, linear, marginal. *Involucre* formed of the reflexed margin of the frond, and frequently dilated into a membrane (sometimes double, as in *Pt. aquilina*).—*Fertile* fronds *unchanged, except in the segments being more contracted:* veins *forked, free, in the only British species.*

Pteris (§ Ornithopteris) *aquilina ;* caudex running long and deep underground; stipites erect, remote, tawny; fronds ample, subdeltoid, coriaceous, tripinnate, glabrous or hairy beneath; primary divisions long-petioled; ultimate pinnæ sessile; pinnules spreading, linear, more or less approximate, entire or hastate, or deeply pinnatifid; segments oblong or linear, ultimate ones more or less elongated; involucre double, membranaceous, more or less villous and ciliated (inner one the smaller, sometimes obsolete).

Pteris aquilina. *Linn. Sp. Pl. p.* 1533. *Sw. Syn. Fil. p.* 100. *Willd. Sp. Pl. v.* 5. *p.* 402. *Ag. Sp. Gen. Pterid. p.* 49. *Sm. Engl. Bot. t.* 1679. *Engl. Fl. v.* 4. *p.* 318. *Hook. and Arn. Brit. Fl. ed.* 8. *p.* 592. *Hook. Sp. Fil. v.* 2. *p.* 196. *t.* 141 *A and B (and see copious remarks on this species in note p.* 195). *Moore, Brit. Ferns, Nat. Print. t.* 44.

Allosorus aquilinus. *Pr. Tent. Pterid. p.* 153.

Pteris caudata. *Schkh. Fil. t.* 95, 96. *Hook. and Arn. Bot. of Beech. Voy. p.* 455 *(not Linn.).*

Pteris recurvata. *Wall. Cat. n.* 113, *and* Pt. firma, *ejusd. n.* 100.

Hab. The most common of all Ferns in open heaths, woods, and thickets, and upon elevated mountains throughout England, Scotland, and Ireland: in open situations seldom attaining a large size; but in favourable spots, far exceeding the height of a man, and forming a favourite haunt of deer.

The commonness of this plant renders it less an object of interest than its merits deserve. It was called *aquilina* by Linnæus, from a fancied resemblance to the imperial eagle[*] on a transverse section of the base of the stipes. This appearance is due to the vascular bundles of tissue being arranged in a peculiar, sinuose manner, around the central cellular substance, which is of a different colour from the rest of the interior, and indeed

[*] In England it is considered to bear a faithful resemblance to King Charles in the Oak.

contains the mucilage which has rendered a variety of this species, common in New Zealand, to be employed as an article of food, as related in the Introductory Notice to this volume; and till better food was introduced, the consumption of *Fern-root* was there very great. The peasantry in England employ the stems of the *Brake* or *Bracken* for another purpose, by procuring an alkali from the burnt ashes, which they mix with water and form into balls. These latter are made hot in the fire, and then used to make lye for scouring linen (*Withering*).

The involucre of this Fern does in general, but not always, constitute a *double* membrane, first detected by Mr. Thomas Smith (see note in Sp. Fil. v. 2. p. 195), hardly of sufficient importance or constancy to constitute a generic distinction.

In regard to geographical distribution, our herbarium is inundated with samples from all parts of the world, in all latitudes, from Lapland in 67° north, to Akaroa, in the south of New Zealand, and in tropical as well as temperate and subarctic regions. It is true the plant has gone under different names, according as it has been found in different and remote countries. A more than sufficiently full list of stations and synonyms has been given by us in the 'Species Filicum,' *l.c.*

PLATE 38. Portion of a caudex and stipes and young frond of *Pteris aquilina*, Linn.,—*natural size*. Fig. 1. Fertile segment,—*magnified*. 2. Portion of the involucre,—*more magnified*. 3. Portion with the involucre laid open, showing its double nature and the capsular receptacle,—*more magnified*.

PLATE 39.

CRYPTOGRAMME CRISPA, *Br.*

Curled Rock-Brake, or Parsley Fern.

Gen. Char. Sori roundish or oblong, submarginal, soon confluent. *Involucre* formed by the revolute margin of the pinnules, which in a young state meet at the back. *Veins* forked. *Fertile fronds* dissimilar to the sterile ones.

CRYPTOGRAMME *crispa;* caudex short, thick, scaly; stipites tufted, numerous; fronds of two kinds, submembranaceous, triangular-ovate; *sterile ones* bipinnate; pinnules bi-tripinnatifid, segments cuneate or oblong, rarely elliptical and pinnatifido-serrate, often bidentate; *fertile fronds* on longer stipites, bipinnate, tripinnate below; pinnules linear-oblong (rarely elliptical), obtuse, entire, narrowed at the base; involucres in age quite spreading from the copious confluent sori.

CRYPTOGRAMME crispa. *Brown in Richard's App. to Frankl. First Journ. p.* 54. *Hook. Gen. Fil. t.* 113. *Hook. and Arn. Brit. Fl. ed.* 8. *p.* 402. *Hook. Sp. Fil. v.* 2. *p.* 128.

PHOROLOBUS crispus. *Desv. in Mém. Soc. Linn. Par. p.* 291. *t.* 11. *Fée, Gen. Fil. p.* 130. *t.* 6 D.

ALLOSORUS crispus. *Bernh. in Schrad. N. Journ. Bot.* 1800. *v.* 1. *pt.* 2. *p.* 536. *Pr. Tent. Pterid. p.* 152. *Metten. Moore, Brit. Ferns, Nat. Print. t.* 8.

ALLOSORUS minutus. *Turcz. Phl. Imag. et Descr. Fl. Ross. p.* 9. *t.* 3.

PTERIS crispa. *Linn. MS., fide Sw., Eng. Bot. t.* 1160. *Sw. Syn. Fil. p.* 101. *Schk. Fil. p.* 90. *t.* 98. *Willd. Sp. Pl. v.* 5. *p.* 395. *Sw. Eng. Fl. v.* 4. *p.* 319.

OSMUNDA crispa. *Linn. Sp. Pl. p.* 1522.

PTERIS Stelleri, *Gmel.* Allosorus, *Rupr.*

Hab. Rocks, especially such as are loose, and stone walls. "Frequent on the mountains (up to 2–3000 feet of elev.) of Scotland and the northern provinces, with a few outlying stations on the much lower hills of the Severn and Peninsula," *H. Watson.* Ireland; mountainous countries in the north; abundant in the Mourne Mountains, *Mackay.*

This elegant Fern is so totally unknown in all the south and middle of England, that botanists who visit the north-west of England and many parts of Scotland and Ireland are struck with its great beauty. It adorns many rocks and stone walls among the English lakes. In Ireland it would appear to be wholly confined to the mountainous countries of the north.

Upon the Continent it is general throughout middle and northern Europe, in mountain regions and moist districts as far north as Lapland, and east to Lake Baikal and Siberia; south to the Pyrenees, Sierra Nevada, etc., in Spain; elev. 8–9000 feet; and to Mount Olympus, in Asia Minor (*Sibthorpe*). I have in this work only noticed the European form of this plant. Some of the most able of botanists have considered as distinct a state of this, with generally broader fertile pinnules, abundant in the mountains of Northern India (*C. Brunoniana*, Wall.), and another found in the Rocky Mountains of North America, and extending thence to California and British Columbia (*C. acrostichoides*, Br.); but I am satisfied that the views I have expressed of their specific identity are correct; indeed, I possess some Scottish specimens which are almost identical with those from India and North America; and from the United States and from British Columbia I have specimens quite agreeing with the common European form.

PLATE 39. *Allosorus crispus*, Br., with fertile and barren fronds,—*natural size*. Fig. 1. Pinnule of a sterile frond. 2. Fertile pinnule. 3. Portion of a fertile frond, with the involucre spread open, showing the venation and sori:—*more or less magnified*.

PLATE 40.

BLECHNUM BOREALE, *Sw.*

Northern Hard-Fern.

Gen. Char. Sori dorsal, linear, continuous, parallel with and usually near the costa. *Involucres* of the same shape as the sori.

BLECHNUM *boreale;* caudex stout, ascending; fronds tufted, of two kinds, lanceolate, attenuated at the base, coriaceo-membranaceous; *sterile ones* on very short stipites, pectinato-pinnatifid; the segments linear-oblong, very compact: *fertile ones* on long stipites, pinnated; pinnæ remote, contracted, linear; sori, when young, intramarginal, in age appearing to cover the whole surface of the under side of the pinnules.

BLECHNUM boreale. *Sw. Syn. Fil. p.* 115. *Sm. Eng. Bot. t.* 1159; *Eng. Fl. v.* 4. *p.* 316. *Schk. Fil. t.* 110. *Schlecht. Adumbr. Fil. Cap. p.* 38. *Hook. and Arn. Brit. Fl. ed.* 8. *p.* 592. *Willd. Sp. Pl. v.* 5. *p.* 408.

LOMARIA borealis. *Link.*

STEGANIA borealis. *Br.*

SPICANTA borealis. *Pr. Epim. Bot. p.* 114.

BLECHNUM Spicant. *Sm. Mem. Acad. Roy. Turin, v.* 5. *p.* 411. *Moore, Brit. Ferns, Nat. Print. t.* 43 C.

OSMUNDA Spicant. *Linn. Sp. Pl. p.* 1522.

LOMARIA Spicant. *Desv. in Berol. Mag. v.* 5. *p.* 325. *Presl, Tent. Pterid. p.* 142. *Fée, Gen. Fil. p.* 68. *Hook. Sp. Fil. v.* 3. *p.* 14. *Pappe and Rawson, Syn. Fil. Afr. Austr. p.* 29.

Hab. Woods, heaths, and hedge-banks; abundant in England, Scotland, and Ireland, especially in a poor light soil.

Clear and distinct as are the true species of *Blechnum* (with the sori and involucre running close to the midrib of the pinnule) and of *Lomaria* (with involucre formed by a reflexed membranaceous margin of the pinna), yet it is well known there are many intermediate gradations, which render it difficult to decide to which genus they should belong; and hence Mettenius and others have united the two genera into one. The present species is an example. The fertile pinnæ are narrow, and if they be examined in a younger state, there will be seen a portion of parenchyme at the margin, outside the involucre, showing that the latter is not formed by the inflection of the margin. In a more advanced state the margin seems obliterated, and then the species appears a *Lomaria*. On account of its general habit and dimorphous fronds, I have preferred, in the 'Species Filicum,' to place it in *Lomaria*, but in the present work, exclusively confined to British Ferns, it may be more convenient to retain the name adopted by the generality of English authors. It is the only species of either genera found in Britain, and it is certainly a very graceful plant, especially common in our northern heaths and moors; and not in Britain only, but almost throughout Europe, from Norwegian Lapland to Spain and the islands of the Mediterranean, Crete, etc. It is found in Middle Russia, in Madeira, the Azores, and Teneriffe, which appears to be its southern limit in the northern hemisphere. Eastward it extends to the Caucasian provinces, and is found in Kamtchatka. A slight variety is found in Japan, but it does not appear to inhabit any part of America, save the north-west, British Columbia, and as far north as the Russian province of Sitka. These specimens are of a larger size than the European form. The South African locality requires confirmation. A forked and very distorted form of the barren fronds of this is occasionally met with.

PLATE 40. Caudex, with a tuft of sterile and fertile fronds,—*natural size*. Fig. 1. Sterile segment of a frond. 2. Fertile pinna, with a young intramarginal involucre. 3. Section. 4. Portion of the same, more advanced. 5. Fertile pinna, with involucre submarginal. 6. Portion of the same, in a more advanced state,—*all more or less magnified*.

PLATE 41.

ADIANTUM CAPILLUS-VENERIS, *L.*

Maiden-hair Fern.

Gen. Char. Sori roundish or transversely oblong, marginal. *Involucres* formed each of a separate reflexed portion or lobe of the margin of the frond, opening inwards, bearing on the under side the capsules on veins which are continued from the frond.—Veins *forked and free in the British species.*

ADIANTUM *Capillus-Veneris;* caudex creeping, scaly; stipites crowded, slender, ebenous, and glossy; fronds ovate in circumscription, a span to a foot long, thin, membranaceous, very delicate, tri-quadripinnate; pinnules half an inch long, and as much broad, flabellato-cuneate or obliquely subrhomboid, on long, very slender, black petioles, the superior margin deeply and irregularly inciso-lobate; sori as broad as the lobe, transversely oblong or subreniform.

ADIANTUM Capillus-Veneris. *Linn. Sp. Pl. p.* 1558. *Sw. Syn. Fil. p.* 124. *Jacq. Misc. v.* 2. *p.* 77. *t.* 7. *Willd. Sp. Pl. v.* 5. *p.* 449. *Sm. Engl. Bot. t.* 1564; *Engl. Fl. v.* 4. *p.* 320. *Hook. and Arn. Brit. Fl. ed.* 8. *p.* 593. *Moore, Brit. Ferns, Nat. Print. t.* 45.

Hab. Moist rocks and walls, south and west of England and Ireland, generally near the sea: rare. Jersey and probably other of the Channel Islands. Ilfracombe, Watermouth, Brixham, and Mewstone Bay, Devon; Carclew, Penzance, and various places between St. Ives and Hayle, Cornwall; Cheddar Cliffs, Somerset. Barny Island, Porthkerry, Aberthaw and Dunraven, Glamorganshire. The Isle of Man appears to be its northern limit. In Ireland, the South Isles of Arran, and near Roundstone, Galway; near Tralee, Kerry, and Ballyranghan, Clare, are recorded localities.

This may be reckoned among the rarities of our native Ferns. Chiefly in the southern districts of our island the species seems to have attained its northern limits; for in warmer temperatures, in almost every part of the globe, it is a frequent denizen: Europe, Asia, Africa, and America, as more fully recorded in our 'Species Filicum,' v. 2. p. 36. In the south of Europe it is extremely abundant, and in France, where it is known by the name of *Capillaire,* travellers cannot fail to have seen it luxuriating at the mouths of wells, and often considerably down the wells, lining them with a dense mass of velvety green. It is a plant too of some notoriety, having, from the time of Dioscorides, been more or less used in conjunction with the *Asplenium Adiantum-nigrum*, and more recently with the American Maiden-hair Fern, *Adiantum pedatum*, L., for medicinal purposes. The fronds of our common Maiden-hair are sold in herb-shops, in the dried state, when if rubbed, they are slightly odorous; the taste is sweetish and bitterish, and they contain tannic or gallic acid, bitter extractive, and a volatile oil, and have been chiefly used as pectorals in chronic catarrhs, and in the form of a syrup. But as the active properties of this Fern are, to say the least, very dubious, it is rejected in modern practice, and the *Sirop de Capillaire* is now prepared exclusively of clarified syrup, flavoured with orange-flower water; and this, Pereira tells us, is sanctioned by the Prussian and Hamburg pharmacopœias, giving formulæ for a *syrupus florum aurantii*, to be used "in loco syrupi capillorum Veneris."

PLATE 41. Fertile plant of *Adiantum Capillus-Veneris*, L.,—*natural size*. Fig. 1. Pinnule, with sori,—*magnified*. 2. Apex of the lobe of a fertile pinnule, with the involucre forced back, and some of the capsules removed, showing that the receptacles of these capsules are on the veins which run up from the pinnule into the involucre,—*more magnified*.

W.F.n.r. del et lith.

Vincent Brooks, Imp

PLATE 42.

TRICHOMANES RADICANS, *Sw.*

Rooting Bristle-Fern.

Gen. Char. Involucre subcylindrical, entire or nearly so (not two-lipped). *Capsules* sessile, with a broad, entire, oblique ring, surrounding on a columnar *receptacle*. *Receptacle* of the sori usually exserted in the form of a bristle.

Obs. The Fern here to be described, together with the subjects of the two following Plates, belong to a group which differs so much in the fructification, as well as in the nature and texture of the fronds, from other Ferns, that some botanists exclude them from true Ferns altogether, and constitute a separate family under the name of *Hymenophyllaceæ* (well named from the delicate texture of the frond, from ὑμην, *a membrane*, and φυλλον, *a leaf*). Indeed the genus *Loxsoma* (see the figure of the rare *L. Cunninghami*, Br., figured in a late number, Plate 31, of the 'Garden Ferns') exhibits a fructification corresponding with *Trichomanes*, but with the entire habit and texture in its fronds of the true Ferns. I cannot subscribe therefore to such a separation, and prefer considering them as a group, under the name of *Hymenophylleæ*. The three species now alluded to are all that are known of the group in the temperate regions of Europe, but in the warmer parts of the world the species are very numerous, and much admired for their delicacy and beauty.

TRICHOMANES *radicans*, Sw.; caudex very long, creeping, tomentose and scaly; fronds ovate or oblong, acuminate, rather firm, membranaceous, bi-triquadripinnatifid, dark-green, primary divisions ovate or lanceolate, cuneate at the base, the segments oblong, obtuse, often bifid; involucres solitary in the axils of the superior segments, margined, cylindrical, entire at the mouth; receptacles of the sori much exserted beyond the involucre; rachis strongly winged.

TRICHOMANES radicans. *Sw. Fl. Ind. Occ. p.* 1736; *Syn. Fil. p.* 143. *Willd. Sp. Pl. v.* 5. *p.* 513. *Hook. Sp. Fil. v.* 1. *p.* 125 (*not Hook. and Grev. Ic. Fil.* 218). *Hook. and Arn. Brit. Fl. ed.* 8. *p.* 593. *Moore, Brit. Ferns, Nat. Print. t.* 48. *Pr. Hymenoph. p.* 16. *f.* 2 B.

TRICHOMANES scandens. *Hedw. Fil. cum ic.* (*excl. most of the synonyms*).

TRICHOMANES speciosum. *Willd. Sp. Pl. v.* 5. *p.* 514.

TRICHOMANES pyxidiferum. *Huds. Fl. Angl. p.* 461 (*not Linn.*). *Bolton, Fil. Brit. p.* 561. *t.* 30.

TRICHOMANES brevisetum. *Br. in Hort. Kew. ed.* 2. *v.* 5. *p.* 529. *Sm. Eng. Fl. v.* 4. *p.* 324.

TRICHOMANES alatum. *Hook. in Fl. Lond. N. S. v.* 4. *t.* 53 (*not Sw.*).

TRICHOMANES europæum. *Sm. in Rees's Cycl.*

HYMENOPHYLLUM alatum. *Sm. in E. Bot.* 147 (*not Schk. Fil. t.* 135 *b.*). *Willd. Sp. Pl. v.* 5. *p.* 526.

HYMENOPHYLLUM Tunbridgense. β, *Sm. Fl. Brit. p.* 1142.

Var. β. *Andrewsii;* fronds lanceolate; sori very copious; receptacles of the sori longer; involucres more winged. *Newm. Brit. Ferns, ed.* 3. *p.* 292.

TRICHOMANES Andrewsii. *Newm. l.c. ed.* 2. *p.* 14.

Hab. Wet rocks in mountainous countries; chiefly in Ireland. Ireland: Hermitage Glen and Powerscourt, county Wicklow; near Youghal, Cork, and Bantry, and in other places in that county; Turk Waterfall, Cromaglaun Mountain, Mount Eagle, near Dingle, Iveragh, etc., county Kerry. Formerly abundant at Bellbank, near Bingsley, Yorkshire, but not now found there. Var. β. Glouin Curragh, Iveragh, Kerry, *W. Andrews, Esq.*

Like the subject of the last Plate (*Adiantum Capillus-Veneris*), this is a local plant, though plentiful in some parts of Ireland. Further south however, in Europe, and extending even into the tropics (especially if mountains) it is abundant, in the African North Atlantic islands, in various parts of Asia, North and South America, and the West Indian and the Sandwich Islands. A more full list of localities than it is here needful or desirable to give, will be found in the 'Species Filicum,' *l.c.*, and also of the synonyms; for the different names are almost as numerous as are the different places of growth. It was long supposed to be peculiar to the British Islands.

The plant itself is one of great beauty, even in its ordinary state, and is much sought for and prized by Fern-cultivators; but the var. *Andrewsii* is especially beautiful, having elongated and often drooping fronds, with copious fructifications, rendered more conspicuous by the very much exserted receptacles, all turning or curved upwards as it were towards the strongest light.

PLATE 42. Fertile plant of *Trichomanes radicans*, Sw. Fig. 1. Pinnatifid segment, with a sorus,—*magnified*. 2. Sorus, with the involucre cut through vertically, showing the capsules attached to the long columnar receptacle,—*more magnified*. 3. Front; and 4, side view of a sessile capsule, showing the broad, entire ring:—*still more magnified*.

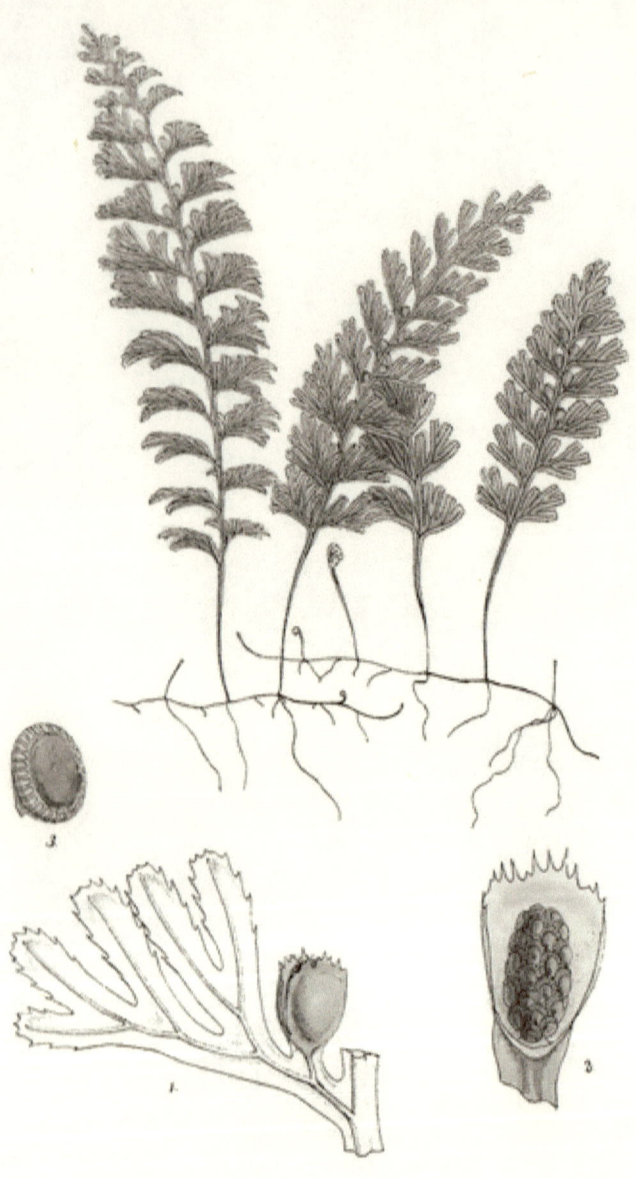

Plate 43.

HYMENOPHYLLUM Tunbridgense, *Sm.*

Tunbridge Filmy-Fern.

Gen. Char. Involucre of the same texture as the frond, 2-valved, opening vertically. *Capsules* sessile, with a broad entire oblique ring, situated on a columnar *receptacle* generally shorter than the involucre.

HYMENOPHYLLUM *Tunbridgense*; fronds tender, soft, pinnate; pinnæ distichous, vertical, pinnatifid; the segments linear, undivided, or bifid, and as well as the axillary solitary, suborbicular, compressed; involucre spinuloso-serrate; rachis winged.

HYMENOPHYLLUM Tunbridgense. *Sm. Fl. Brit. p.* 1141; *Eng. Bot. t.* 162; *Engl. Fl. v.* 4. *p.* 326. *Sw. Syn. Fil. p.* 147. *Willd. Sp. Fil. v.* 5. *p.* 529. *Hook. Fl. Lond. N. S. t.* 71. *Hook. Sp. Fil. v.* 1. *p.* 95. *Hook. and Arn. Brit. Fl. ed.* 8. *p.* 594. *Moore, Brit. Ferns, Nat. Print. t.* 49 *A. Van den Bosch, Synops. Hymenoph. p.* 63.

TRICHOMANES Tunbridgense. *Linn. Sp. Pl. p.* 1561. *Bolton, Brit. Ferns, p.* 58. *t.* 2. *f.* 17 (*not t.* 31).

Hab. Rare in the south and east of England; yet it was first detected on moist rocks at Tunbridge (whence its specific name), where it now appears to be extinct. More frequent in the hilly and mountain districts in the west of England; very abundant in Wales and in Scotland, clothing the surfaces of rocks in patches of two or three feet in length; often found in company with the following species, *H. Wilsoni*, Hook.

This little delicate Fern was for some time supposed to be peculiar to this country, and for awhile even to the vicinity of Tunbridge. Now it is found in various parts of Europe, and even in tropical regions both of the Old and New World. It must be confessed however that the exotic specimens require to be more carefully examined than they have yet been, before their identity can be determined. In general only small and indifferent specimens are received, or such as are badly prepared.

PLATE 43. Fertile specimens of *Hymenophyllum Tunbridgense*, Sm.,—*natural size*. Fig. 1. Pinna and sorus,—*magnified*. 2. Involucre, with one valve removed, showing the sessile capsules covering the short columnar receptacle,—*more magnified*. 3. Capsule,—*still more magnified*.

W. Fitch, del et lith.   Vincent Brooks, Imp

PLATE 44.

HYMENOPHYLLUM WILSONI, *Hook.*

Mr. Wilson's Filmy-Fern.

HYMENOPHYLLUM *Wilsoni*; fronds rigid, pinnate; pinnæ recurved, subunilateral, wedge-shaped, four- to six-lobed, the segments linear, undivided or bifid, spinuloso-serrate; involucres axillary, solitary, ovate, obtuse, inflated below, entire; rachis slightly margined above.

HYMENOPHYLLUM Wilsoni. *Hook. Brit. Fil. ed.* 1. 1830, *p.* 450. *Wils. in Engl. Bot. Suppl. t.* 2686 (*excellent*). *Hook. and Arn. Brit. Fl. ed.* 8. *p.* 594. *Van den Bosch, Synops. Hymenoph. p.* 61.

HYMENOPHYLLUM unilaterale? *Bory, in Willd. Sp. Pl. v.* 5. *p.* 521. *Moore, Brit. Ferns, Nat. Print. t.* 49 B.

HYMENOPHYLLUM Tunbridgense. *Schk. Fil. p.* 124. *t.* 135 D.

TRICHOMANES Tunbridgense, *Bolt. Fil. Brit. t.* 31 (*not t.* 2. *f.* 17).

Hab. Moist rocky glens in mountain districts: Devon, Cornwall, and north of England, but rare. Wales. Abundant in the Highlands of Scotland, and in Ireland, especially about the Lakes of Killarney; not unfrequently in company with *H. Tunbridgense.*

This *Hymenophyllum* has given rise to much discussion, and to conflicting opinions: first, as to its distinctness from *H. Tunbridgense;* and secondly, as to its identity with the *H. unilaterale*, a Bourbon species of Bory de St. Vincent, in Willdenow's ' Species Plantarum.' In regard to the first point, I think it is hardly possible to see the two kinds, as I have done in the West Highlands of Scotland, frequently growing on the same rock, in separate patches, yet maintaining their respective characters, without being satisfied of their being really different; and in this opinion I am supported by one of the most accurate and most acute Cryptogamic botanists of the present day, Mr. William Wilson, of Warrington, who had the merit of first distinguishing the two, as recorded in the first edition of our ' British Flora.' "So very different in aspect," writes Mr. Wilson (Eng. Bot. Suppl. t. 2686, under *H. Wilsoni*), "is this truly distinct species from the far more elegant *H. Tunbridgense,* that no botanist who has had the good fortune to see them luxuriantly growing in company in the rocky woods which border the wildly sequestered Upper Lake of Killarney, would hesitate to pronounce them two species. It was there that, in the summer of 1829, I first became acquainted with the true *Tunbridgense*, and had at once the gratification of clearing up my doubts concerning the spurious kind, with which, as the common *Hymenophyllum* of North Wales, Cumberland, and Perthshire, I had long been imperfectly familiar, and also of unexpectedly adding another Fern to the 'British Flora.' "It is," continues Mr. Wilson (viz. *H. Wilsoni*), "more rigid than *H. Tunbridgense*, and more coarsely reticulated. *Frond* oblong, on a shorter stalk; the *pinnæ* obliquely attached, and often much recurved; the segments not so evidently toothed at the apex, and their nerve is continued to the apex. *Involucre* with very convex valves, so as to appear compressed in a contrary direction to the convexity: its stalk much bent upwards." To these characters must be added the entire apices of the valves of the involucre.

In regard to the second point of discussion, whether it be identical with the *H. unilaterale* of Bourbon; probably most of those who maintain that opinion have not had the opportunity of seeing authentic specimens of Bory's *unilaterale*. I do not profess to have had this advantage myself. A specimen from Bourbon, so named, has been sent to me by Von Martius; but that (see Sp. Fil. 1. p. 95) I believe to be much more certainly referable to *H. Tunbridgense*. I have therefore hesitated to consider *H. Wilsoni* as certainly the same as *H. unilaterale*, knowing the latter only from Willdenow's description. Let me add, too, that the highest authority on this extensive group of Ferns, Dr. Van den Bosch, maintains, in his 'Synopsis Hymenophyllacearum,' that *H. Tunbridgense, unilaterale,* and *Wilsoni* are three distinct species. And of one thing I am sure, that our knowledge of the exotic species of *Hymenophyllum* and *Trichomanes* is, at present, but in its infancy; we have much to study and much to correct of what has been written.

PLATE 44. Fertile plant of *Hymenophyllum Wilsoni*, Hook.,—*natural size*. Fig. 1. Pinna and sorus,—*magnified*. 3. Sorus,—*more magnified*.

PLATE 45.

OSMUNDA REGALIS.

Osmund Royal, or Flowering Fern.

Gen. Char. Capsules subglobose, subcoriaceous, pedicellate or sessile, reticulated, opening vertically halfway down into two valves, and having on one side towards the apex a very small, incomplete, gibbous *ring. Involucre* none.—*Handsome large* Ferns, *with pinnate or bipinnate* fronds; *the* fertile fronds *or portions that become fertile, much altered, and contracted, and loaded with* capsules. Veins *forked, free.*

OSMUNDA *regalis;* fronds bipinnate, pinnules oblong, nearly entire, sometimes auricled, or more or less auricled or lobed at the base, the inferior ones opposite; fertile panicle bipinnate (in British specimens), occupying the extremity of the frond.

OSMUNDA regalis. *Linn. Sp. Pl. p.* 1521. *Sw. Syn. Fil. p.* 160. *Schk. Fil. p.* 147. *t.* 105. *Willd. Sp. Pl. v.* 5. *p.* 97. *Engl. Bot. v.* 3. *t.* 209. *Hook. in Fl. Lond. t.* 150. *Hook. and Arn. Brit. Fl. ed.* 8. *p.* 595. *Bolt. Fil. Brit. p.* 6. *t.* 5. *Sm. Engl. Fl. v.* 4. *p.* 327. *Moore, Brit. Ferns, Nat. Pr. t.* 50.

OSMUNDA spectabilis. *Willd. Sp. Pl. v.* 5. *p.* 98. *Pursh, Fl. Am. p.* 658.

OSMUNDA palustris. *Schrad. in Goet. Gel. Anz.* 1824, *p.* 866.

OSMUNDA Capensis. *Pr. Pterid. Suppl. p.* 63.

OSMUNDA speciosa. *Wall. Cat. n.* 50.

OSMUNDA Hilsenbergii. *Hook. and Grev. Bot. Misc. v.* 3. *p.* 230. *Kze. Schk. Fil. Suppl.*

OSMUNDA gracilis. *Link, Hort. Berol. p.* 81. *t.* 39.

OSMUNDA Hugeliana. *Pr. Pterid. Suppl.*

OSMUNDA obtusifolia. *Willd. in Kaulf. En. Fil. p.* 43.

OSMUNDA glaucescens. *Link, Fil. Hort. Berol. v.* 2. *p.* 146.

OSMUNDA Leschenaultii. *Wall. Cat. n.* 51.

WATER-FERN, or Osmund the Waterman. *Gerarde, Herball, ed. Johns. p.* 1131.

Hab. Bogs, marshy grounds, at the margins of woods, etc., in various parts of England, Scotland, and Ireland.

We are now come, in the subjects of this and the following Plates, to a set of Plants so different in appearance and structure from true Ferns, that they are called by some *Pseudo-Filices* (or

False Ferns). The present genus is readily recognized by the nature of the capsule: instead of being of a delicate and brittle texture, and more or less surrounded by an elastic jointed ring, and bursting irregularly, here it is of a firm, opaque, and somewhat coriaceous texture, opening vertically by two valves, and furnished only with the rudiment of a ring. This is the only species known in Europe; but it is by no means confined to Europe, as may be judged by the above array of synonyms, which, from the copious specimens in my possession from the four quarters of the globe, I have reason to believe are only slightly modified forms of one and the same species. My herbarium contains specimens from most parts of Europe, to the extreme south; North America, from New Orleans to Canada; from Africa, Algeria in the north, Cape of Good Hope to Natal in the south, and as far as Macalisberg in the south interior; Madagascar, Mauritius, and Bourbon. From tropical America, Mexico, Venezuela, etc.; and various parts of New Granada, through Brazil to the Rio Plata. From India, from Bombay on the west coast, eastward to Khasya, and from various parts of Himalaya, Kumaon to Bhotan. From China, Hongkong, etc.; and Japan, and Tsus-Sima, Gulf of Corea. Dr. Wallich's specimens of his *O. speciosa* have generally, but by no means always, the fronds all barren or all fertile; while those I possess from China and Japan are invariably so.

In no country perhaps are finer specimens produced than in Britain, especially on the west coast of Scotland, near the mouth of the Clyde; and there, including the tussock formed aboveground of the caudex and dense mass of matted fibrous roots, we have measured fronds eleven feet high. From the top of these tussocks or hummocks spring the stipites in clusters, with their ample bipinnated fronds. The pinnæ measure from a span to nearly a foot long in some cases; the pinnules are not unfrequently two and a half inches long, and half an inch broad. The uppermost pinnæ form the panicle of fructification. So far from being "invisible," the conspicuous seed-vessels have given rise to one of the common names of the plant, the "*flowering Fern.*" It is more difficult to discover the origin of the most popular name of the present day, "*Osmund Royal.*" Sir James Smith's conjecture seems to have been generally accepted, from *Osmund*, in Saxon, said to mean "domestic peace." In olden time, as Gerarde assures us, it was called "*Osmund the Waterman;*" and the whitish portion of the root-stock ("which boiled or else stamped, and taken with some kind of liquor, is thought to be good for those that are wounded, dry-beaten, and bruised, or that have fallen from some high place") is called the "*heart of Osmund the Waterman.*" Another name in his day was, "*St.*

Christopher's Herb." Now, as we know St. Christopher was the patron Saint of Watermen, and probably of Water-plants, so St. Osmund might be equally venerated under like circumstances, could we know more of his history than is handed down to us; and a Saint of that name did come over from Normandy in 1066 with William the Conqueror, and one of some celebrity too, for he was made Chancellor of the kingdom, and Bishop of Salisbury, where "he reformed the liturgy for the diocese, which afterwards became general throughout the kingdom, under the name of the Salisbury Liturgy." Such a Saint deserved to have his name handed down to posterity in so truly noble a British Fern.

PLATE 45. Fig. 1, 2, 3, portions of a fertile frond of *Osmunda regalis*, Linn.:—*natural size.* 5. A capsule. 6. Seeds or spores:—*magnified.*

PLATE 46.

OPHIOGLOSSUM VULGATUM, *L.*

Common Adder's-tongue.

Gen. Char. Capsules fleshy, 1-celled, 2-valved, opening transversely, connate, forming a compact 2-ranked *spike. Involucre* none.—Fronds *straight in venation, simple (quite undivided), or palmate, or repeatedly forked, bearing the fertile pedunculated* spike *below the frond, or from its margin.* Stipites *with sheathing scales at the base.* Veins *anastomosing.*

OPHIOGLOSSUM *vulgatum;* terrestrial, caudex or small rooting rhizome; fronds stipitate, undivided, varying from linear-oblong to ovate; fertile spike pedunculate, arising from the base of the frond.

OPHIOGLOSSUM vulgatum. *Linn. Sp. Pl.* p. 1518. *Sw. Syn. Fil.* p. 169. *Schk. Fil.* p. 155. *t.* 153. *Willd. Sp. Fil. v.* 5. p. 58. *Bolt. Fil. Br. v.* 2. p. 3. *Engl. Bot. v.* 2. p. 108. *Hook. Fil. Lond. N.S. a* 78. *Hook. and Arn. Brit. Fl. ed.* 8. p. 595. *Sm. Engl. Fl. v.* 4. p. 329. *Moore, Brit. Ferns, Nat. Pr. t.* 51 *B. and* 51 *C. Pr. Suppl. Tent. Pterid.* p. 49.

OPHIOGLOSSUM Lusitanicum (*a small and narrow-fronded form—see our next Plate,* 47). *Linn. Sp. Pl.* p. 1518. *Lam. Illustr. t.* 861. *f.* 3. *Sw. Syn. Fil.* p. 169. *Willd. Sp. Pl. v.* 5. p. 59. *Hook. and Grev. Ic. Fil. t.* 80, *and in Bot. Misc. v.* 3. p. 218. *Newm. Brit. Ferns, ed.* 3. p. 331. *Presl, Suppl. Tent. Pterid.* p. 50. *Moore, Brit. Ferns, Nat. Pr. t.* 51 *C.*

OPHIOGLOSSUM vulgatum, β. Lusitanicum. *Hook. and Arn. Brit. Fl. ed.* 8. p. 595.

Hab. Old moist pastures, and in woods in various parts of England, Scotland, and Ireland, extending to the extreme north.

The synonyms above given may suffice for illustrating the species of a Fern in a work confined to those of Great Britain. Were it connected with the Ferns of all other countries, I should have felt it my duty to make a far more extended list. Linnæus adopted five species of the genus, exclusive of his *O. scandens* and *O. flexuosum* (long since transferred to *Lygodium,* but including the very distant *O. pendulum* and *O. palmatum*): the three remaining ones are, *O. vulgatum* (fronds ovate), *O. Lusitanicum* (fronds lanceolate), and *O. reticulatum* (fronds cordate). These may be said to include the extreme forms of all countries; and these Swartz increased to seven, in which he was followed by Willde-

now, but by Presl to twenty-five! keeping apart and placing in
two new genera the only truly distinct species, viz. his *Ophio-
derma pendulum* and *Cheiroglossa palmata*. Dr. Hooker had the
boldness to be the first, as stated in the 'British Flora,' *l.c.*, to
declare these to be slightly modified forms of one and the same
species. "The genus," he says, "affords one of the most
striking examples of the proneness of many botanists to make
species on insufficient grounds, and of the fallacy that prevails
with regard to species being confined within narrow limits. I
confidently affirm that were I to show the authors of many of
the so-called species of *Ophioglossum*, preserved in the Hookerian Herbarium, their own specimens, named by themselves,
and substitute '*Britain*' on their tickets for the distant countries from which they were brought, these authors would unhesitatingly pronounce their plants to be *O. vulgatum*. As to the
book-characters of the species, some are founded on erroneous
observations, others are drawn from exceptional varieties or
forms, and not a few present only differences of words and not
of meaning." It is true, one or two of my own formerly recognized species come into this category; but my numerous specimens received from various portions of the globe, Europe, Asia,
Africa, and America, Australia, continents and islands, tropical
and temperate regions, many of them well authenticated species,
have convinced me of my error in having so done. All have the
fronds destitute of any real costa, and all are reticulated; and in
some of the larger and more luxuriant specimens there are free
veins in some of the areoles, more general towards the margin.

PLATE 46. Common British forms of *Ophioglossum vulgatum*, Linn.,—*natural
size* (the right-hand figure is from Orkney, *Mr. J. T. Syme*, and is clearly a form
passing into *O. Lusitanicum*, L.). Fig. 1. Portion of the frond. 2. Portion of
a fertile spike. 3.–Spores:—*more or less magnified*.

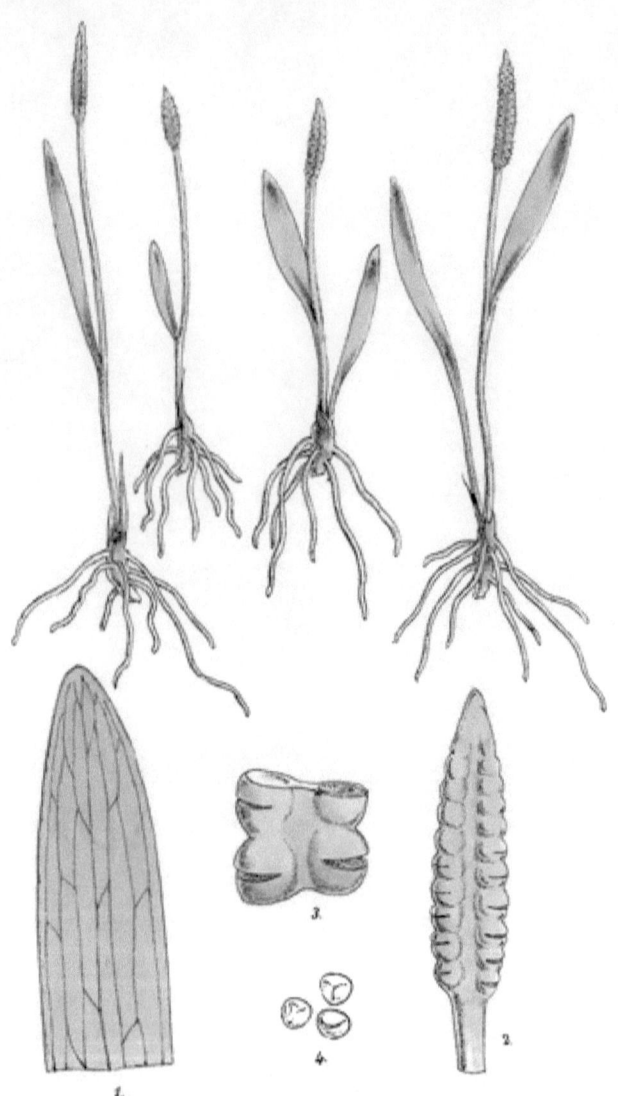

W. Fitch, del. et lith.
Vincent Brooks, Imp.

Plate 47.

OPHIOGLOSSUM vulgatum, *L.*; var. *angustifolium*.

Common Adder's-tongue; narrow-leaved *var.*

Ophioglossum *vulgatum.*
(See specific character and synonyms under Plate 46.)

Var. *angustifolium;* smaller, fronds linear-oblong, areoles of the veins more elongated.

Ophioglossum Lusitanicum. *Linn. Sp. Pl.* p. 1518 (*for the other references, see under* Plate 46).

Hab. Summit of rocks, near Petit Bot Bay, on the south coast of Guernsey, *Mr. G. Wolsey.*

The Channel Islands are remarkable for yielding two Ferns not at present known in any other part of the British Islands, viz. the *Gymnogramme leptophylla,* figured at our Plate 1 of this work, and the subject of our present figure. I wish I could feel as satisfied of the permanency of the species now before us as of that of *Gymnogramme;* but my immense suite of specimens of *Ophioglossum vulgatum,* from all parts of the world, convince me that it is but an extreme form of that species, more frequent indeed nearer or within the tropics than in more northern latitudes: and my specimens from the banks of the Niger, and still further south, Angola, exhibit all the forms of frond between the smallest and narrowest fronds, and decidedly ovato-cordate ones. Indeed, one has but to look at the right-hand figure of our last Plate, and see an Orkney specimen of *O. vulgatum,* which it would be hard to distinguish from *O. Lusitanicum.* I cannot at all agree with Mr. Moore's remarks (Brit. Ferns, Nat. Pr., under this species), who makes its distinguishing characters to depend on "its small size, its thick fleshy texture, and the narrow outline of the sterile branch of its frond; the plants averaging about a couple of inches in height, and rarely exceeding three inches" (hence apparently inferring that it may be fairly allowed to remain separate from *O. vulgatum*);—" unless, indeed, in the Vegetable Kingdom, we must adhere to the rule of combining under the name of a species a lengthened series of widely dissimilar forms, if they happen to be at all seemingly connected, a practice which at the least would be equally inconvenient with the more fashionable mania for subdivision and separation." But truth, and truth alone, should be the object of the researches of the naturalist, however opposed it may be to the views of any particular party. It is true, we do not find free veinlets in the areoles of the frond of *O. Lusitanicum*, but neither do we always see them in the *O. vulgatum*.

PLATE 47. Specimens of *Ophioglossum vulgatum*, L.; var. *angustifolium*, Hook.:—*natural size*. Fig. 1. Portion of a frond. 2. A fertile spike. 3. Portion of a spike, with capsules. 4. Spores:—*more or less magnified*.

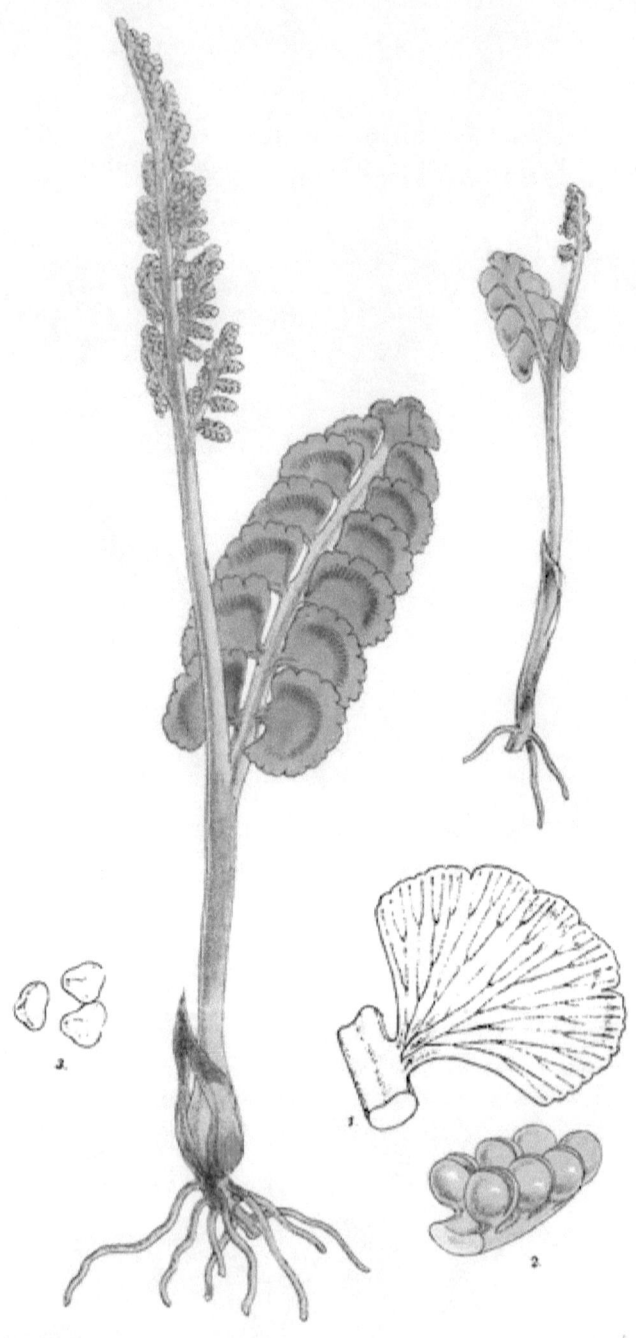

PLATE 48.

BOTRYCHIUM LUNARIA, *Sw.*

Common Moonwort.

Gen. Char. Capsules subglobose, sessile, clustered at the margin and on one side of a pinnated rachis, 1-celled, compressed, opening transversely. *Involucre* none.—Frond, *being a pedunculated* spike *or* panicle *of fructifications.* Veins *forked, free.*

BOTRYCHIUM *Lunaria;* frond oblong, pinnated, pinnæ few, lunate or subflabelliform, crenated or toothed or subpinnatifid; veins radiating, several times dichotomous.

BOTRYCHIUM Lunaria. *Sw. Syn. Fil.* p. 171. *Schk. Fil.* p. 156. *t.* 154. *Willd. Sp. Pl. v.* 5. p. 61. *Hook. in Fl. Lond. Suppl. t.* 66. *Hook. and Arn. Brit. Fl. ed.* 8. p. 596. *Presl, Suppl. Tent. Pterid.* p. 43. *Moore, Brit. Ferns, Nat. Pr.* p. 43. *Sm. Engl. Fl. v.* 4. p. 15.

OSMUNDA Lunaria. *Linn. Sp. Pl.* p. 1519. *Bolt. Fil. Brit.* p. 4. *t.* 4. *Engl. Bot. t.* 318.

β. *Sm.* LUNARIA minor. *Raii Syn.* 129. "*Stalk branched, bearing several leaves and compound spikes, alternately disposed.*" Sm. Eng. Fl. l.c.

γ. *Sm.* LUNARIA racemosa minor, Adianti folio. *Breyn. Cent.* t. 93. "*A slight variety, with more jagged leaves than ordinary.*" Sm. l.c.

δ. *Sm.* LUNARIA minor, foliis dissectis. "*A more spreading habit, with the leaflets pinnatifid.*" Sm. l.c.

Hab. Dry mountain and hilly pastures, and downs near the sea, in various parts of the United Kingdom, from the extreme south to Orkney and Shetland in the north.

Specimens corresponding with the varieties recorded by Smith (though not very clearly defined by him) are not very unfrequent, but appear to me rather malformations, the effect of injury, than varieties worthy of notice. I presume they are included in Mr. Moore's var. *rutaceum*, *B. rutaceum* of continental botanists, and the *B. matricariæfolium*, A. Braun, in Koch's Synopsis, ed. 2. p. 972. Our figures represent the ordinary state of the plant. A very strange figure or monstrosity of it is given by Mr. Newman, Brit. Ferns, ed. 3. p. 324, from a drawing made by Mr. Cruickshank, said to be found on the sands of Barry, Dundee, with four panicles of fructification, and lanceolate and pinnatifid pinnæ, which latter approach the *B. rutaceum*, Sw.; but this must not be confounded with the *B. rutæfolium* of A. Braun and others, which is the *B. matricarioides*, Willd.

The normal form of this is found in various parts of the world, as well as throughout Europe, chiefly in the cooler and temperate regions; in Asiatic Russia, northern India, North America, Fuegia in South America, South Australia, Tasmania, etc.

PLATE 43. Plants of *Botrychium Lunaria*, Sw.,—*natural size*. Fig. 1. Pinna, with a portion of the rachis. 2. Portion of a spikelet, with capsules. 3. Spores: —*more or less magnified*.

Plate 49.

LYCOPODIUM clavatum, *Linn.*

Common Club-Moss, or Wolf's-claw Moss.

Gen. Char. Capsules without a ring, coriaceous, sessile in the axils of the *leaves*, or in distinct *bracts*, 1-celled, 2–3-valved.—Stems *leafy, terrestrial.* Vernation *not circinate.*

Lycopodium *clavatum;* stems very long, creeping, often many feet in length, somewhat distantly and equally branched in a fasciculated manner, fascicles decumbent; leaves densely imbricated, often subsecund, suberect, incurved, terminating in long hair-like points, serrated at the margins, the upper ones mostly entire; spikes in pairs or solitary, cylindrical, on terminal scaly peduncles; bracts cordate, acuminate, sharply serrated.

Lycopodium clavatum. *Linn. Sp. Pl.* p. 1564. *Sw. Syn. Fil.* p. 179. *Willd. Sp. Pl. v.* 5. p. 16. *Sm. Engl. Bot. t.* 224. *Engl. Fl. v.* 4. p. 331. *Hook. and Arn. Brit. Fl. ed.* 3. p. 597. *Spring, Monogr. Lycop.* p. 88, *and Part* 2. p. 42. *Schk. Fil. t.* 162.

Lycopodium inflexum. *Sw. Syn. Fil.* p. 179. *Willd. Sp. Pl. v.* 5. p. 15. *Hook. et Grev. En. Fil. Lycop. in Hook. Bot. Misc. v.* 2. p. 376.

Lycopodium divaricatum. *Wall. Cat. n.* 131. *Hook. et Grev. En. Fil. Lycop. l. c. p.* 377; spikes often 3–6, and there are other differences.

Lycopodium trichiatum. *Bl. En. Fil. Jav.* p. 263.

Lycopodium serpens. *Pr. Reliq. Hænk.* p. 181.

Lycopodium Preslii. *Hook. et Grev. En. Fil. Lycopod. l. c. p.* 377.

Lycopodium piliferum. *Raddi, Fil. Bras.* p. 79. *t.* 3.

Hab. Common in dry heathy and rocky pastures, especially in mountain countries.

This is the most common of our British Club-Mosses, and a widely dispersed species in other countries; throughout Europe and in Asiatic Russia and Siberia; through North America to the extreme west, Behring's Straits, the West Indian Islands, Mexico, Panama, Ecuador, Brazil, and Peru; throughout India (probably there and in all tropical regions as a mountain plant); Malay Islands and Peninsula (*Parish*), Japan, *Thunberg;* Africa, chiefly, I believe, confined to the Cape, Bourbon, Mauritius, and Madagascar. Were exotic specimens at this time specially the objects of consideration, it would not be difficult to find other synonyms referable here, which bear other names in books, and whose variations are in a great measure due to altitude on the mountains, proximity to the Poles, or other modifying circumstances.

The stems of this species run along upon the ground to the length of many feet, and have a slight hold on the soil by means of simple or branched wiry roots. The branches spring in tufts or fascicles of pretty nearly equal lengths, and the stems being very flexible, and the branches very tough and elastic, in the north of Europe the peasantry weave them into doormats of a very useful description, of which samples may be seen in the Museum of the Royal Gardens of Kew. The plant is also employed for dyeing and medicinal purposes, and we have already alluded, in the Introductory Notice, to the use made of the spores of it for producing artificial lightning upon the stage.

PLATE 49. Fertile portion of a plant of *Lycopodium clavatum*, Linn.,—*natural size*. Fig. 1. A leaf,—*magnified*. 2. Bract and 2-valved capsules, including spores,—*magnified*. 3. Spores,—*more highly magnified*.

PLATE 50.

LYCOPODIUM ANNOTINUM.

Interrupted Club-Moss.

LYCOPODIUM *annotinum;* stems long, creeping; branches short, erect, simple or forked, often here and there constricted, as if from a fresh shoot arising from the apex of a former one; leaves subquinquefarious, more or less patent, linear-lanceolate, mucronate, subspinuloso-serrated or entire; spikes terminal, oblong, sessile, cylindrical; bracts broad, cordate, acuminate, the base on each dentato-spinulose.

LYCOPODIUM annotinum. *Linn. Sp. Pl.* p. 1566. *Sw. Syn. Fil.* p. 178. *Willd. Sp. Pl.* v. 5. p. 23. *Schk. Fil.* p. 162. *t.* 162. *Sm. Engl. Bot. t.* 1727. *Engl. Fl.* v. 4. p. 335. *Hook. and Arn. Brit. Fl. ed.* 8. p. 597. *Spring, Monogr. Lycop.* p. 77, and Part 2. p. 36.

LYCOPODIUM juniperifolium. *Lam. and De Cand. Fl. Fr.* v. 2. p. 572.

LYCOPODIUM bryophyllum. *Pr. Reliq. Hænk.* v. 1. p. 81.

LYCOPODIUM Heyneanum. *Wall. Cat. n.* 132.

LEPIDOTIS annotina. *Beauv. Prodr. Æth.* p. 107.

Hab. Stony mountains in the north of England, North Wales, and the Highlands of Scotland; frequent in the Cairngorum mountains.

At the first aspect this has, in its mode of growth and in the copious short branches, a good deal the aspect of *L. clavatum,* but in fruit it may be at once recognized by its sessile (not pedunculated) and shorter spikes, by the more simple branches, and by the different leaves, broader and more lanceolate and acuminated, but never long-hair-pointed as in *L. clavatum.* Although by no means peculiar to Britain, or even to the continent of Europe, it is nevertheless quite confined to the northern hemisphere, and chiefly to the northern or alpine regions there. In Great Britain it is never found in the middle or southern counties, nor in Ireland. In Europe, France is its most southern limit, whereas it extends north through Germany to Scandinavia, and thence westward to Dahuria, Kamtchatka, Behring's Straits, Amur, to the Aleutian Islands, appearing again at Nutka Sound in North-west America, and thence on the east side of the Rocky Mountains to Canada, Newfoundland, and Greenland, Disco Island, etc., *Dr. Lyall.* In the United States it seems to be confined to the White Mountains of Massachusetts (*Tuckerman*) and the Alleghanies (*Drummond*), and my specimens thence are remarkable for the length of the branches, and the slender horizontal or quite reflexed leaves. Dr. Wallich's *Lycopodium Heyneanum*, Wall. Cat. l. c., is undoubtedly our *annotinum*, and, being from Heyne's herbarium, was supposed by Dr. Wallich to be from Malabar, with a mark of interrogation. There are probably no mountains there sufficiently elevated to be likely to afford it; and I should have doubted its being of Indian origin, but that Dr. Hooker detected unquestionably the true plant at Lachen, in Sikkim-Himalaya, elev. 11,000 feet above the sea-level.

PLATE 50. Fertile portion of *Lycopodium annotinum*, Linn.,—*natural size*. Fig. 1, 2. Leaves. 3. Outer, and 4. Inner view of a bractea from the spike:—*magnified*. 5. Spores,—*more magnified*.

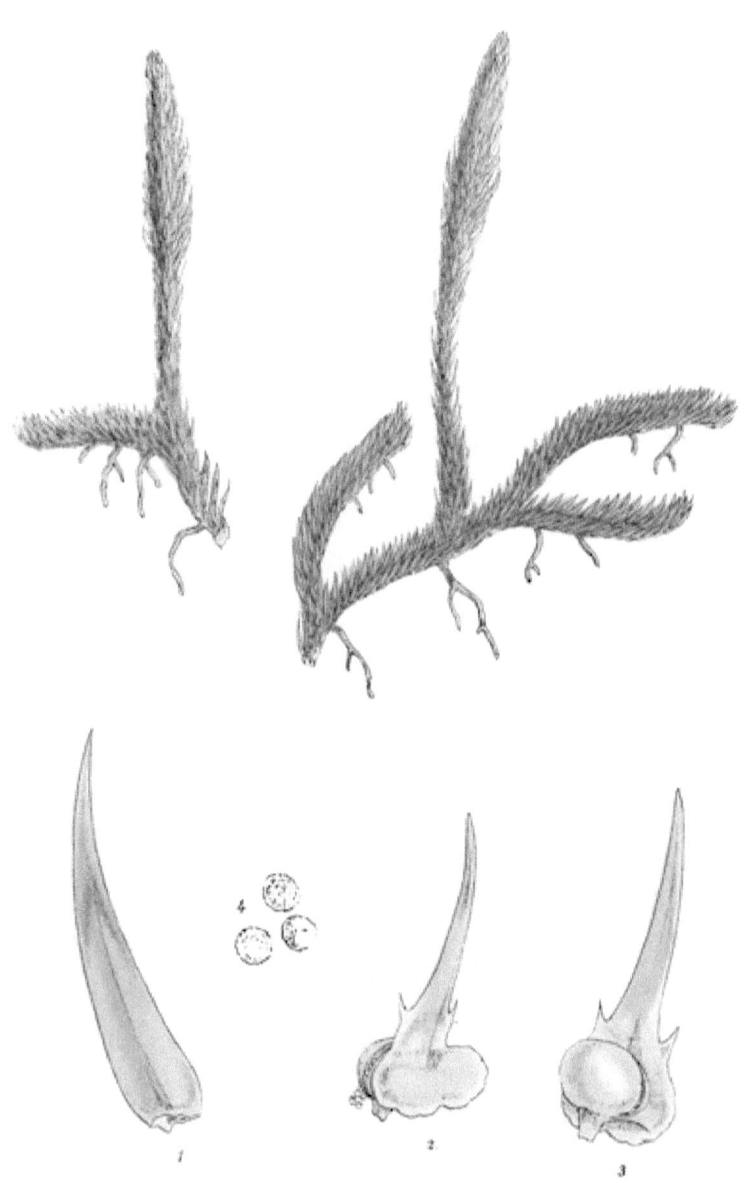

PLATE 51.

LYCOPODIUM INUNDATUM, *Linn.*

Marsh Club-Moss.

LYCOPODIUM *inundatum*; small, stem creeping, short, branched; branches horizontal, also creeping; fertile ones erect; leaves secund on the sterile branches, erect on the fertile ones, lanceolato-subulate, entire, obsoletely 1-nerved; spikes sessile, subfusiform; bracts subulate, remarkably dilated, and cordate and convex at the base, with a spinous tooth on each side.

LYCOPODIUM inundatum. *Linn. Sp. Pl. p.* 1566. *Sw. Syn. Fil. p.* 177. *Willd. Sp. Pl. v.* 5. *p.* 25. *Schk. Fil. t.* 160. *Sm. Eng. Bot. t.* 239. *Engl. Fl. v.* 4. *p.* 332. *Hook. et Arn. ed.* 8. *p.* 597. *Spring, Monogr. Lycop. p.* 74, *and Part* 2. *p.* 6.

LYCOPODIUM Bigelovii. *Oakes and Tuckerman in Sillim. Journ.*

(*L. Carolinianum* and *L. alopecuroides*, and not a few others, supposed species, must be added to this list, if we were to make the exotic synonymy complete.)

LYCOPODIUM palustre. *Lam. Fl. Fr. v.* 1. *p.* 52.

PLANANTHUS inundatus. *Beauv. Prodr. d'Æthéog. p.* 111.

Hab. Moist heathy places occasionally overflowed by water, and boggy ground, in England, Scotland, and Ireland: often overlooked, probably on account of small size and spongy locality; by no means peculiar to mountain districts.

As seen in Great Britain, and in other temperate regions of the earth, in Europe generally, and in some parts of North America, this is a small growing *Club-Moss*, with all the sterile branches lying close to the ground, holding so firmly in the spongy soil by numerous fibres that it is very difficult to collect specimens entire. Our figure here given is among the largest of the normal state of the plant; but in North America, especially in the southern United States, it gradually passes into the larger forms, known as *L. Carolinianum*, Linn., and the still larger *L. alopecuroides*, Linn., which attains its maximum in tropical South America. M. Spring does not indeed seem to recognize this affinity in words; but he does *de facto*, by uniting the *L. Bigelovii* of Oakes and Tuckerman with our European *inundatum*; whereas my authentic specimens prove it to be the *Carolinianum*-form. Some of our specimens of *alopecuroides* have sterile branches, or surculi, and erect and fertile ones of a firm rigid character and are more than a foot or a foot and a half long. In one or another of these states the species is found in tropical and extra-tropical Africa, in Mauritius, Madagascar, Australia (Mouton Island, *L. pallidum*, Mueller), Van Diemen's Land, Ceylon, etc.; but not, as far as I yet know, in India proper.

PLATE 51. Fertile plants of *Lycopodium inundatum*, Linn.,—*natural size*. Fig. 1. Leaf. 2, 3. Back and front view of bracteal scales, with capsules. 4. Spores:—*all more or less magnified*.

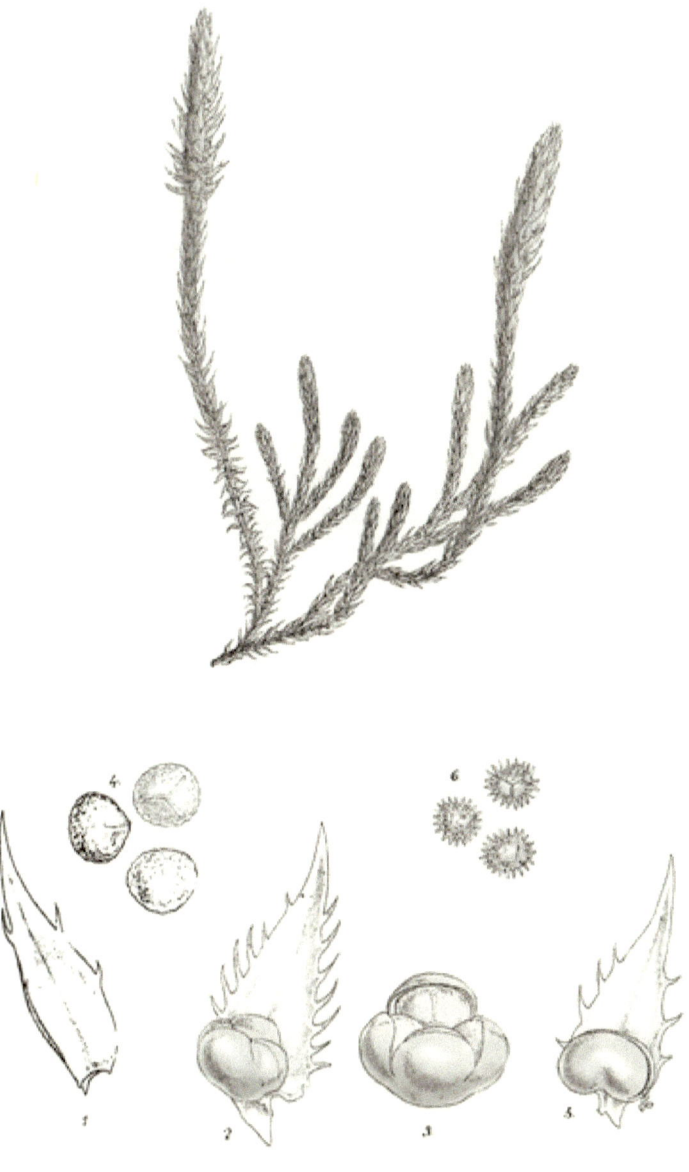

PLATE 52.

LYCOPODIUM SELAGINOIDES.

Lesser Alpine Club-Moss.

LYCOPODIUM *selaginoides*; stems slender, loosely decumbent, sparsely rooting; branches ascending, simple or dichotomous, short; *fertile* branches elongated; leaves lax, broad-lanceolate, acuminate, more or less spinoso-ciliate; spikes terminal, sessile, subcylindrical; bracts resembling the leaves, but larger and more ciliato-spinose; capsules of two kinds; one 2-valved, filled with echinated dust-like spores; the other 3–4-valved, containing 3–4 large globose granules.

LYCOPODIUM selaginoides. *Linn. Sp. Pl. p.* 1565. *Sw. Syn. Fil. p.* 181. *Willd. Sp. Pl. v.* 5, *p.* 28. *Sm. Engl. Bot. t.* 1148. *Engl. Fl. v.* 4, *p.* 332. *Schk. Fil. t.* 165. *Hook. and Arn. Brit. Fl. ed.* 8. *p.* 597.

SELAGINELLA spinosa. *Beauv. Prodr. d'Æthéog. p.* 112. *Spring, Monogr. Lycop. Part* 2. *p.* 59.

SELAGINELLA selaginoides. *Link, Fil. Hort. Berol. p.* 158. *Asa Gray, Man. of Bot. Illust. p.* 604.

LYCOPODIUM ciliatum. *Lam. Fl. Fr. v.* 1. *p.* 32.

Hab. Frequent in moist alpine pastures, in boggy and springy spots in the north of England and Wales, Scotland, and Ireland; but descending to the sandy coasts of the sea-level in Anglesea and Lancashire.

This is the smallest and most delicate of our British *Lycopodia*, and is peculiarly a northern species; or if reaching to the south of Europe, as in the Pyrenees and in Switzerland (whence I have fine specimens from Professor Gouan), is confined to lofty mountains; extending north to Norway, Lapland, and Greenland, and eastward to Siberia. In North America, it is found in Canada, and the east side of the Rocky Mountains: in the United States, only in New Hampshire, Michigan, and about Lake Superior (*Asa Gray*).

Of the British *Lycopodia*, this is the only one that bears two kinds of fructifications—(1) bivalved reniform capsules (*antheridia*), with dust-like spores; and (2) 3–4-lobed and 3–4-valved capsules (*oophoridia*), bearing as many large grains, or seeds, as there are valves. The first of these is characteristic of true *Lycopodium*; the second of *Selaginella*, a group in general so well marked by the jungermannioid and, generally, tetrastichous and dimorphous leaves. But the importance of these genera is much invalidated by the fact that our present plant, together with *Lycopodium rupestre*, *L. uliginosum*, Labill., and a few others, now generally referred to *Selaginella*, have the foliage and habit of *Lycopodium*. The 209 other species of *Selaginella* have dimorphous and jungermannioid foliage.

PLATE 52. Fertile plant of *Lycopodium selaginoides*, Linn.,—*natural size*. Fig. 1. Leaf. 2. Bract, with a four-lobed, four-valved capsule. 3. The four-valved capsule bursting open. 4. Seeds from ditto. 5. Bract, with its two-valved capsule. 6. Spores from the same:—*all more or less highly magnified*.

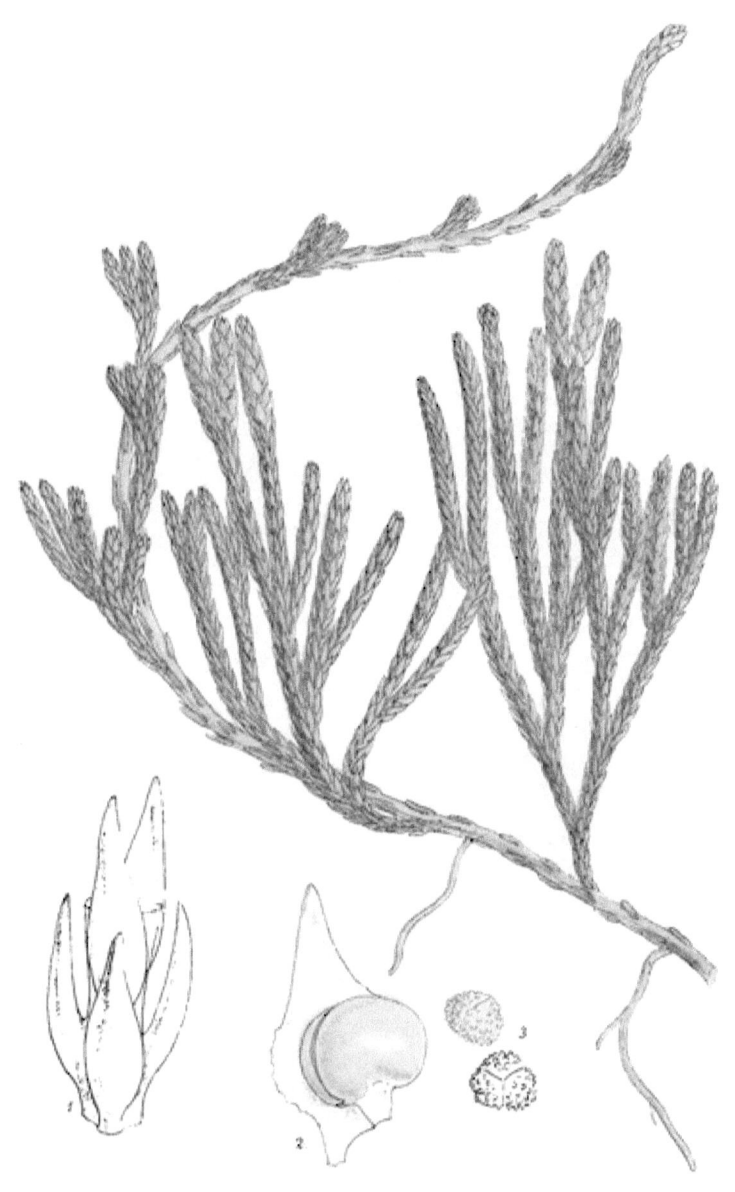

PLATE 53.

LYCOPODIUM ALPINUM, *Linn.*

Savin-leaved Club-Moss.

LYCOPODIUM *alpinum;* stem elongated, creeping, rooting; primary branches distant or approximate, ascending, copiously dichotomous, fastigiate; leaves quadrifarious, erect, imbricated; lateral ones lanceolate, falcate, acute, co-adunato-decurrent at the base, slightly concave, intermediate ones shorter, smaller, subulato-lanceolate, uniform and nearly free on both sides; fertile branches slightly elongated; spikes cylindrical, terminal, solitary, sessile.

LYCOPODIUM alpinum. *Linn. Sp. Pl. p.* 1567. *Fl. Lapp. p.* 417. *t.* 11. *Sw. Syn. Fil. p.* 178. *Willd. Sp. Pl. v.* 5. *p.* 20. *Schk. Fil. t.* 161. *Sm. Eng. Bot. t.* 234. *Hook. and Grev. En. Fil. in Hook. Bot. Misc. v.* 2. *p.* 380. *Sm. Eng. Fl. p.* 335. *Hook. Fl. Bor. Am. v.* 2. *p.* 267. *Hook. and Arn. Brit. Fl. ed.* 8. *p.* 597. *Spring, Monogr. Lycop. part* 1. *p.* 104, *part* 11. *p.* 18.

LYCOPODIUM Chamarense. *Turcz. in Herb. Hook.*

LYCOPODIUM Sitchense. *Ruprecht, Cryptog. Vascul. in Imper. Rossico in Beitr. v.* 2. *Pflanzenkunde d. Russ. Reichs,* 1844–45, *fasc.* 3. *p.* 36?

STACHYGYNANDRUM alpinum. *Presl, Bot. Bem. etc. v.* 3. *p.* 83.

Hab. Elevated mountains, North of England, Wales, Scotland, and Ireland; found as far south as Derbyshire and Somerset.

This is very much a northern species, found indeed in Switzerland, the Pyrenees, and the Vosges, but there on the lofty alps; very general in Siberia and northern Asia, as well as in Norway and Lapland. In North America it appears to be peculiar to Newfoundland, Canada, and the Hudson Bay Territories; rare in the Rocky Mountains, north lat. 53°; not apparently extending to the Pacific side of America, except the *L. Sitchense* of Ruprecht should prove to be the same, which is very probable.

I cannot agree with Spring in his remark, "Il est possible que cette plante ne soit qu'une variété du *L. complanatum*, produite par l'élévation de son habitat." My numerous specimens are uniform in character, and I do not find any of them to pass into that species, which however seems to occupy its place in the United States.

PLATE 54. Fertile plant of *Lycopodium alpinum*, Linn.,—*the natural size.* Fig. 1. Portion of a branch, with leaves. 2. Bracteal leaf, with its capsules. 3. Spores :—*magnified.*

PLATE 54.

LYCOPODIUM Selago, *Linn.*

Fir Club-Moss.

Lycopodium *Selago*; stems four to six inches high, rooting at the base, rigid, dichotomously branched, suberect, tufted; branches obtuse, all densely leafy; leaves uniform, erect, and imbricated or often patent and even reflexed below, lanceolate, subpungently acuminate, rigid, entire; capsules in the axils of the superior and scarcely altered leaves.

Lycopodium Selago. *Linn. Sp. Pl.* p. 1665. *Sw. Syn. Fil.* p. 176. *Willd. Sp. Pl.* v. 5. p. 49. *Kaulf. En. Fil.* p. 19. *Gaudich. in Freyc. Voy. Bot.* p. 289. *Sm. Engl. Bot.* t. 233. *Engl. Fl.* v. 4. p. 333. *Fl. Dan.* t. 104. *Hook. and Arn. Brit. Fl.* ed. 8. p. 597. *Spring, Monogr. Lycop.* p. 19. *Schk. Fil.* t. 159. *Asa Gray, Man. of Bot. Illustr.* p. 603.

Lycopodium recurvum. *Kitaib. in Willd. Sp. Pl.* v. 5. p. 50.

Lycopodium insulare. *Carm. in Linn. Trans.* v. 12. p. 509.

Lycopodium Ceylanicum. *Spring, Monogr. Lycop.* part 1. p. 37, part 2. p. 16.

Lycopodium suberectum. *Lowe in Pl. Azor. in Un. Itin.*

Lycopodium densum. *Lam. Fl. Fr.* v. 1. p. 33.

Lycopodium axillare. *Roxb. in Beats. Fl. of St. Helena,* p. 312.

Lycopodium densum, β. *Hook. fil. Bot. Antarct. Voy.* v. 1. p. 116.

Plananthus Selago. *Beauv. Prodr. d'Æthéog.* p. 100; and P. patens, *ejusd.* p. 101.

Selago foliis facie Abietis. *Raii Syn.* p. 106.

Selago vulgaris, Abietis rubræ facie. *Dill. Musc.* p. 435. t. 56. f. 1.

Muscus terrestris abietiformis. *Raii Syn. ed.* 2. p. 27. *Moris.* v. 3. p. 624. sect. 15. t. 5. f. 9.

Hab. England, Scotland, and Ireland, but chiefly in northern and mountain districts; particularly abundant in the Highland alps. It has been found, though very rarely, in the extreme southern counties, "Cornwall, Dorset, Hants, and Sussex;" and on Felthorpe Bogs, Norfolk, at an elevation little above the level of the sea.

As might be expected, with a plant which in Great Britain prefers the northern and elevated mountain regions, it does not create surprise to learn that it is abundant in the temperate and cold regions of the continent of Europe and northern Asia, and in North America from Carolina (summits of the mountains) to the extreme north, and to Greenland and Spitzbergen, etc., as is really the case: also it inhabits the Falkland Islands in the southern hemisphere, and New Zealand; but one would hardly have looked for it in Madeira, the Azores, St. Helena, Ceylon, Khasya, in Ecuador (at elevations here of 14–1500 feet above the level of the sea), in St. Helena, and Tristan d'Acunha; yet my herbarium includes well-marked specimens from these different localities.

In Scotland, Lightfoot tells us, the Highlanders use this plant instead of alum, to fix colours in dyeing; and that they sometimes take an infusion of it as an emetic and cathartic, though it operates violently, and, unless in a small dose, brings on giddiness and convulsions. "No wonder," adds Sir James Smith, "that a decoction kills the lice of swine and oxen, as Linnæus asserts in 'Flora Suecica.'"

PLATE 54. Fertile plant of *Lycopodium Selago*, Linn.,—*natural size*. Fig. 1 and 2. Stem-leaves. 3. Capsule, with its bractea or floral leaf. 4. Spores:—*magnified*.

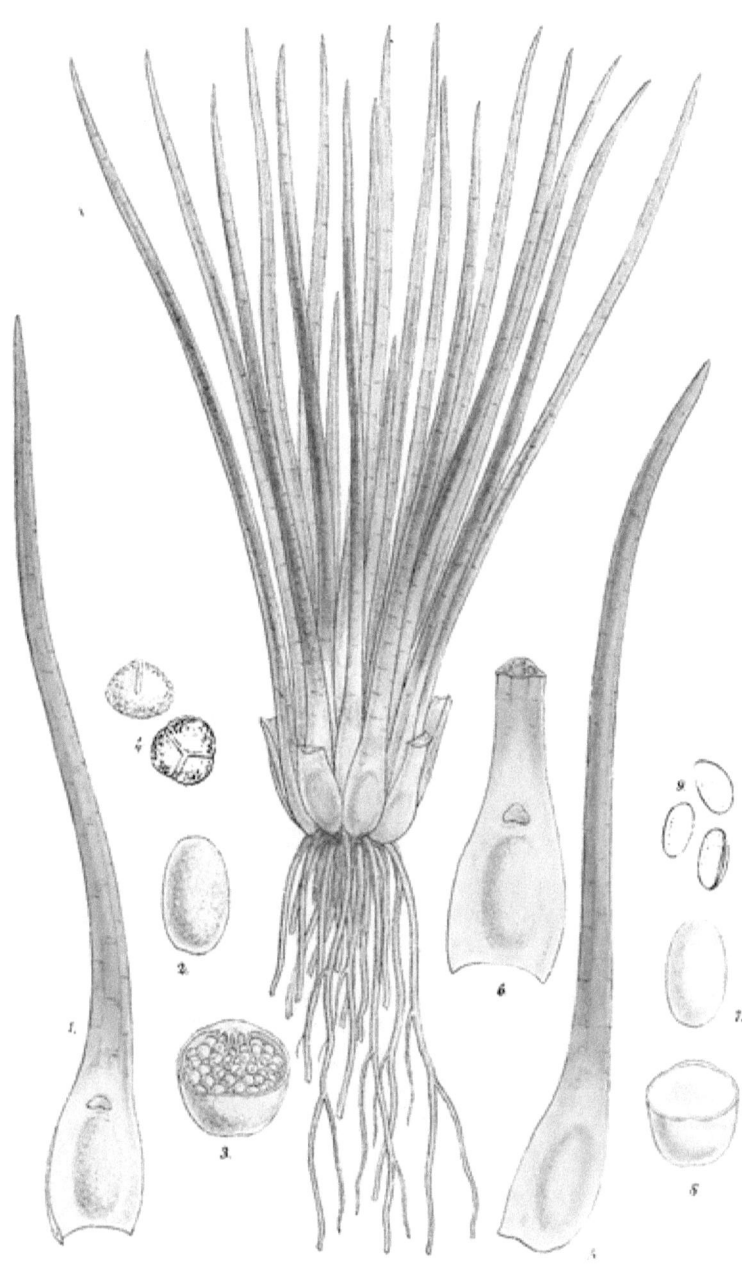

PLATE 55.

ISOETES LACUSTRIS, *Linn.*

Common Quillwort.

Gen. Char. Capsules without a ring, indehiscent, immersed in a cavity of the very dilated base of long subulate radical leaves :—of two kinds : those at the base of the *outer* leaves containing a few large trigonous *spores*, rough with minute points (*oophoridia*); those at the base of the *inner* ones having numerous, minute, oblong granules (*antheridia*) ; in both the contents are seen to be, at least in an early stage, attached to delicate slender filaments.—*More or less aquatic plants, often submerged.*

ISOETES *lacustris;* leaves erect or nearly so, stout, subulate, highly cellular; base of the rhizome destitute of spiny scales; oophoridia smooth.

ISOETES lacustris. *Linn. Sp. Pl. p.* 1563. *Willd. Sp. Pl. v.* 5. *p.* 534. *Engl. Bot. t.* 1084. *Bolt. Fil. Brit. p.* 74. *t.* 41. *Fl. Dan. t.* 191. *Wahl. Fl. Lapp. p.* 26. *Hook. in Fl. Lond. v.* 4. *t.* 121. *Schk. Fil. t.* 172. *Sm. Engl. Fl. v.* 4. *p.* 343. *Hook. and Arn. Brit. Fl. ed.* 8. *p.* 598. *Asa Gray, Man. Bot. Illustr. p.* 606.

ISOETES Engelmanni. *Braun, in Asa Gray, Man. Bot. Illust. p.* 605.

ISOETES riparia. *Engelm. in Asa Gray, Man. Bot. Illustr. p.* 606.

ISOETES setacea. *Bosc, Mém. du Mus. v.* 14. *t.* 6 and 7.

ISOETES velata. *A. Braun, Expl. Alger. t.* 37.

ISOETES Coromandeliana. *Linn. Suppl. p.* 447. *Willd. Sp. Pl. v.* 5. *p.* 535.

CALAMARIA folio breviore et crassiore. *Dill. Musc. p.* 540. *t.* 80. *f.* 1.

Hab. Lakes in mountain districts: England, Wales, Scotland, and Ireland.

This is a very interesting plant, both in structure and in its place of growth,—so unlike any other of the Fern-group, whether true Ferns or which are called Pseudo-Filices, that some botanists reject them altogether ; but, different as the habit of the plant may be, the fructifications too much resemble those of *Lycopodiaceæ* to allow of their being placed far apart. Presl does not admit it among *Filices,* nor does M. Cosson, in his excellent 'Flore des Environs de Paris.' The present species is perhaps much more widely distributed geographically than botanists in general are aware of ; and I cannot but fear that many supposed species of authors must merge into this. In the south of France, and in most warm climates, it bears longer and narrower leaves than with us, and becomes the *Isoetes setacea* of Bosc, *I. velata*, A. Braun. The same variety occurs in Sardinia, Sicily, in Algeria, and in the Madras Peninsula and Afghanistan (*I. Coromandeliana*, Linn.). *I. adspersa* of A. Braun (in Balansa, Pl. d'Algérie) is a fine and very slender-leaved form of the same, as is a specimen of an *Isoetes* in my herbarium from Swan River (*Drummond, n.* 989 and 990); and again from *Barter*, discovered at Nape, tropical Africa (*n.* 1020). The species is common in North America; Dr. Engelmann has found what has been called, one, *I. riparia*, Engelm., and another, *I. Engelmanni*, Braun. From British Columbia and Northern California Mr. Nuttall has sent to me his *Isoetes opaca* (I believe a MS. name), which seems to be identical with our *I. lacustris*, as I do *Isoetes Malinveniana* of De Notaris from Piedmont, and *I. echinospora*, Dene., from Lozera. In South America specimens received from Spruce, Santarem, Brazil, and from the Missions of Duro, Brazil, *Gardner, n.* 5563 (and so named by him), are common forms of our British Quillwort. *Isoetes lacustris*, Metten. in Pl. Lechlerianæ, n. 937, is a short, broad, acuminated-leaved var. from Peru. *Isoetes Andina*, Spruce's MS., from the Quitinian Andes (without number) is probably distinct in the broad, firm, rigid leaves, coriaceous and glossy when dry, scarcely tapering at all, but suddenly acute, and with a very broad rhizome. Another remarkable and I presume very distinct species, from mountain lakes of Tasmania, a good deal resembles this of Mr. Spruce; but many of the leaves are quite obtuse or retuse, and often tipped with a very conspicuous and remarkable gland.

Previous to my knowledge of the two *Isoetides* last mentioned, I had joined Dr. Arnott (see 'British Flora,' *l. c.*) in the remark that "there is probably only one known species of the genus." But since that remark was made, another remarkable *Isoetes* has been discovered, which is figured and described in our next Plate, and I most gladly recall that statement as incorrect.

PLATE 55. Fertile plant of *Isoetes lacustris*, Linn.,—*natural size*. Fig. 1. Front view of a leaf from the centre of the plant, *slightly magnified*, with its capsule. 2. The capsule removed from the leaf. 3. The same cut through transversely. 4. Spores or *antheridia*,—*all more or less magnified*. 5. Back view of an outer leaf. 6. Front view of the base. 7. Capsule removed from the leaf. 8. The same cut through transversely. 9. Minute oblong granules or *oophoridia:—all more or less magnified*.

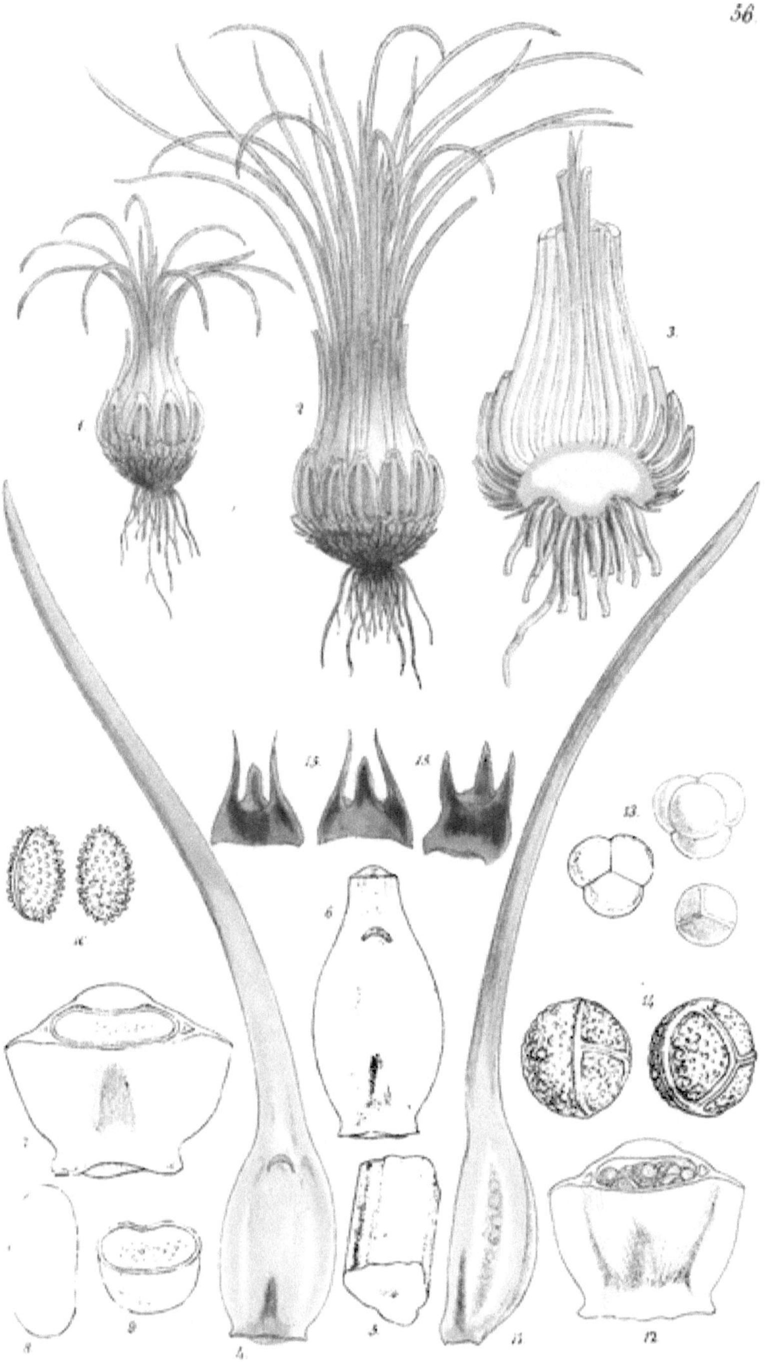

W. Fitch, del. et lith.

Vincent Brooks, Imp.

PLATE 56.

ISOETES DURIEI, *Bory.*

Durieu's Quillwort.

ISOETES *Duriæi*; leaves slender, filiform, subcompactly cellular, the tuft contracted above the bulbiform base, then spreading and recurved; rhizome below the leaves clothed with dark-brown, rigid, pungent, trifid scales; oophoridia strongly granulated.

ISOETES Duriæi. "*Bory, Compt. rendu Acad. Sc. vol.* 18, *June,* 1844." *A. Braun in Bory, Explor. Scientif. de l'Algérie, partie Bot. pl.* 36. *f.* 2 (*no description*). Grenier et Godron, *Fl. de France, v.* 3. *p.* 652.

ISOETES Hystrix. *Wolsey in Phytol. new ser. v.* 5. *p.* 45 (*not of Durieu in Bory, Explor. Scientif. de l'Algérie, pl.* 36. *f.* 1 (*no description*), *and of Grenier and Godron, l. c. p.* 652). *Cosson in Bourgeau, Pl. d'Espagne et de Portugal,* 1853, *n.* 2049.

ISOETES Hystrix *var.* subinermis. *Balansa, Pl. d'Algérie,* 1851, *n.* 27, *and* 1852, *n.* 694; *ejusd. Pl. d'Orient,* 1857, *n.* 1327.

Hab. Damp spots on L'Ancresse common, Guernsey, *Mr. G. Wolsey.*

This first discovery of this species of *Isoetes*, in "lieux incultes et stériles" in the south of France, in Corsica, at Ajaccio (*Requien*), and at Cannes (*Dunal*), could not fail to attract the attention of botanists; and it became still more interesting to British botanists on its discovery in British territory, Guernsey, in June, 1860, by Mr. George Wolsey. The species is only described in one or two works, not easily accessible to a student of British botany, and figured (without description) only in one rare and costly work, on the plants of Algeria; and it is not surprising that it was mistaken for the *I. Hystrix* of Durieu, also an inhabitant of Corsica and Cannes in "pâturages secs, montueux et découverts, jamais dans les terrains inondés." Both are remarkable for blackish-brown, shortly three-spined, imbricating scales on the rhizome, below the leaves, of which there is no trace in *Isoetes lacustris*, nor, as far as I am aware, in any other known species of the genus, save in *I. Hystrix* where these scales are so abundant and so long, that in the figure given in the Algerian Flora, the base of the plant forms a nearly globose ball, an inch and a half in diameter, clothed with long, black, incurved spines, a quarter of an inch long, naturally suggesting the specific name of *Hystrix*. In other respects the two plants have certainly the greatest resemblance to each other, so that Mr. Wolsey is not far wrong in calling the present plant *I. Hystrix*, though Mr. Balansa has probably pursued a better course, in naming our plant *I. Hystrix*, var. *subinermis*; and it is not a little remarkable that the two are found in nearly the same localities both in the south of France and in Algeria. The exotic specimens of *I. Duriæi* in my herbarium are from Limoges, France (M. de Notaris), in "pelouses humides," near the summit of the Sierra de Picota, near Monchique, Algarve, Spain (*Bourgeau*); rocky hills above the village of Kaiageul, near Ouchak in Phrygia (*Balansa*); Algeria, Coteau de Homma (*Mr. Thos. Birch*), Oran, "dans les flaques d'eau," and between Oran and La Senia, "bords des marés" (*Balansa*). True *I. Hystrix* I possess from Algeria, Mostaganem, "clairières des broussailles" (*Balansa*), and from "Straoucli," collected by *Mr. Birch*.

PLATE 50. Fig. 1, 2. Fertile plants of *Isoetes Duriæi*, Bory, with a circle of mature fruits:—*natural size*. 3. Lower portion of the plant, with its rhizome cut through vertically,—*slightly magnified*. 4. An inner leaf, with its fructification in the base. 5. Transverse section of the same above the base. 6. Base:—*more magnified*. 7. Transverse section of the same. 8. Capsules. 9. Section of do. 10. Minute granules, or *antheridia*. 11. Inner leaf, with its fructification in the base. 12. The base, cut through transversely. 13. Young subtetrahedral grains (*oophoridia*). 14. Mature do. 15. Scales from the base of the rhizome; middle one seen from behind, the lateral ones in front:—*more or less magnified*. All the figures are made from specimens kindly sent by Mr. Wolsey.

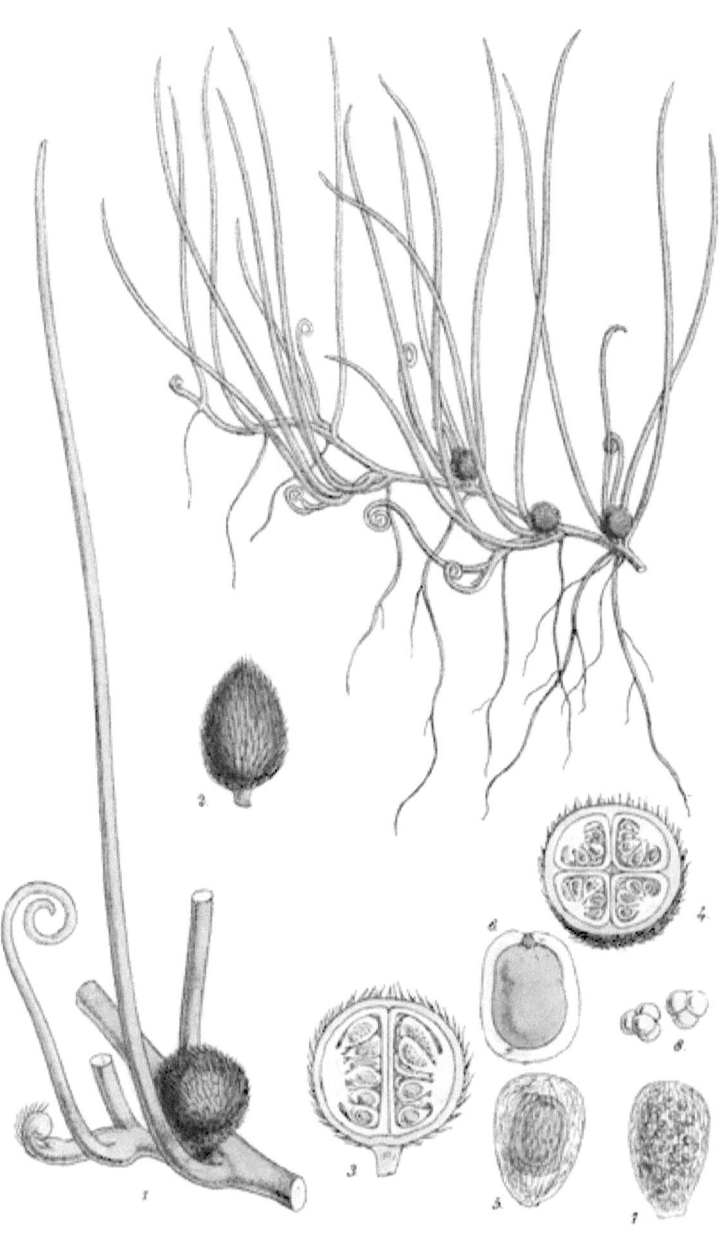

PLATE 57.

PILULARIA GLOBULIFERA, *Linn.*

Pillwort, or Pepper-grass.

Gen. Char. *Fructifications* of two kinds, united in a two- or four-celled globose coriaceous radicular *involucre*, opening by two or four valves at the apex: 1, upper ones in each cell (*antheridia*) pyriform, membranaceous, containing globose granules; 2, lower ones formed of a membranaceous sac enclosing a comparatively large subglobose apiculated crustaceous indehiscent capsule? (*oophoridium*), containing very minute granules, which seem to be united in threes or fours.—*Partially submerged aquatics.* Caudex *slender, filiform, radicant, bearing slender filiform* leaves, *at the base of which are the receptacles.*

PILULARIA *globulifera*; receptacles four-celled.
PILULARIA globulifera. *Linn. Sp. Pl.* p. 1563. *Huds. Angl.* p. 462. *Lightf. Scot.* p. 682. *Fl. Dan.* t. 223. *Boll. Brit. Ferns,* p. 74. t. 40. *Willd. Sp. Pl.* v. 5. p. 534. *Engl. Bot.* t. 521. *Sm. Engl. Fl.* v. 4. p. 342. *Hook. in Fl. Lond.* v. 4. t. 83. *Valent. in Trans. Linn. Soc.* v. 18. p. 483. t. 34 and 35. *Hook. and Arn. Brit. Fl. ed.* 8. p. 598.
PILULARIA palustris juncifolia. *Dill. Musc.* p. 538. t. 72.
GRAMINIFOLIA palustris repens, vasculis granorum piperis æmulis. *Raii Syn.* p. 136.
MUSCUS aureus capillaris palustris, inter foliola folliculis rotundis (ex sententia *D. Doody*) quadripartitis. *Pluk. Almag.* p. 256. *Phyt.* t. 48. f. 1.
PEPPER-GRASS. *Petiv. H. Brit.* t. 9, f. 8.
Hab. Margin of lakes and ponds, and in places that are partially overflowed in England, Scotland, and Ireland: in Great Britain Cornwall is stated to be its southern limit, and Sutherland its northern.

The stations recorded for this curious plant are not numerous, for it is little likely to attract attention. The leaves are slender, like those of some delicate *Scirpus* or *Isolepis;* and the somewhat stouter caudices, yet no bigger than packthread, run along upon the watery ground, and bear the globular fructifications on a very short stalk close to the soil. So rare was this plant considered to be in the early part of the late Sir James Smith's botanical career, that I possess in Gouan's Herbarium specimens sent to the celebrated Professor of Montpellier by Sir James, with the remark, "rarissima planta, tibi ni fallor ignota." It is however more common in France perhaps than in Britain, and occurs in Germany, Sweden, and Norway, and in the middle and south of Russia. It does not appear anywhere in the New World;

but I possess specimens from Swan River (*Drummond*) and from Tasmania (*Mr. Ronald Gunn*).

A very aquatic variety, with long narrow caudex and leaves, partially at least floating upon the water, but without fructification, has been called *P. natans* by Mérat in his Fl. Paris. The same is found in Smoland by Fries, and is his *P. globulifera*, var. *fluitans*.

A very small and extremely delicate *Pilularia* is found in Algeria, of which I possess native specimens from Balansa (n. 210), and others from Professor Braun, "e seminibus culta in Horto Friburgensi, 1848." The leaves scarcely exceed an inch in length, and are as delicate as the most filiform *Ulva*, with fructifications small in proportion. It is the *P. minuta*, Durieu, in Explor. Scientif. de L'Algérie, Partie Bot. t. 38, unfortunately unaccompanied with any description; so that, except the smaller size and the "two-celled" fruit, it is difficult to say how it is to be distinguished from the European species.

P. globulifera has a slender, creeping, filiform, branched *caudex* or *rhizome*, bearing *leaves* circinate in vernation, on the upper side, single or one to two, three, or four in fascicles, and slender fibrous root beneath, opposite to the insertion of the leaves, which are also filiform, yet tapering above, very slender. From the caudex at the base of the leaf the globose *receptacle* appears on a very short footstalk, very hairy at first, at length nearly glabrous; this is subcrustaceous, four-celled, opening at the top by four valves: in the inside, and corresponding with each valve, is a fleshy receptacle, bearing two kinds of membranaceous pellucid *sacs*, the *upper* ones (*antheridia*) pear-shaped, numerous, including subglobose *granules*; the lower part of the cell is occupied by larger membranaceous sacs, including a subglobose glandular body apparently floating in it, slightly constricted near the middle, and crowned with a conical point. This is filled with a grumose substance, composed of particles which appear, under the high power of a microscope, as if formed by a union of three to four granules. Numerous microscopic figures of the contents of these two kinds of fructifications have been published by different authors, but they are by no means in harmony with each other; and we have yet much to learn of their true organization and uses in the economy of the plant.

PLATE 57. Fertile plant of *Pilularia globulifera*, Linn.,—*natural size*. Fig. 1. Portion of a caudex, with leaves and a receptacle. 2. Young receptacle. 3. Perfect receptacle, cut through vertically, showing the two kinds of fructifications. 4. Transverse section of a receptacle. 5. A young, and 6. Mature sac from the lower part of the cell, generally considered to be the female fructification. 7. Sac from the upper part of the cell, considered to be analogous to stamen. 8. 3-4-lobed granules from within the sac:—*all more or less magnified*.

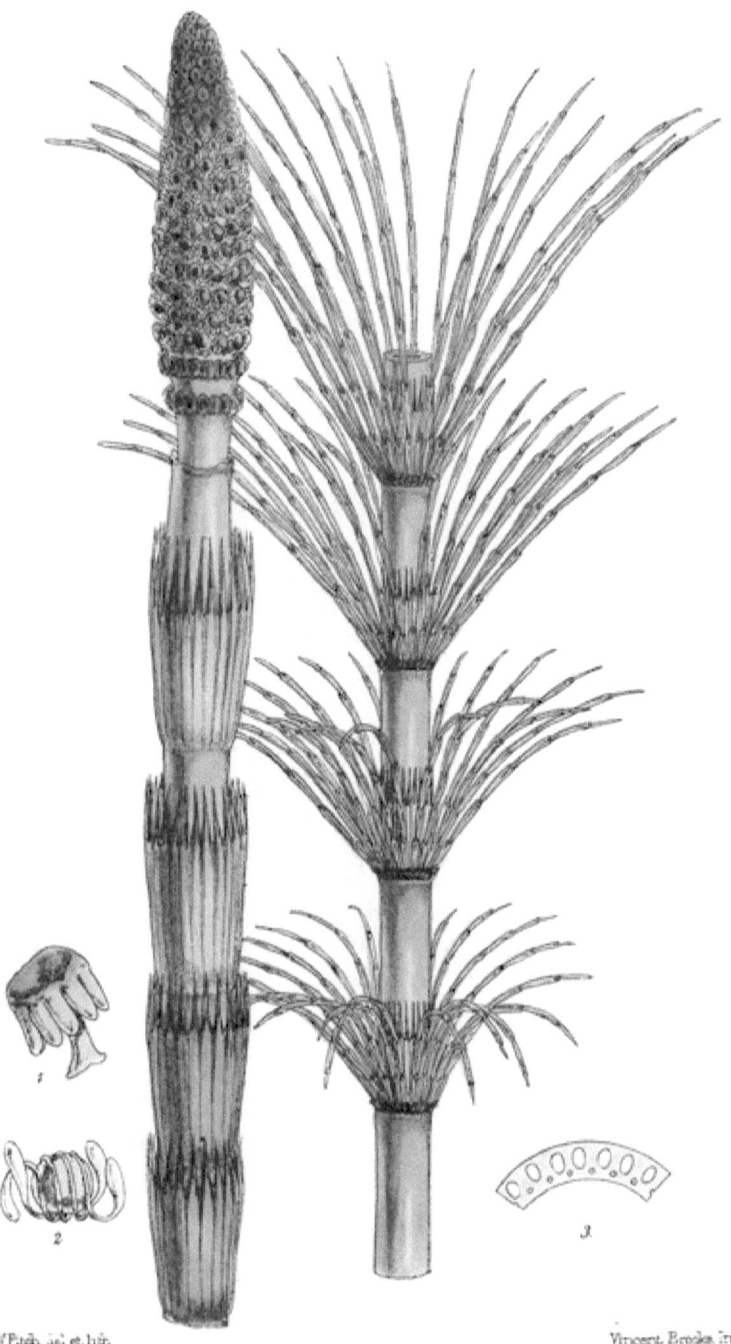

EQUISETUM TELMATEIA, *Ehrh.*

Great Water Horse-tail.

Gen. Char. Fructification terminal, in *spikes* or *catkins*, consisting of peltate polygonous *scales*, on the under side of which are from four to seven *involucres*; these open longitudinally, and contain numerous globose bodies, infolded by four filaments, clavate at their extremities.—*Terrestrial or aquatic.* Stems erect in vernation, *cylindrical, striated or furrowed, leafless, jointed, every* joint *hollow in the centre, and with two circles of lesser cavities in the circumference, terminating in a toothed* sheath, *simple or branched;* branches *more or less whorled.* Cuticle *often rough and abounding in silex, which renders some of the species useful in polishing wood, metals, etc.*

EQUISETUM (§ Vernalia*) *Telmateja;* sterile *stems,* stout, three to six feet long, half an inch wide, smooth (not scabrous), with very numerous (about thirty) striæ, and with erecto-patent simple branches, which have four prominent angles, each with a furrow; sheaths much shorter than the joints; *fertile* stems eight to ten inches long, one-half to three-quarters of an inch wide, including the large, lax sheaths which enclose them; spike two inches and more long.

EQUISETUM Telmateija. *Ehrh. Beitr.* 2. p. 160. *De Cand. Fl. Fr.* 2. p. 581. *Koch. Syn. Fl. Germ. ed.* 2. p. 964. *Newm. Brit. Ferns,* p. 67 *(with figures). Duval-Jouve, in Bull. Soc. Bot. Par.* 5. p. 515. f. 2. *Cosson, Flore des Env. de Paris, ed.* 2. p. 877. *Hook. and Arn. Brit. Fl. ed.* 8. p. 599.

EQUISETUM fluviatile. *Linn. Sp. Pl.* p. 1517. *Bolt. Fil. Brit.* p. 66. *t.* 36, 37. *Willd. Sp. Pl. v.* 5. p. 2. *Engl. Bot. t.* 2022. *Schk. Crypt. t.* 168. *Vauch. Monogr.* p. 35. *t.* 2. *Sm. Engl. Fl.* 4. p. 337.

EQUISETUM eburneum. *Roth. Cat. Bot.* 1. p. 128. *Asa Gray, Man. Bot. Illustr.* p. 586.

EQUISETUM majus. *Raii Syn.* p. 130. *Ger. Em.* 1113. *f.*

Hab. Wet damp ground, sides of clay ditches, clay banks, and swampy bogs, in most English counties; less common in Scotland.

---

* § Vernalia, *Al. Braun.* "Stems of two kinds, the one *fertile,* the other *sterile;* the *fertile* first developing, never green, unbranched, perishing, drying up after the maturity of the spike; *sterile* ones green, furnished with whorled branches, and surviving through the winter." *A. Braun.*—This character does not always hold good; not unfrequently the barren frond, as it is called, bears a spike of fructification, and sometimes the fertile stem becomes branched and is of longer duration.

Sir James Smith justly says of this, certainly the finest of the British Horse-tails, "found here and there in watery places, about the sheltered banks of rivers, where its large, long, branched stems, often six feet high, make a magnificent and Indian-like appearance."

The branches are in dense whorls and very slender. The fertile stems are very different from the sterile, rarely a foot high, very stout, destitute of branches, and covered with large, slightly inflated, lax, striated sheaths, terminated by numerous, subulate, brown, persistent teeth. The species appears to be common on the continent of Europe, extending to Norway and Lapland in the north, particularly abundant in Russia and Siberia, in the southern Taurus, etc. It is found in Madeira, in North Africa, Algeria, but from no country have I received finer and more numerous specimens than from North-west America, from California to 49° of north latitude, in British Columbia (*Dr. Lyall*). Dr. Beck, in his 'Botany of the Northern and Middle States of North America,' is the first, I believe, to record this plant as a native of the United States. He gives, "Buffalo, New York, and the shores of Lake Ontario." Dr. Asa Gray, under the name of *eburneum*, in his 'Flora of the North United States,' gives it as inhabiting the shores of the Great Lakes, and northward; and his description clearly indicates the species he intends. But I presume it is rare, for I have never had the good fortune to receive a specimen, either from the United States, or from Canada, or from the Hudson's Bay possessions, except from the region westward of the Rocky Mountains. In a sample I possess from Germany, a barren, much-branched frond, bears a fertile spike.

PLATE 58. Portion of a sterile and of a fertile stem of *Equisetum Telmateja*, *Ehrh.*,—*natural size*. Fig. 1. Peltate scale, with its involucres, from the spike. 2. A spore, as it is commonly considered, with its spiral clavate filaments. 3. Portion of a transverse section of the stem, to show the lacunes:—*magnified*.

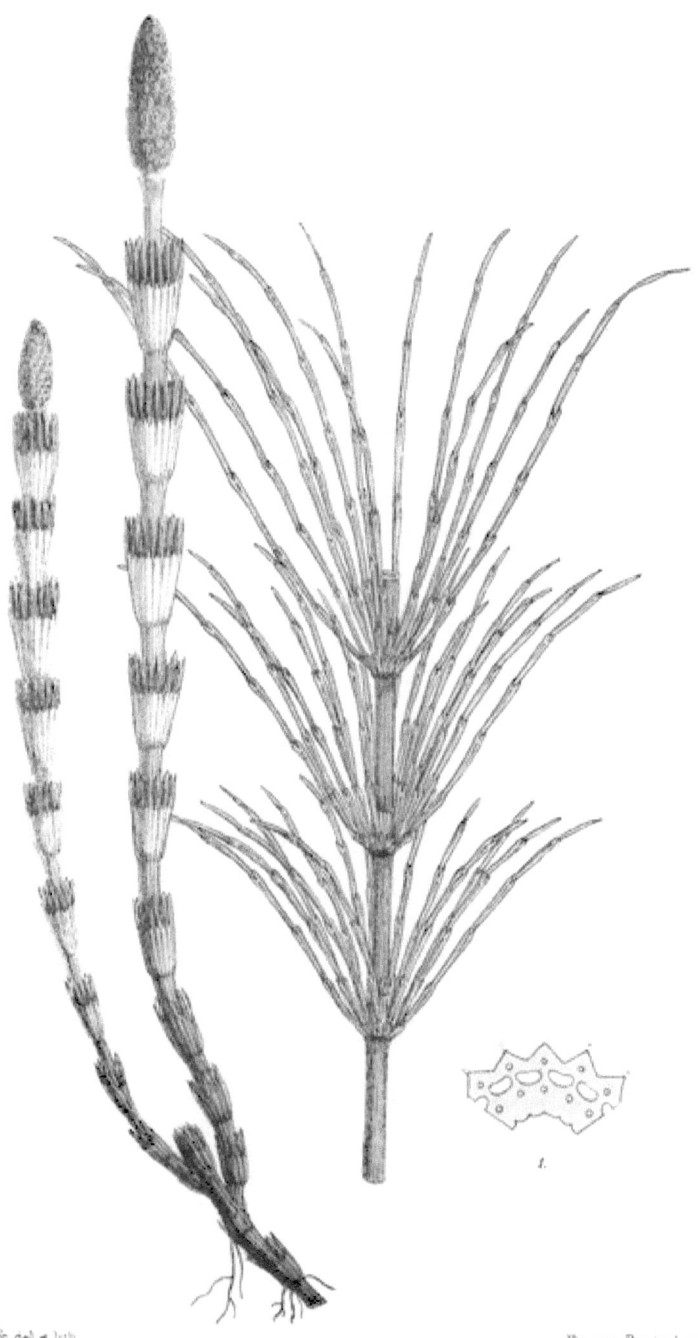

PLATE 59.

EQUISETUM UMBROSUM, *Meyer & Willd.*

Blunt-topped Horse-tail.

EQUISETUM (§ Vernalia) *umbrosum; sterile* frond terminating abruptly at the extremity, its stem (especially upwards) scabrous with prominent points and about twenty striæ; whorls of branches simple, slender, patent; teeth of their sheaths three to four, short, acute, with one rib disappearing before the apex; *fertile* stem without branches, with approximate infundibuliform lax sheaths, pale-coloured, terminated by numerous subulate dark-brown persistent teeth.

EQUISETUM umbrosum. *Meyer, in Willd. Enum. p.* 1063. *Sp. Pl. v.* 5. *p.* 3. *Newm. Brit. Ferns, p.* 63 (*with a figure*). *Hook. et Arn. Brit. Fl. ed.* 8. *p.* 599. *Koch, Syn. Fl. Germ. p.* 975.

EQUISETUM pratense. *Ehrh.* (*not Roth*). *A. Gray, Man. Bot. Illustr. p.* 586. *Benth. Man. p.* 620.

EQUISETUM Drummondii. *Hook. Brit. Fl. ed.* 2. *p.* 451, *and in Engl. Bot. Suppl. p.* 2777.

EQUISETUM Ehrharti, *Mey. Chlor. Hanov. p.* 666; E. pratense, *Ehrh. Beitr. v.* 3. *p.* 77 (*not Roth*), *Hoffm. Phyt. Blätt. p.* 117. *t.* 2; *and* E. sylvaticum β minus, *Retz. Fl. Scand. Suppl. v.* 2. *p.* 12, *are referred hither by Koch.*

Hab. Wet places in England, Scotland, and Ireland, rare? (probably often overlooked or passed by as some other species); Mere Clough, near Manchester; Yorkshire; Northumberland; Westmoreland; Aberdeenshire; near Forfar, and banks of the Isla and Esk, in Forfarshire, extending up the valleys to their sources (*Thos. Drummond*); by the Caledonian Canal; Falls of Moness; Ochills; Campsie Glen; Bonnington woods, Lanarkshire; Woodcock Dale, Linlithgowshire; near Belfast, Ireland, are the localities given in the 8th edition of 'British Flora;' to which Mr. Hewett Watson adds Inverness (*Dr. Graham*).

My attention was first directed to this as a new species of *Equisetum*, or at least new to Britain, many years ago, by the late Mr. Thos. Drummond, who sent me specimens from Forfarshire; and, not being able to satisfy myself that it was a described species, I published it under the name of *E. Drummondii*. But it has since been satisfactorily ascertained to be identical with the *E. umbrosum* of Willdenow (found in Prussian Pomerania), a name which we now adopt. It is most nearly allied to *E. arvense*, but its colour is greener, less glaucous, its stems more rough, with closely-set raised points, its angles and its branches much more numerous, and the mass of branches is singularly blunt at the summit, not tapering into a caudate apex. In general appearance the barren frond resembles *E. sylvaticum*, from which it is at once distinguished by the simple, erecto-patent, not compound, and drooping branches.

Under some or other of the above names (for the synonymy of the *Equisetaceæ* is still very unsettled) the present plant seems of late to be found generally on the continent of Europe, from the southern Alps to Scandinavia, and in the middle and northern United States, and in British North America, from Hudson's Bay to the Rocky Mountains (*Drummond*).

It happens not unfrequently in European and in North American specimens, that the fertile fronds become, if I may so say, sterile ones, by the dying away of the spike and the joints sending out whorls of branches.

PLATE 59. Fertile frond and portion of a sterile stem and branches,—*natural size*. Fig. 1. Portion of a transverse section of the stem, showing the lacunes,—*magnified*.

PLATE 60.

EQUISETUM ARVENSE, *Linn.*

Field Horse-tail.

Equisetum (§ Vernalia) *arvense; sterile* stems slightly scabrous, ending in a long tail-like point, erect or often procumbent, deeply sulcated with twelve to fourteen furrows, copiously branched with simple erecto-patent four-sided branches; *fertile* stems stouter but much shorter than the sterile ones, without branches; sheaths rather distant, tubuloso-infundibuliform, white and scariose, with about twelve brown striæ and as many lanceolate-acuminate sharp brown teeth; peduncle of the oblong-cylindrical spike more or less elongated.

Equisetum arvense. *Linn. Sp. Pl.* p. 1516. *Schk. Fil. v.* 1. p. 167. *Willd. Sp. Pl. v.* 5. p. 1. *Eng. Bot. t.* 2020. *Bolt. Fil.* p. 62. *t.* 34. *Sm. Eng. Fl. v.* 4. p. 339. *Newm. Brit. Ferns*, p. 77 (*with figures*). *Hook. and Arn. Brit. Fl. ed.* 8. p. 600. *Vauch. Monogr. des Presles*, p. 33. *t.* 1. *Duval-Jouve, in Bull. Soc. Bot. v.* 5. *p.* 515. *f.* 1. *Cosson, Fl. des Env. de Paris*, p. 877.

Equisetum arvense, longioribus setis. *Raii Syn.* p. 130.

Hab. Meadows, pastures, and cornfields throughout the kingdom; abundant,—so much so, that it ranks among the *mauvaises herbes*, and is very troublesome to the farmer, not only as difficult to eradicate, but, according to Mr. Curtis, noxious to cattle, especially to kine. Sir James Smith presumes that its action on their intestines may be chiefly mechanical, considering the sharp rough angles and points with which the whole plant abounds, and the abundance of flinty earth in its cuticle, which forms a file, similar to though finer than *E. hyemale*.

Like most plants of wide geographical distribution (and this we receive not only from almost every part of Europe and North America, as far north as the Mackenzie River, from India, chiefly northern, China, etc.), it is liable to vary in size and form and disposition of the branches. The sterile stems are erect or procumbent, the caudate apex is sometimes not developed, and then it approaches very near *E. umbrosum*. Even more than on *E. umbrosum*, the sterile stem is apt to bear a spike of fructification, or the fertile plant throws out branches, and thus apparently becomes perennial.

Plate 60. Fertile frond and upper portion of a sterile frond of *Equisetum arvense*, Linn.,—*natural size*. Fig. Portion of a transverse section of the stem, showing the lacunes,—*magnified*.

PLATE 61.

EQUISETUM SYLVATICUM, *Linn.*

Branched Wood Horsetail.

EQUISETUM (§ Subvernalia*) *sylvaticum;* one to two feet high; barren and fertile fronds with about twelve furrows, fertile ones eventually branched like the sterile; sheaths with three to five long membranaceous obtuse teeth; branches compound, whorled, slender, and much deflexed, their sheaths with subulate long teeth, each one-ribbed to the apex; catkin terminal, obtuse.

EQUISETUM sylvaticum. *Linn. Sp. Pl.* p. 1546. *Schk. Fil. t.* 166. *Sm. Engl. Bot. t.* 1874. *Bolt. Fil.* p. 30. *t.* 32, 33. *Sm. Engl. Fl. v.* 4. *p.* 336. *Vauch. Monogr.* p. 37. *t.* 3. *Duval-Jouve, in Bull. Soc. Bot. v.* 5. *p.* 516. *f.* 3. *Hook. and Arn. Brit. Fl. ed.* 8. *p.* 600. *Coss. and Germ. Fl. Env. Par.* p. 878. *Newm. Brit. Ferns,* p. 59 (*with a figure*). *Gray, Man. of Bot. Ill.* p. 586.

Hab. Frequent in boggy places and wet woods in England, Scotland, and Ireland, from the Isle of Wight in the south to the Hebrides, Orkney, and Shetland, according to Mr. Hewett Watson.

In a genus like that of the *Horsetails* we do not expect much that is beautiful; but our *Equisetum Telmateja*, Pl. 58, and the present are really handsome plants; and the advantage of size in favour of the former is compensated for by the grace and real elegance of the latter. *E. sylvaticum* springs in large patches from the black creeping underground roots or caudices which interlace each other copiously. In the young state, the stems are, as it were, blenched, having no green colour, and are destitute of branches both in the sterile and fertile fronds; soon, however, the fertile ones, as well as the sterile, throw out copious whorls of slender, drooping, compound green branches, and after a time the former cast off their terminal catkins, and both kinds assume a similar appearance, except that the fertile are more obtuse at the apex. A mass of these plants not inaptly resembles a miniature grove of drooping Larches.

The species is common in the middle United States of Ame-

---

* § Subvernalia, *Al. Braun:* "Stems of two kinds, sterile and fertile; the fertile appearing at the same time with the sterile, never green nor branched when young, persistent after the maturity of the spike, throwing out whorls of green branches and then resembling the sterile stems." Our last species, *E. umbrosum* (Plate 60), sometimes assumes the character belonging to this section.

rica, northward to Canada, and westward to British Columbia (*Seemann*). It occupies similar latitudes in temperate Europe, and there is found as far north as Smoland.

PLATE 61. Young fertile frond, and another more fully developing its branches, of *Equisetum* (§ Subvernalia) *sylvaticum*, Linn.,—*natural size*. Fig. 1. Section of a portion of the stem, showing the lacunes. 2. Section of a branch, which has no lacunes,—*magnified*.

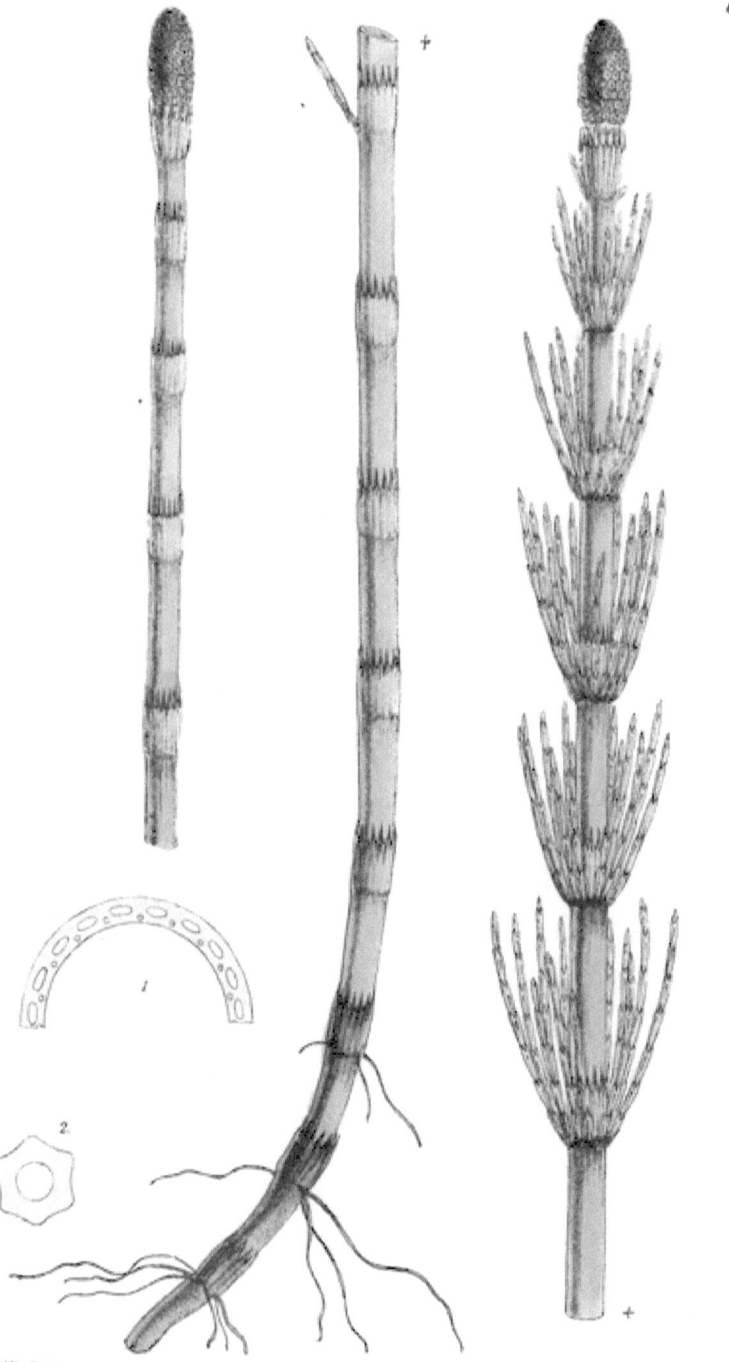

Plate 62.

EQUISETUM LIMOSUM, *Linn.*

Smooth Naked Horsetail.

EQUISETUM (§ Æstivalia*) *limosum;* stems or fronds one and a half to two and even more than three feet high, nearly smooth, striated; striæ about sixteen to eighteen; teeth of the sheaths short, rigid, distinct; branches nearly erect, simple, whorled, often abortive; catkin terminal upon the stem.

EQUISETUM limosum. *Linn. Sp. Pl. p.* 1517. *Willd. Sp. Pl. v.* 5. *p.* 4. *Sm. Engl. Bot. t.* 929. *Boll. Fil. p.* 68. *t.* 38. *Schk. Fil. t.* 171. *Vauch. Monogr. p.* 44. *t.* 8. *Sm. Engl. Fl. v.* 4. *p.* 339. *Duval-Jouve, in Bull. Soc. Bot. p.* 516. *f.* 5. *Hook. and Arn. Brit. Fl. ed.* 8. *p.* 600. *Cosson and Germ. Fl. Env. Par. p.* 880.

EQUISETUM fluviatile. *Fl. Dan. t.* 1184. *Newm. Brit. Ferns, p.* 51. (*It is the E. fluviatile, Linn., according to Fries, in Herb. nostr. and others.*)

EQUISETUM nudum lævius nostras. *Raii Syn. p.* 131. *t.* 5. *f.* 2 *A, B.*

Hab. Wet marshy grounds, in ponds and ditches and sides of rivers, throughout Great Britain.

This is next in point of size to *Equisetum Telmateja,* but very different in aspect and structure, and especially in the presence of catkins on stems that are similar to the barren ones, and in the fewer angles and teeth and fewer branches in whorls; and these latter are often short and imperfect or wanting.

The species seems to be as frequent in the temperate and subarctic districts of Europe and of North America as in Britain. Some of my specimens from each country have, besides the terminal catkin, nearly all the upper whorls of branches terminated by small black spikes. Differences of opinion exist as to this plant being the *fluviatile* of Linnæus. Hartmann, in his Annotationes on the Scandinavian Plants of the Linnæan Herbarium, assents to the two there being the same, but considers *E. fluviatile* the older name ("primum hinc inscriptum"). Fries's "*E. fluviatile, Linn.!*" in my herbarium is the larger and more branched form of our *limosum,* and his "*E. limosum, Linn.!*" is merely a smaller form with fewer branches. I do not at all see

---

* § Æstivalia, *Al. Braun:* "Stems all of one kind and fertile, fully developed at the time of fructification, green, throwing out whorls of branches, which, however, are not universal."

why the name *limosum* should be now disturbed. The surface of the stem is peculiarly smooth in all my specimens.

PLATE 62. Two forms of the plant—one with branches, the other unbranched—of *Equisetum* (§ Hyemalia) *limosum*, Linn., are represented,—*natural size*. Fig. 1. Section of the stem. 2. Section of a branch :—*magnified*.

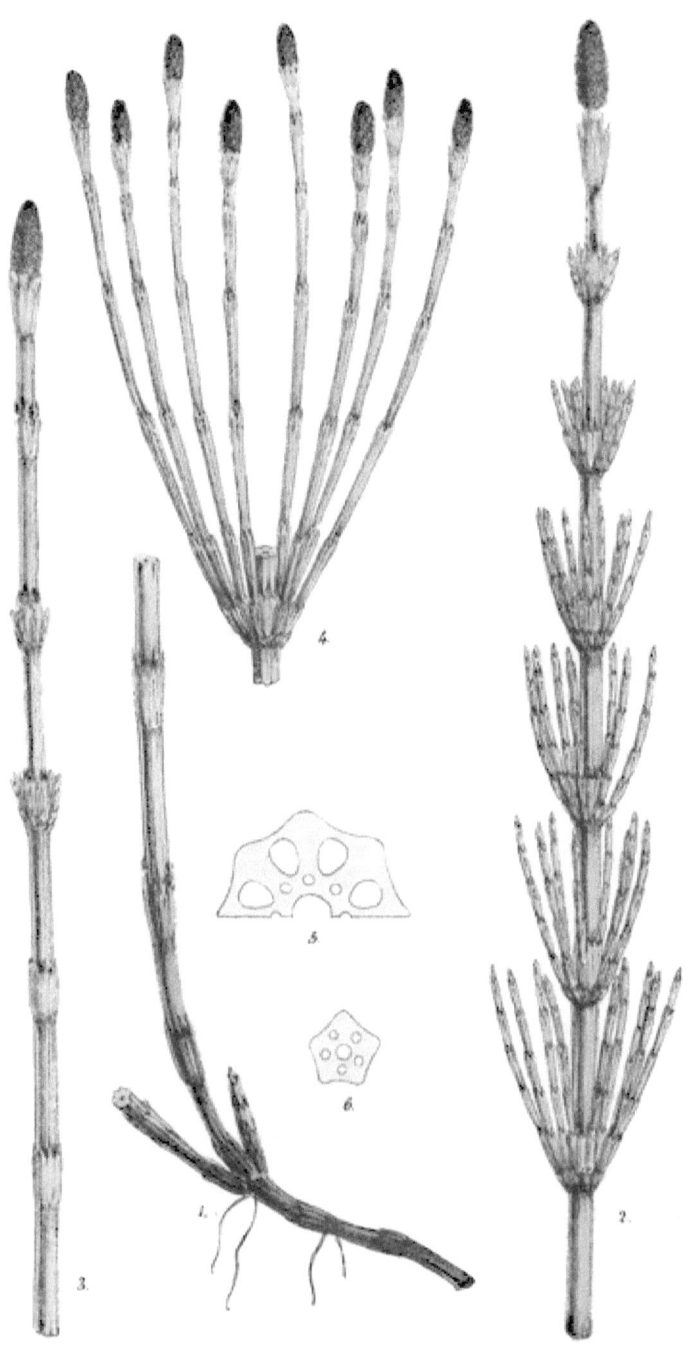

PLATE 63.

EQUISETUM PALUSTRE, *Linn.*

Marsh Horsetail.

EQUISETUM (§ Æstivalia) *palustre*; stems from a foot to a foot and a half high, four- to eight-furrowed, very smooth to the touch; teeth of the sheaths wedge-shaped, acute, brown at the point and membranaceous at the margin; branches simple, whorled, gradually shorter upwards, sometimes wanting; catkins terminal, obtuse.

EQUISETUM palustre. *Linn. Sp. Pl. p.* 1516. *Willd. Sp. Pl. v.* 5. *p.* 5. *Schk. Fil. t.* 169, 170 (*very good*). *Fl. Dan. t.* 1183. *Bolt. Fil. p.* 64. *t.* 35. *Engl. Bot. t.* 2021. *Vauch. Monogr. p.* 30. *t.* 3. *Duval-Jouve, in Bull. Soc. Bot. v.* 5. *p.* 516. *f.* 4. *Sm. Engl. Fl. v.* 4. *p.* 338. *Hook. and Arn. Brit. Fl. ed.* 8. *p.* 600. *Coss. and Germ. Fl. Env. Par. p.* 879. *Newm. Brit. Ferns, p.* 43 (*with figures*).

Var. β. *polystachion*; whorls of branches bearing catkins. *Willd. l. c. Sm. Engl. Fl. l. c.*

Var. γ. *Hook. and Arn. Brit. Fl. l.c. p.* 601.

EQUISETUM palustre minus polystachyon. *Bauh. Pin. p.* 10; *Prodr. p.* 24. *Raii Syn. p.* 131. *t.* 5. *f.* 3.

Hab. Marshy ground; equally common with the two preceding throughout the British dominions.

Mr. Hewett Watson justly observes of this: "A very variable plant; the small and slightly-branched states of which, both alpine and sublittoral, are not distinguished from *E. variegatum* without difficulty in determining to which species the individual examples should be referred." I have experienced the difficulty myself, especially of that small slightly-branched state, figured by Newman, and called var. *nudum*. The stems should be of annual duration, one would presume, in order to belong to the section "*Æstivalia*, persistant *jusqu'à* l'hiver," in contradistinction to the "*Hyemalia*, persistant *pendant* l'hiver;" but though Cosson does place it in that section, he yet calls it *perennial*. The polystachious form is analogous to that noticed under *E. limosum*. The species is common on the continent of Europe, but Dr. Asa Gray does not consider it to be a native of the United States; but I possess specimens gathered by Bourgeau in Palliser's Exploring Journey in British North America, which I am disposed to consider the same; and there is the same or a nearly allied species, of which I possess specimens from all the four quarters of the globe, tropical as well as temperate, which it will be hard to distinguish from it.

PLATE 63. Figs. 1 and 2. Usual form of *Equisetum* (§ Æstivalia) *palustre*, Linn.,—*natural size*. 3. Portion of a young stem or frond, with branches sprouting. 4. Portion of stem, with amentiferous branches. 5. Section of a stem. 6. Section of a branch, showing the lacunes :—*magnified*.

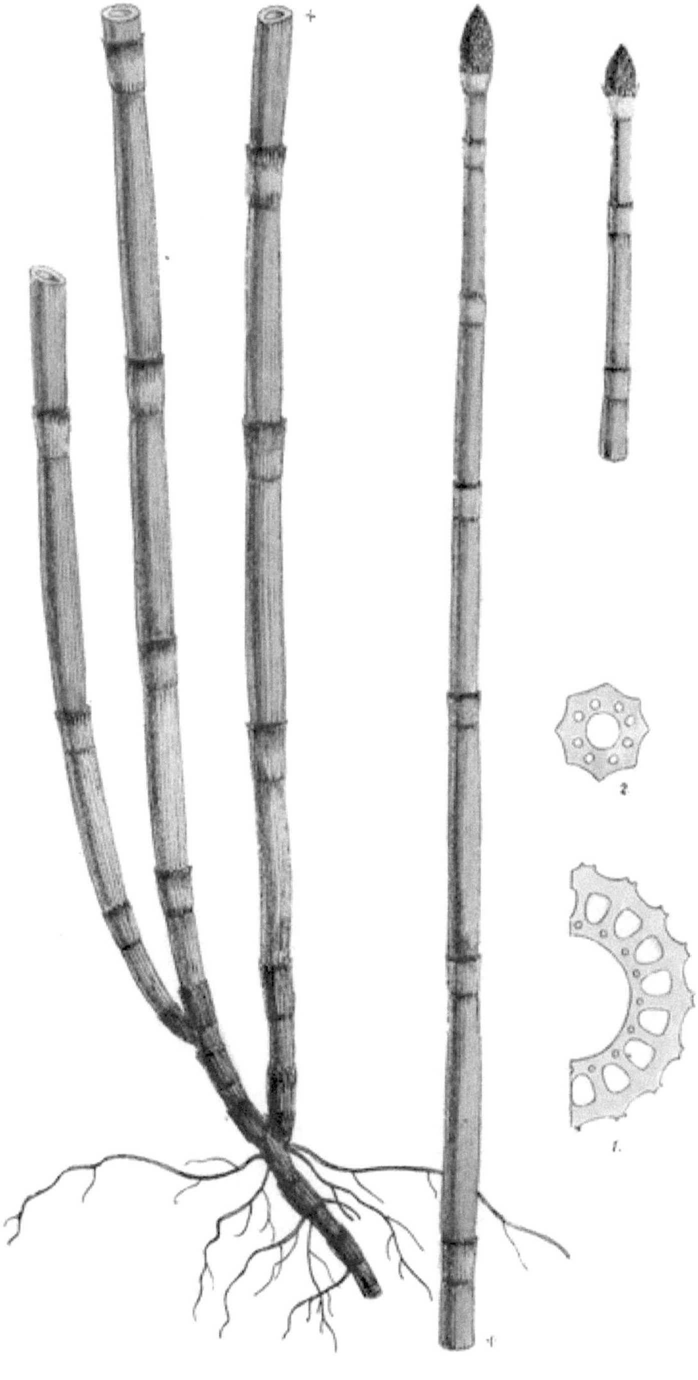

PLATE 64.

EQUISETUM HYEMALE, *Linn.*

Rough Horsetail, or Dutch Rushes.

EQUISETUM (§ Hyemalia*) *hyemale*; stems one to two and even three feet high, glaucous-green, throwing simple branches from the base, very rough to the touch on the surface, furrowed; sheaths black above and below, otherwise whitish, with twelve to eighteen very short black membranous mucronated teeth; the mucro deciduous; catkin terminal, mucronate, or sharply conical at the point.

EQUISETUM hyemale. *Linn. Sp. Pl. p.* 1517. *Willd. Sp. Pl. v.* 5. *p.* 8. *Schk. Fil. t.* 172 *C* (*very good*). *Engl. Bot. t.* 915. *Vanch. Monogr. p.* 46. *t.* 9. *Sm. Eng. Fl. v.* 4. *p.* 339. *Hook. Fl. Lond. t.* 16. *Hook. and Arn. Brit. Fl. ed.* 8. *p.* 601. *Newm. Brit. Ferns, p.* 17. *Gray, Man. of Bot. Illustr. p.* 587.

EQUISETUM nudum. *Raii Syn. p.* 131.

Hab. In boggy woods, but not very general; more frequent in North Britain than in the south, and in Ireland.

Readily distinguished by its size, glaucous colour, rough surface, and simple stems, or only branched at the base (except abnormally so), and never in whorls. It is very much a northern species and upon the continent of Europe, where Mr. Joseph Woods, in his 'Tourist's Flora,' speaks of it as "rare." I possess it from Switzerland and Altai, but probably in both cases from the mountains. It is found in Middle Russia, Scandinavia, and I have received it from Kamtchatka (*Seemann*) and from the Amur (*Maximowicz*). It is said to be a native of Spain, and I have specimens from Tunis, in North Africa, sent me by *Kralik*, and from Turkey (Rumelia); but North America would seem to be the favourite region of this plant. Notwithstanding that Asa Gray speaks of it as a northern plant, and that it is not recorded in Chapman's 'Flora of the Southern States,' I have specimens from as far south as New Mexico, from El Pasco, Western Texas (*C. Wright*), and from San Luis (*Engelmann*). It is sent from various parts of British North America, the Rocky Mountains, etc.; and in California and British North-West America, it

---

* § Hyemalia, *Al. Braun.*: "Stems of one kind, all fertile, perfectly developed at the period of fructification, green, with or without whorls of branches, persistent through the winter."

is not only extremely abundant, but some of my specimens are three to four feet long and more than half an inch in diameter.

The stems are ascertained by analysis to contain full thirteen per cent. of silicious earth, and the ashes have been found to consist of half their weight of silica: hence the extensive use made of this species for polishing wood, brass, ivory, etc.; so that it forms a considerable article of trade, under the name of *Dutch Rushes*. The Dutch dairymaids keep their milkpails beautifully neat and clean by the use of them. The astringent and stimulating properties attributed to them in former days caused them to be employed in our Pharmacopœia, and in a collection of drugs I have lately received from China this is among them.

PLATE 64. Fertile plant of *Equisetum* (§ Hyemalia) *hyemale*,—*natural size*. Figs. 1 and 2. Section of the stem,—*magnified*.

PLATE 65.

EQUISETUM TRACHYODON, *A. Braun.*

Rough-toothed Horsetail.

EQUISETUM (§ Hyemalia) *trachyodon;* stems branched at the base; branches long, flexuose, simple, or again irregularly-branched towards the apex, very scabrous, furrowed; sheaths ultimately wholly black, with six to thirteen narrow, somewhat persistent, subulate teeth; catkins terminal, mucronate.

EQUISETUM trachyodon. *Al. Braun, Regensb. Bot. Zeit. v.* 22. *p.* 308. *Koch, Syn. Fl. Germ. ed.* 2. *v.* 2. *p.* 967. *Duval-Jouve, in Bull. Soc. Bot. v.* 5. *p.* 518. *f.* 8. *Bab. Man. Brit. Fl. ed.* 4. *p.* 416. *Hook. and Arn. Brit. Fl. ed.* 8. *p.* 601.

EQUISETUM Mackaii. *Newm. Brit. Ferns, p.* 25 (*with figure*). *Hook. and Arn. Brit. Fl. ed.* 7 *and* 8.

EQUISETUM elongatum. *Hook. Brit. Fl. ed.* 5, *viz Willd.*

Hab. Colin Glen, Belfast, *Mackay and Whitla;* north of Ireland, in many of the glens, *C. Moore;* banks and inundated portions of banks in the bed of the Dee, Aberdeenshire, *Mrs. Brichan.*

When my attention was first directed to this *Equisetum* by Messrs. Whitla and Mackay, I was disposed to refer it, but as it appears without sufficient reason, to the little-known *E. elongatum* of Willdenow. I afterwards acquiesced in calling it *E. Mackaii* of Newman; and now I believe that Mr. Babington has satisfactorily shown it to be the *E. trachyodon* of Alexander Braun. Still I feel doubtful as to its being a permanently distinct species. It evidently belongs to the same group or division of *Equisetum* as *E. hyemale,* and one might almost look upon it as holding an intermediate place between that and the following species, *E. variegatum;* indeed, Koch (a very careful observer) remarks, l. c., "Sequente (*E. varieg.*) triplo crassius, pars membranacea, dentibus vaginarum imposita, subulata ex ovato-lanceolata basi, in dorso et margine muriculato-scabra, albida linea dorsali fusca, in apicem excurrente." These marks are almost too minute to be practically useful. The same may be said of the lacunes seen under the microscope in the transverse sections of the stem, on which M. Duval-Jouve places great reliance. It is recorded as a native of Germany, and has probably been overlooked elsewhere as some other known species;

nor does it appear in the American Floras; but I have specimens from British North America (*Drummond*), gathered near Cumberland House Fort, and others from Chili (*Macrae*), which I cannot distinguish from it.

PLATE 65. Portions of *Equisetum* (§ Hyemalia) *brachyodon*, Al. Braun, with fertile and barren branches,—*natural size*. Fig. 1. Section of a stem, showing the lacunes,—*magnified*.

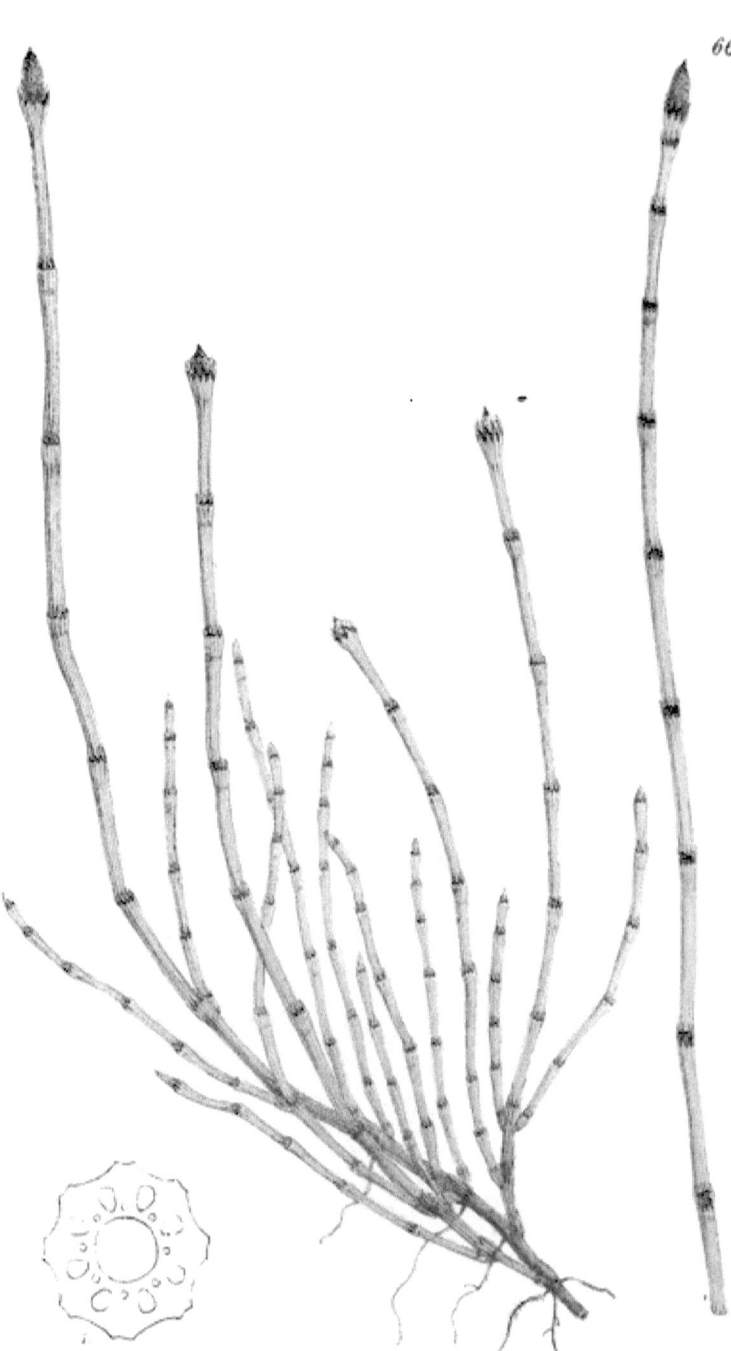

PLATE 66.

EQUISETUM VARIEGATUM, *Schleich.*

Variegated Rough Horse-tail.

EQUISETUM (§ Hyemalia) *variegatum;* small; stems filiform, often decumbent, rough, branched chiefly at the base, with four to ten furrows; sheaths green below, black above, with white or black-edged, membranous, obtuse, somewhat bristle-pointed teeth; catkin terminal, mucronate.

EQUISETUM variegatum. *Schleich. Cat. Pl. Helv.* p. 27. *Willd. Sp. Pl. v.* 5. p. 7. *Engl. Bot. t.* 1987. *Sm. Engl. Flora, v.* 4. p. 340. *Hook. and Arn. Brit. Fl.* ed. 8. p. 601. *Newm. Brit. Ferns,* p. 31, and at p. 39 his var. Wilsoni, (*erect, two to three feet high and smooth*). *Koch, Syn. Fl. Germ.* ed. 2. v. 2. p. 967. (*Under this species Koch brings as a synonym* E. reptans, β variegatum, *Wahl. Lapp.* p. 298.)

EQUISETUM scirpoides? *Mich. Fl. Bor. Am.* p. 281.

Hab. Sandy sea-shores, New Brighton, Cheshire; Bootle and South Port, Lancashire; Portmarnock sands; sands of Barrie, Dundee.—Var. *Wilsoni* (if really belonging to this species), Muckross, Killarney, *W. Wilson.*

That which is usually considered to be the true *Equisetum* appears with us to be confined to *sandy dunes near the sea.* The var. *Wilsoni* of Mr. Newman is found *in water;* enough in itself to produce a considerable difference between the two. But it is quite certain the limits of the species, belonging to the "Hyemalia" group, are far from being well defined, and they require to be studied, if possible, in their fresh state, and by means of copious suites of specimens from different localities. It is better in the meanwhile to doubt than to run headlong into conclusions. Hewett Watson says truly of *E. variegatum,* "While on the one side it makes some approach to *E. palustre,* in the small forms of this latter, on the other side *E. variegatum* shades off through *Wilsoni* and *Mackaii,* almost to *E. hyemale.* I am not suggesting that all these should be united into one species, but that the intervening species (one or more) between *palustre* and *hyemale* is not clearly understood by the technical diagnosis hitherto attempted to be drawn." Dr. Arnott and myself, too, have said in Brit. Flora, "It is very doubtful if the colour of the sheaths or the number of their teeth afford sufficient distinguishing characters; so that Mr. Newman was probably correct when he gave his opinion that all of the group with simple or irregularly-branched stems formed only one species." Some of my American specimens quite accord with the normal form of our plant, and I cannot agree with Koch when he says, "A nostra planta *luculenter* differt *Equisetum scirpoides*, Mich. (*F. reptans*, var. *a*, Wahl. Fl. Lapp. p. 298), caulibus humilioribus dimidio tenuioribus sexangularibus cum vaginis tantum tridentatis, quarum dentes persistunt. Caules *E. scirpoidis* revera tricostati sunt, sed linea impressa, costarum dorsalis ita excavata est, ut strias inter costas sitas æquet."

PLATE 66. Entire plant and a fertile branch of *Equisetum* (§ Hyemalia) *variegatum*, Schleich,—*natural size*. Fig. 1. Section of a stem, to show the lacunes,—*magnified*.

LATIN INDEX.

	Plate
Acropteris	
septentrionalis, Link	26
Acrostichum	
alpinum, Bol.	7
Ilvense, Linn.	8
leptophyllum, De Cand.	1
Ruta-muraria, Lam.	28
septentrionale, Linn.	26
Adiantum	
Capillus-Veneris, *Linn.*	41
Allosorus	
aquilinus, Pr.	38
crispus, Bernh.	39
minutus, Turcz.	39
Asplenium	
Germanicum, Newm.	27
Ruta-muraria, Newm.	28
septentrionale, Newm.	26
Anogramme	
leptophylla, Link and Fée	1
Aspidium	
aculeatum, Benth.	10
" (var. α *lobatum*)	10
" (var. β *intermedium*)	11
" (var. γ *angulare*)	12
aculum, Sw.	20
alpestre, Sw.	6
alpinum, Sw.	24
angulare, Willd.	10
angustum, Willd.	35
argutum, Kaulf.	16
asplenoides, Sw.	35
Bootii, Tuckerman	22
campylopterum, Kze.	19
cristatum, Sw.	17
dentatum, Sw.	33
depastum, Schk.	15
dilatatum, Höll	20
dilatatum, Willd.	19
" (var. *Bootii*, A. Gray)	22

	Plate
A. dilatatum (var. *recurvum*, Bree.)	20
drepanum, Schk.	19
dumetorum, Sm.	21
erosum, Schk.	19
Filix-fœmina, Sw.	35
Filix-mas, Sw.	15
fragile, Sw.	23
lancastriensis, Sw.	17
lobatum, Mett.	10
Lonchitis, *Sw.*	9
montanum, Sw.	25
Oreopteris, *Sw.*	14
paleaceum, Don	15
pallidum, Link	16
Pontederæ, Willd.	23
recurvum, Bree	20
regium, Sw.	24
remotum, A. Braun	22
rhæticum, Sw.	6
rigidum, Sw.	16
" (β *remotum*, A. Braun)	22
spinulosum, Hook. and Arn.	19
" (var. β, Hook. & Arn.)	21
Taygetense, Bory	24
Thelypteris, Sw.	13
Asplenium	
acutum, Bory	33
Adiantum-nigrum, *Linn.*	33
alpestre, Mett.	6
alternifolium, Wulf.	27
argutum, Klfs.	33
Bellottii, Sch.	32
Breynii, Retz	27
Capense, Linn.	33
Ceterach, *Linn.*	36
cuneatum, Sch.	32
cuneifolium, Vis.	33
densum, Brack.	29
dichronum, Kze.	29
elatius, Link	35

ii   LATIN INDEX.

	Plate
A. Filix-fœmina, *Beruh.*	35
fissum, Weinm.	33
fontanum, *Beruh.*	34
Forsteri, Sadl.	32
Germanicum, *Weiss*	27
Gaudichaudianum, Hook.	33
Halleri, Willd.	34
heterochroum, Kze.	29
humile, Bl.	33
incisum, Opitz	33
intermedium, Pr.	30
lanceolatum, *Huds.*	32
" (var. *microdon*, Moore)	32
leptophyllum, Cav.	1
luridum, Sal.	33
marinum, *Linn.*	31
" (var. *microdon*, Moore)	32
melanocaulon, Willd.	29
multicaule, Sch.	33
murorum, Lam.	28
nigrum, Beruh.	33
novum, Sadl.	33
obovatum, Viv.	32
obtusum, Kit.	33
Oreopteris, Linn.	33
productum, Lowe	33
rotundatum, Kls.	32
Ruta-muraria, *Linn.*	28
scolopendrium, Linn.	37
septentrionale, *Hoffm.*	26
Serpentini, Tausch.	33
Silesiacum, Milde	33
tabulare, Schrad.	33
trapeziforme, Huds.	31
Trichomanes ramosum, Bauhin	30
Trichomanes, *Linn.*	29
trichomanoides, Cav.	29
umbrosum, Vill.	30
viride, *Huds.*	30
Athyrium	
angustum, Pr.	35
asplenioides, Desv.	35
Filix-fœmina, Sw.	35
fontanum, Roth.	34
Halleri, Roth.	34
lanceolatum, Heufl.	32
Michauxii, Spr.	35
ovatum, Newm.	35
rhæticum, Roth.	6
tripinnatum, Rupr.	35
Blechnum	
boreale, *Sw.*	40
Spicant, Sm.	40
Botrychium	
Lunaria, *Sw.*	18

	Plate
Calamaria, Dill.	55
Ceterach	
alpinum, De Cand.	7
officinarum, Desv.	36
Cryptogramme	
crispa, *Br.*	39
Ctenopteris	
vulgaris, Newm.	2
Cyathea	
alpina, Sm.	24
dentata, Sm.	23
fragilis, Sm.	23
incisa, Sm.	24
montana, Sm.	25
regia, Forst.	24
Cystea	
angustata, Sm.	23
dentata, Sm.	23
fragilis, Sm.	23
regia, Sm.	24
Cystopteris	
Allioni, Newm.	25
alpina, *Desv.*	24
dentata, Hook.	23
Dickieana, Sim.	23
fragilis, *Beruh.*	23
" (var. α vulgaris)	23
" (var. β dentata)	23
" (var. γ Dickieana)	23
montana, Beruh.	25
myrrhidifolia, Newm.	25
regia, Presl	24
Dryopteris	
dilatata, A. Gray	19
rigida, A. Gray	22
Thelypteris, A. Gray	13
Equisetum	
arvense, *Linn.*	60
Drummondii, Hook.	59
Ehrharti, Mey.	59
eburneum, Roth.	58
elongatum, Hook.	64
fluviatile, Linn.	58
hyemale, *Linn.*	64
limosum, *Linn.*	62
Mackaii, Newm.	64
majus, Raii	58
nudum, Raii	64
palustre, *Linn.*	63
pratense, Ehrh.	59
scirpoides, Mich.	66
sylvaticum, *Linn.*	61
Telmateja, *Ehrh.*	58
trachyodon, *A. Braun.*	65
umbrosum, *Meyer and Willd.*	59

LATIN INDEX.

	Plate
E. variegatum, *Schleich.*	66
Wilsoni, Newm.	66
Grammitifolia	
palustris repens, Raii	37
Grammitis	
Ceterach, Sw.	36
leptophylla, Sw.	1
Gymnogramme	
Ceterach, Sp.	36
leptophylla, Desv.	1
Gymnocarpium	
Dryopteris, Newm.	4
Phegopteris, Newm.	3
Robertianum, Newm.	5
Gymnopteris	
Ceterach, Bernh.	36
Hemestheum	
montanum, Newm.	14
Hemionites	
leptophylla, Lag.	1
Pozoi, Moore	1
Hymenophyllum	
alatum, Sm.	42
Tunbridgense, Sm.	43
Tunbridgense, Schk.	43
Wilsoni, Hook.	44
unilaterale?, Bory	44
Isoetes	
Coromandeliana, Linn.	55
Duriæi, Bory	56
Engelmanni, Braun	55
Hystrix, Wolsey	56
,, (var. subinermis, Bal.)	56
lacustris, Linn.	55
riparia, Eng.	55
setacea, Bosc.	55
velata, A. Braun	55
Lastrea	
æmula, Brack.	20
concava, Newm.	20
cristata, Presl	17
,, (var. spinulosa, Moore)	18
dilatata, Pr.	19
,, (var. collina, Moore)	21
,, (var. dumetorum, Moore)	21
,, (var. maculata, Moore)	21
Dryopteris, Newm.	4
Filix-mas, Pr.	15
Foenisecii, Wats	20
maculata, Deakin	21
multiflora, Newm.	19
,, (var. collina, Newm.)	21
Oreopteris, Pr.	14
remota, Moore	22
rigida, Pr.	16

	Plate
L. Robertiana, Newm.	5
rufidula, Pr.	8
spinulosa, Pr.	18
Thelypteris, Pr.	13
Lepidotis	
annotina, Beauv.	50
Lomaria	
borealis, Link	40
Spicant, Sm.	40
Lophodium	
Callipteris, Newm.	17
collinum, Newm.	21
Fœnisecii, Newm.	20
glandulosum, Newm.	18
recurvum, Newm.	20
spinosum, Newm.	18
uliginosum, Newm.	18
Lycopodium	
alpinum, Linn.	53
annotinum, Linn.	50
axillare, Roxb.	54
Bigelovii, Oakes	51
bryophyllum, Pr.	50
Ceylanicum, Spr.	54
Chamærense, Turcz.	53
ciliatum, Lam.	52
clavatum, Linn.	49
densum, Lam.	54
divaricatum, Wall.	49
Heyneanum, Wall.	50
inflexum, Sw.	49
inundare, Carm.	54
inundatum, Linn.	51
juniperifolium, Lam.	50
palustre, Lam.	51
piliferum, Raddi	49
Preslii, Hook. and Grev.	49
recurvum, Kit.	54
selaginoides, Linn.	53
Selago, Linn.	54
serpens, Pr.	49
suberectum, Lowe	54
Sitchense, Rup.	53
trichiatum, Bl.	49
Nephrodium	
asplenoides, Mich.	35
cristatum, Mich.	17
Filix-fœmina, Mich.	35
Filix-mas, Rich.	15
Fœnisecii, Lowe	20
Oreopteris, Desv.	14
pallidum, Bory	16
remotum, Hook.	22
rigidum, Desv.	16
rufidulum, Mich.	8

	Plate
N. spinulosum, *Sw.*	20
,, (var. æmulum)	20
,, (var. bipinnatum)	18
,, (var. dilatatum)	19
,, (var. dumetorum)	21
Thelypteris, *Desv.*	13
Notopleurum	
Ceterach, Newm.	36
Ophioglossum	
Lusitanicum, Linn.	47
vulgatum, *Linn.*	46
,, (var. angustifolium)	47
Osmunda	
Capensis, Pr.	45
crispa, Linn.	39
glaucescens, Link	45
gracilis, Link	45
Hilzenbergii, Hook. and Grev.	45
Hugeliana, Pr.	45
Leschenaultii, Wall.	45
leptophylla, Lam.	1
Lunaria, Linn.	48
obtusifolia, Willd.	45
palustris, Sch.	45
regalis, Linn.	45
speciosa, Wall.	45
spectabilis, Willd.	45
Spicant, Linn.	40
Phegopteris	
alpestris, Mett.	6
calcarea, Fée	5
Dryopteris, Fée	4
polypodioides, Fée	3
vulgaris, Mett.	5
Phorolobus	
crispus, Desv.	39
Phyllitis	
Scolopendrium, Newm.	37
Pilularia	
globulifera, *Linn.*	57
palustris juncifolia, Dill.	57
Plananthus	
inundatus, Beauv.	51
Selago, Beauv.	54
Polypodium	
aculeatum, Linn.	10
aculeatum, Huds.	11
æmulum, Sol.	20
alpestre, Hoppe	6
alpinum, Wulf.	24
Arcouicum, Sm.	7
Arcouicum, With	8
australe, Fée	2
calcareum, Pursh.	4
calcareum, Sm.	5

	Plate
P. Cambricum, Linn.	2
connectile, Mich.	3
cristatum, Bolt.	19
cristatum, Linn.	17
dentatum, Dicks.	23
dentigerum, Wall.	35
dilatatum, Hoffm.	19
Dryopteris, Dicks.	5
Dryopteris, *Linn.*	4
Filix-femina, Linn.	35
Filix-mas, Linn.	15
flexile, Moore	6
fontanum, Linn.	34
fragile, Linn.	23
hyperboreum, Sm.	7
Ilvense, With.	7
Ilvense, Sw.	8
leptophyllum, Linn.	1
Lonchitis, Linn.	9
montanum, Lam.	25
myrrhidifolium, Vill.	25
Oreopteris, Ehrh.	14
Phegopteris, *Linn.*	3
regium, Linn.	24
rhæticum, Dicks.	23
rhæticum, Linn.	35
rhæticum, Vill.	6
rigidum, Hoffm.	16
Robertianum, *Hoffm.*	5
tanacetifolium, Hoffm.	19
Thelypteris, Huds.	14
Virginianum, Linn.	2
vulgare, *Linn.*	2
Polystichum	
aculeatum, Roth	11
angulare, Presl	12
montanum, Roth	14
cristatum, Roth	17
Dryopteris, Roth	4
Lonchitis, Roth	9
Phegopteris, Roth	3
spinosum, Roth	18
Pseudathyrium	
alpestre, Newm.	6
flexile, Newm.	6
Pteris	
aquilina, *Linn.*	38
crispa, Linn.	39
caudata, Schkh.	38
recurvata, Wall.	38
Stelleri, Gmel.	39
Scolopendrium	
alternifolium, Roth.	27
Ceterach, Sym.	36
officinarum, Sw.	37

S. *Phyllitis*, Roth	37
vulgare, *Sw.*	37
Selaginella	
selaginoides, Link	52
spinosa, Beauv.	52
Spicanta	
borealis, Pr.	40
Stegania	
borealis, Br.	40
Stachygynandrum	
alpinum, Pr.	53
Tarachia	
lanceolata, Pr.	32
Thelypteris	
palustris, Schott	13
Trichomanes	
alatum, Hook.	42
T. *Andrewsii*, Newm.	42
brevisetum, Br.	42
europæum, Sm.	42
pyxidiferum, Huds.	42
radicans, Sw.	42
scandens, Hedw.	42
speciosum, Willd.	42
Tunbridgense, Bolt.	41
Tunbridgense, Linn.	43
Woodsia	
hyperborea, Br.	7
alpina, Gray	7
Ilvensis, Benth.	7
Ilvensis, Br.	8
Rajana, Newm.	8

ENGLISH INDEX.

	Plate
Adder's-tongue, Common	46
Adder's-tongue, Common (narrow-leaved)	47
Bladder Fern, Alpine	24
Bladder Fern, Brittle	23
Bladder Fern, Mountain	25
Brake or Bracken, Common	38
Bristle Fern, Rooting	42
Buckler Fern, Crested	17
Buckler Fern, Distant-leaved	22
Buckler Fern, Male	15
Buckler Fern, Marsh	13
Buckler Fern, Mountain	14
Buckler Fern, Prickly (*ornatum*)	20
Buckler Fern, Prickly (bipinnate)	18
Buckler Fern, Prickly (*dumetorum*)	21
Buckler Fern, Prickly (tripinnate)	19
Buckler Fern, Rigid	16
Ceterach, Common	36
Club Moss, Common	49
Club Moss, Fir	54
Club Moss, Interrupted	50
Club Moss, Lesser Alpine	52
Club Moss, Marsh	51
Club Moss, Savin-leaved	53
Dutch Rushes	64
Filmy Fern, Tunbridge	43
Filmy Fern, Mr. Wilson's	44
Flowering Fern	45
Gymnogram, Small Annual	1
Hard-Fern, Northern	40
Holly Fern, Alpine	9
Horse-tail, Blunt-topped	59
Horse-tail, Branched Wood	61
Horse-tail, Common	37
Horse-tail, Field	60
Horse-tail, Great Water	58
Horse-tail, Marsh	63
Horse-tail, Rough	64
Horse-tail, Rough-toothed	65

	Plate
Horse-tail Smooth Naked	62
Horse-tail, Variegated	66
Lady Fern	35
Maiden-hair Fern	41
Moonwort, Common	48
Oak Fern, Tender Three-branched	4
Osmund Royal	45
Osmund the Waterman	45
Parsley Fern	39
Pepper-grass	57
Pillwort	57
Polypody, Alpine	6
Polypody, Common	2
Polypody, Pale Mountain	3
Polypody, Rigid Three-branched	5
Polypody, Tender Three-branched	4
Quillwort, Common	55
Quillwort, Durieu's	56
Rock Brake, Curled	39
Shield Fern, Alpine	9
Shield Fern, Prickly (angular)	12
Shield Fern, Prickly (intermediate)	11
Shield Fern, Prickly (lobed)	10
Spleenwort, Alternate-leaved	27
Spleenwort, Black	33
Spleenwort, Common	29
Spleenwort, Forked	26
Spleenwort, Green	30
Spleenwort, Lanceolate	32
Spleenwort, Maiden-hair	29
Spleenwort, Scaly	36
Spleenwort, Sea	31
Spleenwort, Short-fruited	35
Spleenwort, Smooth Rock	34
Wall Rue	28
Water-Fern	45
Wolf's-claw Moss	49
Woodsia, Oblong	8
Woodsia, Round-leaved	7

LIST OF WORKS

PUBLISHED BY L. REEVE & CO.

L. REEVE AND CO.'S NEW SERIES OF NATURAL HISTORY FOR BEGINNERS.

*** A good introductory series of books on Natural History for the use of students and amateurs is still a *desideratum*. Those at present in use have been too much compiled from antiquated sources; while the figures, copied in many instances from sources equally antiquated, are far from accurate, the colouring of them having become degenerated through the adoption, for the sake of cheapness, of mechanical processes.

The present series will be entirely the result of original research carried to its most advanced point; and the figures, which will be chiefly engraved on steel, by the artist most highly renowned in each department for his technical knowledge of the subjects, will in all cases be drawn from actual specimens, and coloured separately by hand.

Each work will treat of a department of Natural History sufficiently limited in extent to admit of a satisfactory degree of completeness.

The following are now ready:—

BRITISH INSECTS; a Familiar Description of the Form, Structure, Habits, and Transformations of Insects. By E. F. STAVELEY. Crown 8vo, 16 Coloured Steel Plates, engraved from Natural Specimens expressly for the work by E. W. ROBINSON, and numerous Wood-Engravings by E. C. RYE, 14s.

BRITISH BUTTERFLIES AND MOTHS; an Introduction to the study of our Native LEPIDOPTERA. By H. T. STAINTON. Crown 8vo, 16 Coloured Steel Plates, containing Figures of 100 Species, engraved from Natural Specimens expressly for the work by E. W. ROBINSON, and Wood-Engravings, 10s. 6d.

BRITISH BEETLES; an Introduction to the Study of our Indigenous COLEOPTERA. By E. C. RYE. Crown 8vo, 16 Coloured Steel Plates, comprising Figures of nearly 100 Species, engraved from Natural Specimens, expressly for the work, by E. W. ROBINSON, and 11 Wood-Engravings of Dissections by the Author, 10s. 6d.

BRITISH BEES; an Introduction to the Study of the Natural History and Economy of the Bees indigenous to the British Isles. By W. E. SHUCKARD. Crown 8vo, 16 Coloured Steel Plates, containing nearly 100 Figures, engraved from Natural Specimens, expressly for the work, by E. W. ROBINSON, and Woodcuts of Dissections, 10s. 6d.

BRITISH SPIDERS; an Introduction to the Study of the ARANEIDÆ found in Great Britain and Ireland. By E. F. STAVELEY. Crown 8vo, 16 Plates, containing Coloured Figures of nearly 100 Species, and 40 Diagrams, showing the number and position of the eyes in various Genera, drawn expressly for the work by TUFFEN WEST, and 44 Wood-Engravings, 10s. 6d.

BRITISH GRASSES; an Introduction to the Study of the Grasses found in the British Isles. By M. PLUES. Crown 8vo, 16 Coloured Plates, drawn expressly for the work by W. FITCH, and 100 Wood-Engravings, 10s. 6d.

BRITISH FERNS; an Introduction to the Study of the Ferns, LYCOPODS, and EQUISETA indigenous to the British Isles. With Chapters on the Structure, Propagation, Cultivation, Diseases, Uses, Preservation, and Distribution of Ferns. By MARGARET PLUES. Crown 8vo, 16 Coloured Plates, drawn expressly for the work by W. FITCH, and 55 Wood-Engravings, 10s. 6d.

BRITISH SEAWEEDS; an Introduction to the Study of the Marine ALGÆ of Great Britain, Ireland, and the Channel Islands. By S. O. GRAY. Crown 8vo, 16 Coloured Plates, drawn expressly for the work by W. FITCH, 10s. 6d.

Other Works in preparation.

BOTANY.

THE NATURAL HISTORY OF PLANTS. By H.
BAILLON, President of the Linnæan Society of Paris, Professor of Medical
Natural History and Director of the Botanical Garden of the Faculty of
Medicine of Paris. Translated by MARCUS M. HARTOG, Trinity College,
Cambridge. Super-royal 8vo. Vol. I., with 503 Wood Engravings, 25s.

Of the accuracy and excellence of this great work, the position of the author,
as a Botanist of the first rank, and an original investigator, is a sufficient
guarantee. Its popular readable style will commend it to all those who desire
to become acquainted with the wonderful variety of form and structure found in
the vegetable kingdom, but are deterred by the technicalities of other botanical
works. The Illustrations, unequalled for beauty, clearness, and accuracy, and
abundant in sectional detail of Flower, Fruit, and Seed, add greatly to the value
as well as to the attractiveness of the work. The Geographical Distribution
and the useful or noxious properties of Plants are duly noted at the end of each
family. In the Notes will be found full references to authorities and such
other matter as the advanced botanist may require. The First Volume, contains the Families RANUNCULACEÆ, DILLENIACEÆ, MAGNOLIACEÆ, ANONACEÆ, MONIMIACEÆ, and ROSACEÆ. The second volume is in the press, and
the continuation will keep pace with the French Edition.

DOMESTIC BOTANY; an Exposition of the Structure and
Classification of Plants, and of their uses for Food, Clothing, Medicine,
and Manufacturing Purposes. By JOHN SMITH, A.L.S., ex-Curator of
the Royal Botanic Gardens, Kew. Crown 8vo, pp. 560, with 16 Coloured
Plates and Wood Engravings, 16s.

A handy book of the Vegetable Kingdom, containing a large amount of interesting information, relative to the uses of Plants to man in this country, as
well as in those where they grow.

HANDBOOK OF THE BRITISH FLORA; a Description of the Flowering Plants and Ferns indigenous to, or naturalized in, the
British Isles. For the Use of Beginners and Amateurs. By GEORGE
BENTHAM, F.R.S., President of the Linnean Society. New Edition, Crown
8vo, 680 pp., 12s.

Distinguished for its terse and clear style of description; for the introduction
of a system of Analytical Keys, which enable the student to determine the family
and genus of a plant at once by the observation of its more striking characters;
and for the valuable information here given for the first time of the geographical
range of each species in foreign countries.

**HANDBOOK OF THE BRITISH FLORA, ILLUSTRATED
EDITION;** a Description (with a Wood-Engraving, including dissections, of
each species) of the Flowering Plants and Ferns indigenous to, or naturalized in, the British Isles. By GEORGE BENTHAM, F.R.S., President of
the Linnean Society. Demy 8vo, 2 vols., 1155 pp., 1295 Wood-Engravings,
from Original Drawings by W. FITCH, £3. 10s.

An illustrated edition of the foregoing Work, in which every species is accompanied by an elaborate Wood-Engraving of the Plant, with dissections of its
leading structural peculiarities.

BRITISH WILD FLOWERS, Familiarly Described in the Four Seasons. A New Edition of 'The Field Botanist's Companion.' By THOMAS MOORE, F.L.S. One volume, Demy 8vo, 424 pp. With 24 Coloured Plates, by W. FITCH, 16s.

An elegantly-illustrated volume, intended for Beginners, describing the plants most readily gathered in our fields and hedgerows, with the progress of the seasons. Dissections of the parts of the flowers are introduced among the Figures, so that an insight may be readily obtained not only of the Species and name of each plant, but of its structure and characters of classification.

BRITISH GRASSES; an Introduction to the Study of the Gramineæ of Great Britain and Ireland. By M. PLUES. Crown 8vo, 100 Wood-Engravings, 6s.; with 16 Coloured Plates by W. FITCH, 10s. 6d.

One of the 'New Series of Natural History,' accurately describing all the Grasses found in the British Isles, with introductory chapters on the Structure, Cultivation, Uses, etc. A Wood-Engraving, including dissections, illustrates each Species; the Plates contain Coloured figures of 43 Species.

CURTIS'S BOTANICAL MAGAZINE, comprising New and Rare Plants from the Royal Gardens of Kew, and other Botanical Establishments. By Dr. J. D. HOOKER, F.R.S., Director of the Royal Gardens. Royal 8vo. Published Monthly, with 6 Plates, 3s. 6d. coloured. Vol. XXVI. of the Third Series (being Vol. XCVI. of the entire work) now ready, with a new GENERAL INDEX of the 26 volumes, 43s. The INDEX separately, 1s. A complete set of the THIRD SERIES may be had; also a copy of the Second Series, 18 years' issue in 17 vols., new, in cloth.

Descriptions and Drawings, beautifully coloured by hand, of newly-discovered plants suitable for cultivation in the Garden, Hothouse, or Conservatory.

THE FLORAL MAGAZINE, containing Figures and Descriptions of New Popular Garden Flowers. By the Rev. H. HONYWOOD DOMBRAIN, A.B. Imperial 8vo. Published Monthly, with 4 Plates, 2s. 6d. coloured. Vols. I. to V., each, with 64 coloured plates, £2. 2s. Vols. VI. to IX., 48 coloured plates, 31s. 6d. each.

Descriptions and Drawings, beautifully coloured by hand, of new varieties of Flowers raised by the nurserymen for cultivation in the Garden, Hothouse, or Conservatory.

OUTLINES OF ELEMENTARY BOTANY, as Introductory to Local Floras. By GEORGE BENTHAM, F.R.S., President of the Linnean Society. Demy 8vo, pp. 45, 2s. 6d.

LAWS OF BOTANICAL NOMENCLATURE adopted by the International Botanical Congress, with an Historical Introduction and a Commentary. By ALPHONSE DE CANDOLLE. 2s. 6d.

A SECOND CENTURY OF ORCHIDACEOUS PLANTS,
selected from the subjects published in Curtis's 'Botanical Magazine' since the issue of the 'First Century.' Edited by JAMES BATEMAN, Esq., F.R.S. Complete in 1 Vol., royal 4to, 100 Coloured Plates, £5. 5s.

During the fifteen years that have elapsed since the publication of the 'Century of Orchidaceous Plants,' now out of print, the 'Botanical Magazine' has been the means of introducing to the public nearly two hundred of this favourite tribe of plants not hitherto described and figured, or very imperfectly so. This volume contains a selection of 100 of the most beautiful and best adapted for cultivation. The descriptions are revised and in many cases re-written, agreeably with the present more advanced state of our knowledge and experience in the cultivation of Orchidaceous plants, by Mr. Bateman, the acknowledged successor of Dr. Lindley as the leading authority in this department of botany and horticulture.

MONOGRAPH OF ODONTOGLOSSUM, a Genus of the
Vandeous Section of Orchidaceous Plants. By JAMES BATEMAN, Esq., F.R.S. Imperial folio. Parts I. to IV., each with 5 Coloured Plates, and occasional Wood Engravings, 21s.

Designed for the illustration, on an unusually magnificent scale, of the new and beautiful plants of this favoured genus of *Orchidaceæ*, which are being now imported from the mountain-chains of Mexico, Central America, New Granada, and Peru.

SELECT ORCHIDACEOUS PLANTS. By ROBERT WARNER, F.R.H.S.
With Notes on Culture by B. S. WILLIAMS. In Ten Parts, folio, each, with 4 Coloured Plates, 12s. 6d.; or, complete in one vol., cloth gilt, £6. 6s.
Second Series, Parts I. to VII., each, with 3 Coloured Plates, 10s. 6d.

THE RHODODENDRONS OF SIKKIM-HIMALAYA;
being an Account, Botanical and Geographical, of the Rhododendrons recently discovered in the Mountains of Eastern Himalaya from Drawings and Descriptions made on the spot, by Dr. J. D. HOOKER, F.R.S. By Sir W. J. HOOKER, F.R.S. Folio, 30 Coloured Plates, £4. 14s. 6d.

Illustrations on a superb scale of the new Sikkim Rhododendrons, now being cultivated in England, accompanied by copious observations on their distribution and habits.

THE TOURIST'S FLORA; a Descriptive Catalogue of the
Flowering Plants and Ferns of the British Islands, France, Germany, Switzerland, Italy, and the Italian Islands. By JOSEPH WOODS, F.L.S. Demy 8vo, 504 pp., 18s.

Designed to enable the lover of botany to determine the names of any wild plants he may meet with while journeying in our own country and the countries of the Continent most frequented by tourists. The author's aim has been to make the descriptions clear and distinct, and to comprise them within a volume of not inconvenient bulk.

GENERA PLANTARUM, ad Exemplaria imprimis in Herbariis Kewensibus servata definita. By GEORGE BENTHAM, F.R.S., President of the Linnean Society, and Dr. J. D. HOOKER, F.R.S., Director of the Royal Gardens, Kew. Vol. I. Part I. pp. 454. Royal 8vo, 21s. Part II., 14s.; Part III., 15s.; or Vol. I. complete, 50s.

This important work comprehends an entire revision and reconstruction of the Genera of Plants. Unlike the famous 'Genera Plantarum' of Endlicher, which is now out of print, it is founded on a personal study of every genus by one or both authors. The First Vol. contains 82 Natural Orders and 2544 Genera.

FLORA VITIENSIS; a Description of the Plants of the Viti or Fiji Islands, with an Account of their History, Uses, and Properties. By Dr. BERTHOLD SEEMANN, F.L.S. Royal 4to, Parts I. to IX, each, 10 Coloured Plates, 15s. To be completed in 10 Parts.

This work owes its origin to the Government Mission to Viti, to which the author was attached as naturalist. In addition to the specimens collected, the author has investigated all the Polynesian collections of Plants brought to this country by various botanical explorers since the voyage of Captain Cook.

FLORA OF THE ANTARCTIC ISLANDS. By Dr. J. D. HOOKER, F.R.S. Royal 4to, 2 vols., 574 pp., 200 Plates, £10. 15s. coloured. Published under the authority of the Lords Commissioners of the Admiralty.

The 'Flora Antarctica' illustrates the Botany of the southern districts of South America and the various Antarctic Islands, as the Falklands, Kerguelen's Land, Lord Auckland and Campbell's Island, and 1370 species are enumerated and described. The plates, beautifully coloured, illustrate 370 species, including a vast number of exquisite forms of Mosses and Seaweeds.

FLORA OF TASMANIA. By Dr. J. D. HOOKER, F.R.S. Royal 4to, 2 vols., 972 pp., 200 Plates, £17. 10s., coloured. Published under the authority of the Lords Commissioners of the Admiralty.

The 'Flora of Tasmania' describes all the Plants, flowering and flowerless, of that Island, consisting of 2203 Species, collected by the Author and others. The Plates, of which there are 200, illustrate 412 Species.

ON THE FLORA OF AUSTRALIA, its Origin, Affinities, and Distribution; being an Introductory Essay to the 'Flora of Tasmania.' By Dr. J. D. HOOKER, F.R.S. 128 pp., quarto, 10s.

FLORA OF THE BRITISH WEST INDIAN ISLANDS. By Dr. GRISEBACH, F.L.S. Demy 8vo, 806 pp., 37s. 6d. Published under the auspices of the Secretary of State for the Colonies.

Containing complete systematic descriptions of the Flowering Plants and Ferns of the British West Indian Islands, accompanied by an elaborate index of reference, and a list of Colonial names.

FLORA OF TROPICAL AFRICA. By DANIEL OLIVER, F.R.S., F.L.S. Vols. I. and II., 20s. each. Published under the authority of the First Commissioner of Her Majesty's Works.

This important and much-needed work embodies the researches of a long list of explorers, the results of whose labours have been accumulating at the Royal Gardens, Kew, and other museums, for many years past. The present volume contains the Orders *Ranunculaceæ* to *Connaraceæ*.

HANDBOOK OF THE NEW ZEALAND FLORA; a Systematic Description of the Native Plants of New Zealand, and the Chatham, Kermadec's, Lord Auckland's, Campbell's, and Macquarrie's Islands. By Dr. J. D. HOOKER, F.R.S. Demy 8vo. Part I., 16s.; Part II., 14s.; or complete in one vol., 30s. Published under the auspices of the Government of that colony.

A compendious account of the plants of New Zealand and outlying islands, published under the authority of the Government of that colony. The first Part contains the Flowering Plants, Ferns, and Lycopods; the Second the remaining Orders of *Cryptogamia*, or Flowerless Plants, with Index and Catalogues of Native Names and of Naturalized Plants.

FLORA AUSTRALIENSIS; a Description of the Plants of the Australian Territory. By GEORGE BENTHAM, F.R.S., President of the Linnean Society, assisted by FERDINAND MUELLER, F.R.S., Government Botanist, Melbourne, Victoria. Demy 8vo. Vols. I. to V., 20s. each. Published under the auspices of the several Governments of Australia.

The materials for this great undertaking, the present volumes of which contain three thousand closely-printed pages, are derived not only from the vast collections of Australian plants brought to this country by various botanical travellers, and preserved in the herbaria of Kew and of the British Museum, including those hitherto unpublished of Banks and Solander, of Captain Cook's first Voyage, and of Brown in Flinders', but from the very extensive and more recently collected specimens preserved in the Government Herbarium of Melbourne, under the superintendence of Dr. Ferdinand Mueller. The descriptions are written in plain English, and are masterpieces of accuracy and clearness.

FLORA HONGKONGENSIS; a Description of the Flowering Plants and Ferns of the Island of Hongkong. By GEORGE BENTHAM, P.L.S. With a Map of the Island. Demy 8vo, 550 pp., 16s. Published under the authority of Her Majesty's Secretary of State for the Colonies.

The Island of Hongkong, though occupying an area of scarcely thirty square miles, is characterized by an extraordinarily varied Flora, partaking, however, of that of South Continental China, of which comparatively little is known. The number of Species enumerated in the present volume is 1056, derived chiefly from materials collected by Mr. Hinds, Col. Champion, Dr. Hance, Dr. Harland, Mr. Wright, and Mr. Wilford.

CONTRIBUTIONS TO THE FLORA OF MENTONE, AND TO A WINTER FLORA OF THE RIVIERA, INCLUDING THE COAST FROM MARSEILLES TO GENOA. By J. Traherne Moggridge. Royal 8vo. In 4 Parts, each, with 25 Coloured Plates, 15s. or complete in one Vol. 63s.

In this work a full page is devoted to the illustration of each Species, the drawings being made by the author from specimens collected by him on the spot, and they exhibit in vivid colours the beautiful aspect which many of our wild flowers assume south of the Alps.

ILLUSTRATIONS OF THE NUEVA QUINOLOGIA OF PAVON, with Observations on the Barks described. By J. E. Howard, F.L.S. With 27 Coloured Plates by W. Fitch. Imperial folio, half-morocco, gilt edges, £6. 6s.

THE QUINOLOGY OF THE EAST INDIAN PLANTATIONS. By J. E. Howard, F.L.S. Folio, 3 Coloured Plates, 21s.

REVISION OF THE NATURAL ORDER HEDERACEÆ, being a reprint, with numerous additions and corrections, of a series of papers published in the 'Journal of Botany, British and Foreign.' By Berthold Seemann, Ph.D., F.L.S. 8vo, 7 Plates. 10s. 6d.

ILLUSTRATIONS OF THE GENUS CAREX. By Francis Boott, M.D. Part IV. Folio, 189 Plates, £10.

ICONES PLANTARUM. Figures, with brief Descriptive Characters and Remarks, of New and Rare Plants, selected from the Author's Herbarium. By Sir W. J. Hooker, F.R.S. New Series, Vol. V. Royal 8vo, 100 plates, 31s. 6d.

FERNS.

BRITISH FERNS; an Introduction to the study of the Ferns, Lycopods, and Equiseta indigenous to the British Isles. With Chapters on the Structure, Propagation, Cultivation, Diseases, Uses, Preservation, and Distribution of Ferns. By M. Plues. Crown 8vo, 55 Wood-Engravings, 6s.; with 16 Coloured Plates by W. Fitch, 10s. 6d.

One of the 'New Series of Natural History for Beginners,' accurately describing all the Ferns and their allies found in Britain, with a Wood-Engraving of each Species, and Coloured Figures of 32 of the most interesting, including magnified dissections showing the Venation and Fructification.

THE BRITISH FERNS; or, Coloured Figures and Descriptions, with the needful Analyses of the Fructification and Venation, of the Ferns of Great Britain and Ireland, systematically arranged. By Sir W. J. HOOKER, F.R.S. Royal 8vo, 66 Plates, £2. 2s.

The British Ferns and their allies are illustrated in this work, from the pencil of Mr. FITCH. Each Species has a Plate to itself, so that there is ample room for the details, on a magnified scale, of Fructification and Venation. The whole are delicately coloured by hand. In the letterpress an interesting account is given with each species of its geographical distribution in other countries.

GARDEN FERNS; or, Coloured Figures and Descriptions, with the needful Analyses of the Fructification and Venation, of a Selection of Exotic Ferns, adapted for Cultivation in the Garden, Hothouse, and Conservatory. By Sir W. J. HOOKER, F.R.S. Royal 8vo, 64 Plates, £2. 2s.

A companion volume to the preceding, for the use of those who take an interest in the cultivation of some of the more beautiful and remarkable varieties of Exotic Ferns. Here also each Species has a Plate to itself, and the details of Fructification and Venation are given on a magnified scale, the Drawings being from the pencil of Mr. FITCH.

FILICES EXOTICÆ; or, Coloured Figures and Description of Exotic Ferns, chiefly of such as are cultivated in the Royal Gardens of Kew. By Sir W. J. HOOKER, F.R.S. Royal 4to, 100 Plates, £6. 11s.

One of the most superbly illustrated books of Foreign Ferns that has been hitherto produced. The Species are selected both on account of their beauty of form, singular structure, and their suitableness for cultivation.

FERNY COMBES; a Ramble after Ferns in the Glens and Valleys of Devonshire. By CHARLOTTE CHANTER. *Third Edition*. Fcp. 8vo, 8 coloured plates by FITCH, and a Map of the County, 5s.

MOSSES.

HANDBOOK OF BRITISH MOSSES, containing all that are known to be Natives of the British Isles. By the Rev. M. J. BERKELEY, M.A., F.L.S. Demy 8vo, pp. 360, 24 Coloured Plates, 21s.

A very complete Manual, comprising characters of all the species, with the circumstances of habitation of each; with special chapters on development and structure, propagation, fructification, geographical distribution, uses, and modes of collecting and preserving, followed by an extensive series of coloured illustrations, in which the essential portions of the plant are repeated, in every case on a magnified scale.

SEAWEEDS.

BRITISH SEAWEEDS; an Introduction to the Study of the Marine Algæ of Great Britain, Ireland, and the Channel Islands. By S. O. Gray. Crown 8vo, 6s.; with 16 Coloured Plates, drawn expressly for the work by W. Fitch, 10s. 6d.

One of L. Reeve and Co.'s 'New Series,' briefly but accurately describing, according to the classification of the best and most recent authorities, all the Algæ found on our coasts.

PHYCOLOGIA BRITANNICA; or, History of British Seaweeds, containing Coloured Figures, Generic and Specific Characters, Synonyms and Descriptions of all the Species of Algæ inhabiting the Shores of the British Islands. By Dr. W. H. Harvey, F.R.S. New Edition. Royal 8vo, 4 vols., 765 pp., 360 Coloured Plates, £7. 10s.

This work, originally published in 1851, is still the standard work on the subject of which it treats. Each Species, excepting the minute ones, has a Plate to itself, with magnified portions of structure and fructification, the whole being printed in their natural colours, finished by hand.

PHYCOLOGIA AUSTRALICA; a History of Australian Seaweeds, comprising Coloured Figures and Descriptions of the more characteristic Marine Algæ of New South Wales, Victoria, Tasmania, South Australia and Western Australia, and a Synopsis of all known Australian Algæ. By Dr. Harvey, F.R.S. Royal 8vo, 5 vols., 300 Coloured Plates, £7. 13s.

This beautiful work, the result of an arduous personal exploration of the shores of the Australian continent, is got up in the style of the 'Phycologia Britannica' by the same author. Each Species has a Plate to itself, with ample magnified delineations of fructification and structure, embodying a variety of most curious and remarkable forms.

NEREIS AUSTRALIS; or, Algæ of the Southern Ocean, being Figures and Descriptions of Marine Plants collected on the Shores of the Cape of Good Hope, the extratropical Australian Colonies, Tasmania, New Zealand, and the Antarctic Regions. By Dr. Harvey, F.R.S. Imperial 8vo, 50 Coloured Plates, £2. 2s.

A selection of Fifty Species of remarkable forms of Seaweed, not included in the 'Phycologia Australica,' collected over a wider area.

FUNGI.

OUTLINES OF BRITISH FUNGOLOGY, containing Characters of above a Thousand Species of Fungi, and a Complete List of all that have been described as Natives of the British Isles. By the Rev. M. J. BERKELEY, M.A., F.L.S. Demy 8vo, 484 pp., 24 Coloured Plates, 30s.

Although entitled simply 'Outlines,' this is a good-sized volume, of nearly 500 pages, illustrated with more than 200 Figures of British Fungi, all carefully coloured by hand. Of above a thousand Species the characters are given, and a complete list of the names of all the rest.

THE ESCULENT FUNGUSES OF ENGLAND. Containing an Account of their Classical History, Uses, Characters, Development, Structure, Nutritious Properties, Modes of Cooking and Preserving, etc. By C. D. BADHAM, M.D. Second Edition. Edited by F. CURREY, F.R.S. Demy 8vo, 152 pp., 12 Coloured Plates, 12s.

A lively classical treatise, written with considerable epigrammatic humour, with the view of showing that we have upwards of 30 Species of Fungi abounding in our woods capable of affording nutritious and savoury food, but which, from ignorance or prejudice, are left to perish ungathered. "I have indeed grieved," says the Author, "when reflecting on the straitened condition of the lower orders, to see pounds of extempore beefsteaks growing on our oaks, in the shape of *Fistulina hepatica*; Puff-balls, which some have not inaptly compared to sweetbread; *Hydna*, as good as oysters; and *Agaricus deliciosus*, reminding us of tender lamb-kidney." Superior coloured Figures of the Species are given from the pencil of Mr. FITCH.

ILLUSTRATIONS OF BRITISH MYCOLOGY, comprising Figures and Descriptions of the Funguses of interest and novelty indigenous to Britain. By Mrs. T. J. HUSSEY. Royal 4to; First Series, 90 Coloured Plates, £7. 12s. 6d.; Second Series, 50 Coloured Plates, £4. 10s.

This beautifully-illustrated work is the production of a lady who, being an accomplished artist, occupied the leisure of many years in accumulating a portfolio of exquisite drawings of the more attractive forms and varieties of British Fungi. The publication was brought to an end with the 140th Plate by her sudden decease. The Figures are mostly of the natural size, carefully coloured by hand.

CLAVIS AGARICINORUM: an Analytical Key to the British Agaricini, with Characters of the Genera and Subgenera. By WORTHINGTON G. SMITH, F.L.S. Six Plates. 2s. 6d.

SHELLS AND MOLLUSKS.

ELEMENTS OF CONCHOLOGY; an Introduction to the Natural History of Shells, and of the Animals which form them. By LOVELL REEVE, F.L.S. Royal 8vo, 2 vols., 478 pp., 62 Coloured Plates, £2. 16s.

Intended as a guide to the collector of shells in arranging and naming his specimens, while at the same time inducing him to study them with reference to their once living existence, geographical distribution, and habits. Forty-six of the plates are devoted to the illustration of the genera of shells, and sixteen to shells with the living animal, all beautifully coloured by hand.

CONCHOLOGIA ICONICA; or, Figures and Descriptions of the Shells of Mollusks, with remarks on their Affinities, Synonymy, and Geographical Distribution. By LOVELL REEVE, F.L.S. Demy 4to, published monthly in Parts, 8 Plates, carefully coloured by hand, 10s.

Of this work, comprising illustrations of Shells of the natural size, nearly 2300 Plates are published, but the plan of publication admits of the collector purchasing it at his option in portions, each of which is complete in itself. Each genus, as the work progresses, is issued separately, with Title and Index; and an Alphabetical List of the published genera, with the prices annexed, may be procured of the publishers on application. The system of nomenclature adopted is that of Lamarck, modified to meet the exigencies of later discoveries. With the name of each species is given a summary of its leading specific characters in Latin and English; then the authority for the name is quoted, accompanied by a reference to its original description; and next in order are its Synonyms. The habitat of the species is next given, accompanied, where possible, by particulars of soil, depth, or vegetation. Finally, a few general remarks are offered, calling attention to the most obvious distinguishing peculiarities of the species, with criticisms, when necessary, on the views of other writers. At the commencement of the genus some notice is taken of the animal, and the habitats of the species are worked up into a general summary of the geographical distribution of the genus.

CONCHOLOGIA ICONICA IN MONOGRAPHS.

Genera.	Plates.	£	s	d	Genera.	Plates.	£	s	d
ACHATINA	23	1	9	0	BULLA	6	0	8	0
ACHATINELLA	6	0	8	0	BULLIA	4	0	5	6
ADAMSIELLA	2	0	3	0	CALYPTRAEA	8	0	10	6
AKERA	1	0	1	6	CANCELLARIA	18	1	3	0
AMPHIDESMA	7	0	9	0	CAPSA	1	0	1	6
AMPULLARIA	28	1	15	6	CAPSELLA	2	0	3	0
ANASTOMA	1	0	1	6	CARDITA	9	0	11	6
ANATINA	4	0	5	6	CARDIUM	22	1	8	0
ANCILLARIA	12	0	15	6	CARINARIA	1	0	1	6
ANCULOTUS	6	0	8	0	CASSIDARIA	1	0	1	6
ANODON	37	2	7	0	CASSIS	13	0	16	6
ANOMIA	8	0	10	6	CASTALIA	3	0	4	0
APLUSTRUM	1	0	1	6	CERITHIDEA	4	0	5	6
APLYSIA	10	0	13	0	CERITHIUM	20	1	5	6
ARCA	17	1	1	6	CHAMA	9	0	11	6
ARGONAUTA	4	0	5	6	CHAMOSTRAEA	1	0	1	6
ARTEMIS	10	0	13	0	CHITON	33	2	2	0
ASPERGILLUM	4	0	5	6	CHITONELLUS	1	0	1	6
ATYS	5	0	6	6	CHONDROPOMA	11	0	14	0
AVICULA	18	1	3	0	CIRCE	10	0	13	0
BUCCINUM	14	0	18	0	COLUMBELLA	37	2	7	0
BULIMUS	89	5	12	0	CONCHOLEPAS	2	0	3	0

Genera	Plates	£	s.	d.		Genera	Plates	£	s.	d.
Conus	55	5	11	0		Navicella & Latia	8	0	10	6
Corbula	5	0	5	6		Nemita	12	1	4	0
Crania	1	0	1	6		Neritina	37	2	7	0
Crassatella	3	0	4	0		Niso	1	0	1	6
Crenatula	2	0	3	0		Oliva	30	1	16	0
Crepidula	5	0	6	6		Oniscia	1	0	1	6
Cuccibulum	7	0	9	0		Orbicula	1	0	1	6
Cucullea	1	0	1	6		Ovulum	14	0	18	0
Cyclophorus	20	1	5	0		Paludina	11	0	14	0
Cyclostoma	23	1	9	0		Paludomus	3	0	4	0
Cyclotus	9	0	11	6		Partula	4	0	5	6
Cymbium	26	1	13	0		Patella	42	2	13	0
Cyprea	27	1	14	6		Pecten	35	2	4	6
Cyprecardia	2	0	3	0		Pectunculus	9	0	11	6
Cytherea	10	0	13	0		Pedum	1	0	1	6
Delphinula	5	0	6	6		Perna	6	0	8	0
Dione	12	0	15	6		Phasianella	6	0	8	0
Dolabella	2	0	3	0		Pholas	3	0	4	0
Doladnifera	1	0	1	6		Pinna	34	2	3	0
Dolium	8	0	10	6		Pirena	2	0	3	0
Donax	9	0	11	6		Placunanomia	3	0	4	0
Eburna	1	0	1	6		Pleiodon	1	0	1	6
Emato	3	0	4	0		Plecobranchus	1	0	1	6
Eulima	6	0	8	0		Pleurotoma	40	2	10	6
Fasciolaria	7	0	9	6		Potamides	1	0	1	0
Ficula	1	0	1	6		Psammobia	8	0	10	6
Fissurella	16	1	0	6		Psammotella	1	0	1	6
Fusus	21	1	6	6		Pterocera	6	0	8	0
Galatea	6	0	8	0		Pterocyclos	5	0	6	6
Glauconome	1	0	1	6		Purpura	13	0	16	6
Halia	1	0	1	6		Pyramidella	6	0	8	0
Haliotis	17	1	1	6		Pyrazus	1	0	1	6
Haminea	5	0	6	6		Pyrula	9	0	11	6
Harpa	4	0	5	6		Ranella	8	0	10	6
Helix	210	13	5	0		Nicinula	6	0	8	0
Hemipecten	1	0	1	6		Rostellaria	3	0	4	6
Hemisinus	6	0	8	0		Sanguinolaria	1	0	1	6
Hinnites	1	0	1	6		Scarabus	3	0	4	0
Hipponyx	1	0	1	6		Scutus	2	0	3	0
Hydatina	2	0	3	0		Sigaretus	5	0	6	6
Hyria	5	0	6	6		Smeulopsis	2	0	3	0
Ianthina	5	0	6	6		Siphonaria	7	0	9	0
Io	3	0	4	0		Solarium	3	0	4	0
Iredina	2	0	3	0		Solettellina	4	0	5	6
Isocardia	1	0	1	6		Spondylus	18	1	3	0
Lampania	2	0	3	0		Strombus	19	1	4	0
Leiostraca	3	0	4	0		Struthiolaria	1	0	1	6
Leptopoma	8	0	10	6		Tapes	13	0	16	6
Lingula	2	0	3	0		Telescopium	1	0	1	6
Lithodomus	5	0	6	6		Tellina	58	3	13	6
Littorina	18	1	3	0		Terebra	27	1	14	6
Lucina	11	0	14	0		Terebellum	1	0	1	6
Lutraria	5	0	6	6		Terebratula & Rhynchonella	11	0	14	0
Mactra	21	1	6	6		Thracia	3	0	4	0
Malleus	3	0	4	0		Tornatella	4	0	5	6
Mangelia	8	0	10	6		Tridacna	8	0	10	6
Marginella	27	1	14	6		Trigonia	1	0	1	6
Melania	62	3	14	6		Triton	20	1	5	6
Melanopsis	3	0	4	0		Trochita	3	0	4	0
Melatoma	3	0	4	0		Trochus	16	1	0	6
Mesoe	3	0	4	0		Tugalia	1	0	1	6
Mesalia & Eglisia	1	0	1	6		Tugonia	1	0	1	6
Mesodesma	4	0	5	6		Turbinella	13	0	16	6
Mita	1	0	1	6		Turbo	13	0	16	6
Mitra	39	2	9	6		Turritella	11	0	14	0
Modiola	11	0	14	0		Tympanotonos	2	0	3	0
Monoceros	4	0	5	6		Umbrella	1	0	1	6
Murex	37	2	7	0		Unio	96	6	1	0
Myadora	1	0	1	6		Venus	26	1	13	0
Mycetopus	4	0	5	6		Vertagus	5	0	6	0
Myochama	1	0	1	6		Vitrina	10	0	13	0
Mytilus	11	0	14	0		Voluta	22	1	8	0
Nassa	29	1	17	0		Vulsella	2	0	3	6
Natica	30	1	18	0		Zizyphinus	8	0	10	6
Nautilus	6	0	8	0						

CONCHOLOGIA INDICA; being Illustrations of the Land and Freshwater Shells of British India. Edited by SYLVANUS HANLEY, F.L.S., and WILLIAM THEOBALD, of the Geological Survey of India. 4to, Part I. and II., each, with 20 Coloured Plates, 20s.

For want of a comprehensive book of reference, the land and freshwater shells of British India are less known in Europe and America than those of countries less frequented by travellers. To meet this acknowledged want, this first attempt at a special conchology of our Indian empire has been essayed.

THE EDIBLE MOLLUSKS OF GREAT BRITAIN AND IRELAND, with the modes of cooking them. By M. S. LOVELL. Crown 8vo, 5s.; with 12 Coloured Plates, 8s. 6d.

INSECTS.

BRITISH INSECTS. A Familiar Description of the Form, Structure, Habits, and Transformations of Insects. By E. F. STAVELEY, Author of "British Spiders." Crown 8vo, with 16 beautifully Coloured Steel Plates and numerous Wood Engravings, 14s.

"This little work is planned on the supposition that the reader knows nothing scientifically of the insect world, but that he has exercised some degree of observation on such common species as must have come before him. From this it is attempted to lead him on to a general idea of the structure and classification of insects."—*Preface.*

BRITISH BEETLES; an Introduction to the Study of our Indigenous COLEOPTERA. By E. C. RYE. Crown 8vo, 16 Coloured Steel Plates, comprising Figures of nearly 100 Species, engraved from Natural Specimens, expressly for the work, by E. W. ROBINSON, and 11 Wood-Engravings of Dissections by the Author, 10s. 6d.

This little work forms one of a New Series designed to assist young persons to a more profitable, and, consequently, more pleasurable observation of Nature, by furnishing them in a familiar manner with so much of the science as they may acquire without encumbering them with more of the technicalities, so confusing and repulsive to beginners, than are necessary for their purpose. In the words of the Preface, it is "somewhat on the scheme of a *Delectus*; combining extracts from the biographies of individual objects with principles of classification and hints for obtaining further knowledge."

BRITISH BEES; an Introduction to the Study of the Natural History and Economy of the Bees indigenous to the British Isles. By W. E. SHUCKARD. Crown 8vo, 16 Coloured Steel Plates, containing nearly 100 Figures, engraved from Natural Specimens, expressly for the work, by E. W. ROBINSON, and Woodcuts of Dissections, 10s. 6d.

A companion volume to that on British Beetles, treating of the structure, geographical distribution and classification of Bees and their parasites, with lists of the species found in Britain, and an account of their habits and economy.

BRITISH BUTTERFLIES AND MOTHS; an Introduction to the Study of our Native Lepidoptera. By H. T. Stainton. Crown 8vo, 16 Coloured Steel Plates, containing Figures of 100 Species, engraved from Natural Specimens expressly for the work by E. W. Robinson, and Wood-Engravings, 10s. 6d.

Another of the 'New Series of Natural History for Beginners and Amateurs,' treating of the structure and classification of the Lepidoptera.

BRITISH SPIDERS; an Introduction to the Study of the Araneidæ found in Great Britain and Ireland. By E. F. Staveley. Crown 8vo, 16 Plates, containing Coloured Figures of nearly 100 Species, and 40 Diagrams, showing the number and position of the eyes in various Genera, drawn expressly for the work by Tuffen West, and 44 Wood-Engravings, 10s. 6d.

One of the 'New Series of Natural History for Beginners,' and companion volume to the 'British Beetles' and 'British Bees.' It treats of the structure and classification of Spiders, and describes those found in Britain, with notes on their habits and hints for collecting and preserving.

CURTIS'S BRITISH ENTOMOLOGY. Illustrations and Descriptions of the Genera of Insects found in Great Britain and Ireland, containing Coloured Figures, from nature, of the most rare and beautiful species, and, in many instances, upon the plants on which they are found. Royal 8vo, 8 vols., 770 Plates, coloured, £21.

Or in separate Monographs.

Orders.	Plates.	£	s.	d.	Orders.	Plates.	£	s.	d.
Aphaniptera	2	0	2	0	Hymenoptera	125	4	0	0
Coleoptera	256	8	0	0	Lepidoptera	193	6	0	0
Dermaptera	1	0	1	0	Neuroptera	13	0	9	0
Dictyoptera	1	0	1	0	Omaloptera	6	0	4	6
Diptera	104	3	5	0	Orthoptera	5	0	4	0
Hemiptera	32	1	1	0	Strepsiptera	3	0	2	6
Homoptera	21	0	14	0	Trichoptera	9	0	6	6

'Curtis's Entomology,' which Cuvier pronounced to have "reached the ultimatum of perfection," is still the standard work on the Genera of British Insects. The Figures executed by the author himself, with wonderful minuteness and accuracy, have never been surpassed, even if equalled. The price at which the work was originally published was £43. 16s.

INSECTA BRITANNICA; Vol. III., Diptera. By Francis Walker, F.L.S. 8vo, with 10 Plates, 25s.

ANTIQUARIAN.

SACRED ARCHÆOLOGY; a Popular Dictionary of Ecclesiastical Art and Institutions, from Primitive to Modern Times. Comprising Architecture, Music, Vestments, Furniture Arrangement, Offices, Customs, Ritual Symbolism, Ceremonial Traditions, Religious Orders, etc., of the Church Catholic in all Ages. By MACKENZIE E. C. WALCOTT, B.D. Oxon., F.S.A., Præcentor and Prebendary of Chichester Cathedral. Demy 8vo, 18s.

Mr. Walcott's 'Dictionary of Sacred Archæology' is designed to satisfy a great and growing want in the literature of the day. The increased interest taken by large classes of the community in the Ecclesiastical History, the Archæology, the Ritual, Artistic, and Conventual Usages of the early and middle ages of Christendom has not been met by the publication of manuals at all fitted by their comprehensiveness, their accuracy, and the convenience of their arrangement to supply this highly important demand. To combine in one the varied and general information required by the cultivated reader at large with the higher and more special sources of knowledge of which the student of ecclesiastical lore has need, is the object which has been kept in view in the compilation now offered to the public. In no work of the kind has the English public, it is confidently believed, had presented to it so large and varied a mass of matter in a form so conveniently arranged for reference. One valuable feature to which attention may be invited is the copious list of authorities prefixed to Mr. Walcott's Dictionary. The student will here find himself put readily upon the track for following up any particular line of inquiry, of which the Dictionary has given him the first outlines.

A MANUAL OF BRITISH ARCHÆOLOGY. By CHARLES BOUTELL, M.A. Royal 16mo, 398 pp., 20 Coloured Plates, 10s. 6d.

A treatise on general subjects of antiquity, written especially for the student of archæology, as a preparation for more elaborate works. Architecture, Sepulchral Monuments, Heraldry, Seals, Coins, Illuminated Manuscripts and Inscriptions, Arms and Armour, Costume and Personal Ornaments, Pottery, Porcelain and Glass, Clocks, Locks, Carvings, Mosaics, Embroidery, etc., are treated of in succession, the whole being illustrated by 20 attractive Plates of Coloured Figures of the various objects.

SHAKESPEARE'S SONNETS, Facsimile, by Photo-Zincography, of the First Printed edition of 1609. From the Copy in the Library of Bridgewater House, by permission of the Right Hon. the Earl of Ellesmere. 10s. 6d.

BEWICK'S WOODCUTS. Impressions of Upwards of Two Thousand Woodblocks, engraved, for the most part, by THOMAS and JOHN BEWICK; including Illustrations of various kinds for Books, Pamphlets, and Broadsides; Cuts for Private Gentlemen, Public Companies, Clubs, etc.; Exhibitions, Races, Newspapers, Shop Cards, Invoice Heads, Bar Bills, etc. With an Introduction, a Descriptive Catalogue of the Blocks, and a List of the Books and Pamphlets illustrated. By the Rev. T. HUGO, M.A., F.R.S.L., F.S.A. In one large handsome volume, imperial 4to, gilt top, with full length steel Portrait of Thomas Bewick. £6. 6s.

Among these Cuts, distributed in 247 Plates, will be found the Engravings of a large number of the most celebrated Works illustrated by these Artists, and a unique assemblage of Cuts for Private Gentlemen, Public Societies and Companies, Amusements, Newspapers, Shop Cards, Invoices, Bar Bills, and other miscellaneous purposes. The Volumes referred to are, in general, rare and costly, while of most of the Miscellaneous Engravings very few impressions are known to exist. Not only to Bewick Collectors, but to all persons interested in the progress of Art, and especially of Wood Engraving, this Volume, exhibiting chronologically the Works of the Fathers of that Art in England, cannot fail to be of the highest interest.

THE BEWICK COLLECTOR AND SUPPLEMENT. A Descriptive Catalogue of the Works of THOMAS and JOHN BEWICK, including Cuts, in various states, for Books and Pamphlets, Private Gentlemen, Public Companies, Exhibitions, Races, Newspapers, Shop Cards, Invoice Heads, Bar Bills, Coal Certificates, Broadsides, and other miscellaneous purposes, and Wood Blocks. With an Appendix of Portraits, Autographs, Works of Pupils, etc. The whole described from the Originals contained in the Largest and most Perfect Collection ever formed, and illustrated with 292 Cuts from Bewick's own Blocks. By the Rev. THOMAS HUGO, M.A., F.S.A., the Possessor of the Collection. 2 vols. demy 8vo, price 42s.; imperial 8vo (limited to 100 copies), with a fine Steel Engraving of Thomas Bewick, £4. 4s. The SUPPLEMENT, with 180 Cuts, may be had separately; price, small paper, 21s.; large paper, 42s.; also, the Portrait on imperial folio, price 7s. 6d.

MAN'S AGE IN THE WORLD ACCORDING TO HOLY SCRIPTURE AND SCIENCE. By an ESSEX RECTOR. Demy 8vo, 264 pp., 8s. 6d.

The Author, recognizing the established facts and inevitable deductions of Science, seeks an interpretation of the Sacred Writings, consistent alike with their authenticity, when rightly understood, and with the exigencies of Science. He treats in successive Chapters of The Flint Weapons of the Drift,—The Creation,—The Paradisiacal State,—The Genealogies,—The Deluge,—Babel and the Dispersion; and adds an Appendix of valuable information from various sources.

THE ANTIQUITY OF MAN; An Examination of Sir Charles Lyell's recent Work. By S. R. PATTISON, F.G.S. Second Edition. 8vo, 1s.

MISCELLANEOUS.

ON INTELLIGENCE. By H. TAINE, D.C.L. Oxon. Translated from the French by T. D. HAYE, and revised, with additions, by the Author. Part I. 8s. 6d. Part II. 10s. or, complete in One Volume, 18s.

"In the first part, the elements of knowledge have been determined; by consecutive reductions we have arrived at the most simple elements, and have passed from these to the physiological changes which are the condition of their origin. In the second part, we have first described the mechanism and general effect of their combination; then, applying the law we have discovered, we have examined the elements, formation, certitude, and range of the principal kinds of our knowledge, from that of individual things to that of general things, from the most special perceptions, previsions, and recollections, up to the most universal judgments and axioms."—*Preface.*

THE BIRDS OF SHERWOOD FOREST; with Observations on their Nesting, Habits, and Migrations. By W. J. STERLAND. Crown 8vo, 4 Plates. 7s. 6d. coloured.

THE NATURALIST IN NORWAY; or, Notes on the Wild Animals, Birds, Fishes, and Plants of that Country, with some account of the principal Salmon Rivers. By the Rev. J. BOWDEN, LL.D. Crown 8vo, 8 Coloured Plates. 10s. 6d.

CALIPHS AND SULTANS; being Tales omitted in the ordinary English Version of 'The Arabian Nights Entertainments,' freely rewritten and rearranged. By S. HANLEY, F.L.S. 6s.

LIVE COALS; or, Faces from the Fire. By L. M. BUDGEN, "Acheta," Author of 'Episodes of Insect Life,' etc. Dedicated, by Special Permission, to H.R.H. Field-Marshal the Duke of Cambridge. Royal 4to, 35 Original Sketches printed in colours, 42s.

The 'Episodes of Insect Life,' published in three series some years since, won from the late Prince Consort a graceful acknowledgment in the presentation to the Author of a copy of a book, 'The Natural History of Deeside,' privately printed by command of Her Majesty the Queen. The above Work comprises a series of Thirty-five highly imaginative and humorous Sketches, suggested by burning Coals and Wood, accompanied by Essays, descriptive and discursive, on :—The Imagery of Accident—The Fire in a New Light—The Fire an Exhibitor—The Fire a Sculptor.

SUNSHINE AND SHOWERS; their Influences throughout Creation. A Compendium of Popular Meteorology. By ANDREW STEINMETZ, Esq. Crown 8vo, Wood Engravings, 7s. 6d.

This Work not only treats fully all the leading topics of Meteorology, but especially of the use of the Hygrometer, for which systematic Rules are now for the first time drawn up. Among other interesting and useful subjects, are chapters on Rainfall in England and Europe in general—Wet and Dry Years—Temperature and Moisture with respect to the health of Plants and Animals—The Wonders of Evaporation—Soil Temperature—The Influence of Trees on Climate and Water Supply—The Prognostication of the Seasons and Harvest—The Characteristics and Meteorology of the Seasons—Rules of the Barometer—Rules of the Thermometer as a Weather Glass—Popular Weather-casts—Anemometry—and finally, What becomes of the Sunshine—and what becomes of the Showers.

THE REASONING POWER IN ANIMALS. By the Rev. J. S. WATSON, M.A. 480 pp. Crown 8vo, 9s.

The object of the above treatise is to trace the evidences of the existence in the lower animals of a portion of that reason which is possessed by man. A large number of carefully-selected and well-authenticated anecdotes are adduced of various animals having displayed a degree of intelligence distinct from instinct, and called into activity by circumstances in which the latter could have been no guide.

METEORS, AEROLITES, AND FALLING STARS. By Dr. T. L. PHIPSON, F.C.S. Crown 8vo. 25 Woodcuts and Lithographic Frontispiece, 6s.

A very complete summary of Meteoric Phenomena, from the earliest to the present time, including the shower of November, 1866, as observed by the Author.

MANUAL OF CHEMICAL ANALYSIS, Qualitative and Quantitative; for the Use of Students. By Dr. HENRY M. NOAD, F.R.S. Crown 8vo, pp. 663, 109 Wood Engravings, 16s. Or, separately, Part I., 'QUALITATIVE,' New Edition, New Notation, 6s.; Part II., 'QUANTITATIVE,' 10s. 6d.

A Copiously-illustrated, Useful, Practical Manual of Chemical Analysis, prepared for the Use of Students by the Lecturer on Chemistry at St. George's Hospital. The illustrations consist of a series of highly-finished Wood-Engravings, chiefly of the most approved forms and varieties of apparatus.

PHOSPHORESCENCE; or, the Emission of Light by Minerals, Plants, and Animals. By Dr. T. L. PHIPSON, F.C.S. Small 8vo, 225 pp., 30 Wood Engravings and Coloured Frontispiece, 5s.

An interesting account of the various substances in nature—mineral, vegetable, and animal—which possess the remarkable property of emitting spontaneous light.

THE ZOOLOGY OF THE VOYAGE OF H.M.S. SA-
MARANG, under the command of Captain Sir Edward Belcher, C.B., during
the Years 1843-46. By Professor Owen, Dr. J. E. Gray, Sir J. Richardson, A. Adams, L. Reeve, and A. White. Edited by Arthur Adams,
F.L.S. Royal 8vo, 257 pp., 55 Plates, mostly coloured, £3. 10s.

In this work, illustrative of the new species of animals collected during the
surveying expedition of H.M.S. Samarang in the Eastern Seas in the years 1843-
1846, there are 7 Plates of Quadrupeds, 1 of Reptiles, 10 of Fishes, 24 of Mollusca and Shells, and 13 of Crustacea. The Mollusca, which are particularly interesting, include the anatomy of *Spicula* by Professor Owen, and a number of
beautiful Figures of the living animals by Mr. Arthur Adams.

TRAVELS ON THE AMAZON AND RIO NEGRO;
with an Account of the Native Tribes, and Observations on the Climate,
Geology, and Natural History of the Amazon Valley. By ALFRED R.
WALLACE. Demy 8vo, 541 pp., with Map and Tinted Frontispiece, 18s.

A lively narrative of travels in one of the most interesting districts of the
Southern Hemisphere, accompanied by Remarks on the Vocabularies of the
Languages, by Dr. R. G. LATHAM.

A SURVEY OF THE EARLY GEOGRAPHY OF
WESTERN EUROPE, as connected with the First Inhabitants of Britain,
their Origin, Language, Religious Rites, and Edifices. By HENRY LAWES
LONG, Esq. 8vo, 6s.

THE GEOLOGIST. A Magazine of Geology, Palæontology,
and Mineralogy. Illustrated with highly finished Wood-Engravings.
Edited by S. J. MACKIE, F.G.S., F.S.A. Vols. V. and VI., each, with numerous Wood-Engravings, 18s. Vol. VII., 9s.

THE STEREOSCOPIC MAGAZINE. A Gallery for the
Stereoscope of Landscape Scenery, Architecture, Antiquities, Natural History, Rustic Character, etc. With Descriptions. 5 vols., each complete
in itself and containing 50 Stereographs, £2. 2s.

THE ARTIFICIAL PRODUCTION OF FISH. By Pis-
CARIUS. Third Edition. 1s.

EVERYBODY'S WEATHER-GUIDE. The Use of Me-
teorological Instruments clearly Explained, with Directions for Securing at
any time a probable Prognostic of the Weather. By A. STEINMETZ, Esq.
Author of 'Sunshine and Showers,' etc. 1s.

SERIALS.

THE NATURAL HISTORY OF PLANTS. By Professor Baillon, with numerous Wood Engravings. Monthly, 2s. 6d.

THE BOTANICAL MAGAZINE. Figures and Descriptions of New and Rare Plants of interest to the Botanical Student, and suitable for the Garden, Stove, or Greenhouse. By Dr. J. D. Hooker, F.R.S. Published monthly, with 6 Coloured Plates, 3s. 6d. Annual Subscription, post free, 42s. in advance.

THE FLORAL MAGAZINE. Figures and Descriptions of New Popular Flowers for the Garden, Stove, or Conservatory. By the Rev. H. H. Dombrain. Published monthly, with 4 Coloured Plates, 2s. 6d. Annual Subscription, post free, 31s. 6d. in advance.

CONCHOLOGIA ICONICA. By Lovell Reeve, F.L.S., in Double Parts, with 16 Coloured Plates, 20s.

CONCHOLOGIA INDICA. The Land and Freshwater Shells of British India. In Parts, with 20 Coloured Plates, 20s.

A MONOGRAPH OF ODONTOGLOSSUM. By James Bateman, F.R.S. Imperial folio, 5 Coloured Plates, 21s.

SELECT ORCHIDACEOUS PLANTS. By Robert Warner. 3 Coloured Plates, 10s. 6d.

RECENTLY PUBLISHED.

DOMESTIC BOTANY. By J. Smith, 16s.

ON INTELLIGENCE. By H. Taine. 18s.

THE NATURAL HISTORY OF PLANTS. By Professor Baillon. Vol. I. 25s.

BRITISH INSECTS. By E. F. Staveley. 14s.

THE FLORA OF TROPICAL AFRICA. By D. Oliver. Vol. II., 20s.

CONCHOLOGIA INDICA. Part II. 20s.

FLORA AUSTRALIENSIS. By G. Bentham. Vol. V. 20s.

BEWICK'S WOODCUTS. By the Rev. T. Hugo. Imp. 4to. £6. 6s.

NOAD'S QUALITATIVE ANALYSIS. New Edition, 6s.

STERLAND'S BIRDS OF SHERWOOD FOREST. 7s. 6d.

BOWDEN'S NATURALIST IN NORWAY. 10s. 6d.

WALCOTT'S SACRED ARCHÆOLOGY. 18s.

FORTHCOMING WORKS.

THE NATURAL HISTORY OF A FLOWERING PLANT. By Prof. Dyer.

THE YOUNG COLLECTOR'S HANDY BOOK OF BOTANY. By the Rev. H. P. Dunster. [*Just ready.*

THE YOUNG COLLECTOR'S HANDY BOOK OF RECREATIVE SCIENCE. By the Rev. H. P. Dunster.

MONOGRAPH OF ODONTOGLOSSUM. By James Bateman, Esq. Part V.

FLORA VITIENSIS. By Dr. Seemann. Part X.

FLORA OF INDIA. By Dr. Hooker and Dr. Thomson.

THE LAND AND FRESHWATER SHELLS OF BRITISH INDIA. By S. Hanley and Wm. Theobald. Part III.

NATURAL HISTORY OF PLANTS. By Prof. Baillon. Vol. II.

LONDON.
L. REEVE & CO., 5, HENRIETTA STREET, COVENT GARDEN.

PRINTED BY TAYLOR AND CO., LITTLE QUEEN STREET, W.C.

www.ingramcontent.com/pod-product-compliance
Lightning Source LLC
Chambersburg PA
CBHW022046230426
43672CB00008B/1087